REFORM, ETHICS AND LEADERSHIP IN PUBLIC SERVICE

Reform, Ethics and Leadership in Public Service

A *Festschrift* in honour of Richard A. Chapman

Edited by
MICHAEL HUNT
BARRY J. O'TOOLE

Ashgate

Aldershot • Brookfield USA • Singapore • Sydney

Published by
Ashgate Publishing Limited
Gower House
Croft Road
Aldershot
Hants GU11 3HR
England

Ashgate Publishing Company
Old Post Road
Brookfield
Vermont 05036
USA

British Library Cataloguing in Publication Data
Reform, ethics and leadership in public service:
  a festschrift in honour of Richard A. Chapman
  1. Civil service – Great Britain
  2. Civil service ethics – Great Britain
  I. Hunt, Michael, 1947– II. O'Toole, Barry J.
  351.4'1

Library of Congress Catalog Card Number: 98-072854

ISBN 1 84014 107 7

Typeset by Owain Hammonds Associates,
Ebeneser, Bont-goch, Talybont, Ceredigion, Wales SY24 5DP. Telephone (01970) 832014.

Printed in Great Britain by the Ipswich Book Company, Suffolk

Contents

Preface

The purpose of this book is to pay respect to a person widely regarded as the doyen of the study of public administration in Britain, Richard A. Chapman, who retired from the University of Durham in 1996. To that end we commissioned a number of his friends and colleagues, from this country and abroad, to write chapters based on subjects derived from the three themes which we consider to have formed the core of Professor Chapman's considerable scholarship, namely 'reform', 'ethics' and 'leadership' in public service. Thus, whilst this work is a *festschrift*, we have not adopted a traditional approach to its compilation. In particular, we have not asked Professor Chapman's immediate colleagues in the Department of Politics in Durham to offer contributions (although two of the present authors, Greenaway and O'Toole, have worked in that department). Rather, we have approached colleagues and friends whose specialist interests are in some way linked with those of Professor Chapman, in particular with the three themes mentioned. This does not mean that we have concentrated on public administration in the narrow sense that so many so often seem to conceive it these days. That would be to betray the spirit of Professor Chapman's contribution, since he has always had a much wider view of his subject than many others of our colleagues. His is a view which has always included biographical, comparative, historical, philosophical and sociological approaches, and our concern has been to reflect this broad conception of public administration. The contributions, therefore, reflect these perspectives. Nevertheless, each essay is focused on one of the three themes of 'reform', 'ethics' and 'leadership' in public service, and it is in this way that we have adopted the unconventional or non-traditional approach to the *festschrift* form referred to above. However, each contribution is a work of scholarship in its own right, and the book *is not* an exhaustive survey of the three themes identified. At the same time, the book *itself* does stand as a contribution to the literature of public administration since it does explore the relationships between the three themes.

The people we have asked to make these contributions are all friends of Professor Chapman, two of some thirty or more years standing (Professor Morris and Dr Jack). Some are former students (Dr Jack and Dr O'Toole).

Others have produced major works with him (Dr Greenaway and Mr Hunt). Some have worked closely with him in the Public Administration Committee, which he has served with great distinction throughout his career (Dr Barberis, Mr Hunt and Dr O'Toole). Others he knows because of his connections with scholarship overseas (Professor Rohr and Mr Warrington). All have benefited from his encouragement and the enthusiasm he has always shown towards his subject. Each of the essays is thus a personal tribute to someone who has influenced the author's approach to their work and their subject.

It remains for us to pay our special thanks to Professor Chapman. First, and specifically in relation to this *festschrift*, we must thank him for confirming the accuracy of our recollection of some of the anecdotes and significant memories which we have heard before, either in his teaching or from more informal meetings. Secondly, and more importantly, we must thank him for the encouragement he has given, the enthusiasm for his subject – which has inspired our own approaches – and for his friendship. He is a person we hold in the highest possible regard, and we dedicate this book to him in that spirit.

MH and BO'T, Sheffield and Glasgow, January 1998

Acknowledgements

The Editors are grateful to the following publishers for permission to reproduce copyright material; Routledge for a table from *Management in Government* (1972) by Desmond Keeling, and Financial Times Management for extracts from *Organisation and Management in the Public Sector* (first edition, 1991) by Allan Lawton and Aidan Rose.

List of contributors

Peter Barberis is Reader in Politics at Manchester Metropolitan University. He is the author of a number of books and articles on the civil service including the first book on Britain's permanent secretaries *The Elite of the Elite* (Dartmouth Publishing, 1996). He has also edited *The Whitehall Reader* (Open University Press, 1996) and *The Civil Service in an Era of Change* (Dartmouth Publishing, 1997).

David L. Dillman received his Ph.D. from the University of Massachusetts, Amherst and since 1984 has been Professor of Political Science at Abilene Christian University, Abilene, Texas, USA. He has written widely on leadership in the American civil service.

John Greenaway is Lecturer in Politics at the University of East Anglia. He has written and researched on reform of the British civil service from an historical perspective and was co-author with Richard Chapman of *The Dynamics of Administrative Reform* (Croom Helm, 1980). He is currently working on a study of alcohol and British politics 1830-1960.

Michael Hunt is Senior Lecturer in Public Administration at Sheffield Hallam University. He was joint editor, with Professor Chapman, of *Open Government: a study of the prospects of open government within the limitations of the British political system,* (Croom Helm, 1987) and has subsequently published work on open government and on public service ethics. He is the current editor of *Teaching Public Administration.*

Malcolm Jack has written widely on eighteenth-century English and French literature and philosophy, publishing his study *Corruption and Progress: The Eighteenth-Century Debate* in 1989. He is a reviewer for learned journals in the USA as well as in the UK. He is editor of the correspondence of Lady Mary Wortley Montagu, of an anthology of William Beckford's prose (published by Penguin Classics) and of *The Episodes To Vathek*. His latest book, *William Beckford: An English Fidalgo* was published in New York in 1996.

David S. Morris is a Professor at Sheffield Business School, a Senior Research Fellow of the Atlantic Council and holds visiting professorships at the University of Leicester and the Universidade do Algarve. He has published in a variety of areas and has a particular interest in the implementation of Total Quality Management within both public and private sector organisations.

Barry J. O'Toole is Reader in Politics at the University of Glasgow, having previously taught at the Universities of Durham, Loughborough and Liverpool. He has written widely on the British civil service, in particular on the ethics of public officials. His publications include *Private Gain and Public Service* (Routledge 1989), *The Next Steps: Improving Management in Government?* (edited with Grant Jordan), and numerous articles in scholarly journals. He is editor of the journal of the Joint University Council Public Administration Committee, *Public Policy and Administration*.

John A. Rohr is Professor of Public Administration at Virginia Polytechnic Institute and State University. He has researched on both ethics in the public service and on constitutionalism. His publications include *To Run a Constitution: the Legitimacy of the Administrative State* (University Press of Kansas, 1986), *Ethics for Bureaucrats: An Essay on Law and Values* (Marcel Dekker, 2nd Ed., 1988), and *Founding Republics in France and America: A Study in Constitutional Governance* (University Press of Kansas, 1995).

Edward Warrington is a Lecturer at the University of Malta doing research into the civil services of Malta, Barbados and Fiji. Previously a member of the Administrative Class of the Malta Civil Service he was Secretary of the Public Management Reform Commission between 1988 and 1990. His previous publications have concerned the governance of micro states, and administrative reform.

1 The Ethic of Public Service: The Contribution of Richard A. Chapman to the Study of Public Administration

Barry J. O'Toole and Michael Hunt

Richard Chapman is the leading scholar of the British civil service. His long and distinguished career has been devoted to helping others understand how that service evolved, how it operates today and what values underpin its work. He has enhanced that understanding not only by his writing and teaching, but also through the sterling work he has done in promoting scholarship in public administration, primarily, but not exclusively, as a long standing servant of the Joint University Council (JUC), and of its Public Administration Committee (PAC) in particular. The public administration community is fortunate indeed to have had such a stalwart and selfless member. That community remains fortunate in that, while Professor Chapman has officially retired from the University of Durham, he will continue to be an active participant in its affairs. However, it is his formal retirement on 30 September 1996 which has provided the opportunity for this *festschrift*. It is a celebration of Professor Chapman's contribution to the study of public administration.

Richard Arnold Chapman was born on 15 August 1937, the only child of Grace and George Chapman. His father was a postman, and the young Chapman was brought up in a modest semi-detached house in Bexleyheath. His father was away for most of the Second World War, and, apart from the war, his childhood was ordinary and uneventful, as was his early education. He failed his 11+ examination and spent his first two years of secondary education at Bexleyheath Secondary Modern School, where he was very happy. However, because of the enlightened education policy of Kent County Council, which provided the opportunity for pupils aged 13+ to transfer to grammar schools as well as to technical schools, he spent the remaining years of his secondary education at Dartford Grammar School, which he left when he was 16.

On leaving school Richard Chapman became a civil servant, in the Air

Ministry. This was an important formative experience in his life, and had enormous influence on his future career. The reason was that it was during his time at the Air Ministry, as a Clerical Officer, that the report on the Crichel Down case was published. Every civil servant received a Treasury Circular from Sir Edward Bridges, the then Head of the Home Civil Service, in which he told them to 'read and take to heart' the comments made by the internal committee of officials which considered the future of the civil servants implicated in the case. The committee had written: 'In present times the interests of the private citizen are affected to a great extent by the actions of Civil Servants ... [they] should constantly bear in mind that the citizen has a right to expect ... that his personal feelings, no less than his rights as an individual, will be sympathetically and fairly considered' (quoted in Chapman, 1988a, p.304). Richard Chapman did indeed take this warning to heart, and has often used it as an example of the values of civil servants.

While at the Air Ministry Richard Chapman demonstrated the capacity for hard work which has been one of the hallmarks of his career. He was determined to advance up the civil service hierarchy, and sought admission to the then Executive Class, as an Executive Officer, through the open competition. In those days, the examination consisted of a series of academic tests, roughly equivalent to taking 'A' levels. In order to be able to pass the examination a great deal of effort was required, and the young Chapman attended evening classes on four nights of each week – as well as working the five and a half days which was then required of full-time civil servants. He passed the examination, and submitted a request to be posted to the Ministry of Pensions and National Insurance.

Chapman's career was interrupted by the requirements of National Service, which he undertook in the Royal Air Force between 1956 and 1958. He became engaged in personnel selection work at the Ground Officer Selection Centre (GOSC) at RAF Uxbridge. His future life was enormously influenced by his experiences during this period. First, he acquired his life-long antipathy to all facets of war, which, combined with his religious allegiance, has latterly manifested itself in what might be described as 'pragmatic pacifism'. Secondly, because of the work he was assigned, which involved the psychometric testing of potential RAF officers, he became extremely interested in personnel selection, and in particular in 'leadership'. This is a fascination which has inspired much of his scholarship. Thirdly, because of the close proximity he had with people who had had university education, he developed a desire to go to university himself. His experience in dealing with people who were thought to be officer material led him to the belief that he was no less intelligent than they were. He decided to take three 'A' levels, part-time, while still a corporal in the RAF, in British Constitution, Economics and Economic History, all of which he passed. Fourthly, he had direct experience of the operation of the convention of ministerial responsi-

2

bility, which he remains convinced is a valuable pillar of our system of government.

This latter point deserves special attention through an example which Chapman sometimes used in his teaching. Candidates for officer selection would arrive at RAF Uxbridge to undertake three days of tests. The first test, an intelligence test, being taken after supper, at about 7.30 p.m. Sometimes, of course, candidates were late, especially on Sundays, and thus unable to take the first test. The people who were responsible for administering and marking this test, led by Corporal Chapman, worked out an arrangement, agreed with their superior officers, whereby those who missed the Sunday evening test would be able to take that test at the conclusion of the test series, but they would only sit the test if it was clear from the results of the other tests that they were capable of passing the series. This seemed a common-sense arrangement, and worked well. Until, that is, a particular candidate felt that he had been unfairly treated. He had been late for the Sunday test but was not afforded the opportunity to sit it at the end of the series because his performance in the other tests had indicated that he would be a clear failure. The candidate's father knew his local M.P. well and complained. The M.P. wrote to the then Secretary of State for Air, Mr George Ward. The Ministry swung into action, with the ultimate effect that Corporal Chapman was brought before his Group Captain who, naturally enough, wanted to know 'What the hell is going on?' The Group Captain had to write a report for the Minister, who could then reply to the M.P., who could then deal with his constituent. The moral of this story is quite simple: even the most humble of Her Majesty's servants may inadvertently affect the rights of individual citizens; furthermore, even minor administrative arrangements may have political consequences. The convention of ministerial responsibility is designed to ensure that when this happens the individual citizen can obtain redress. More importantly, it means that public servants will, or should, always bear in mind that the Minister can, and sometimes does, become involved in what appear to be the most minor of decisions. Richard Chapman never forgot this lesson in the practice of public administration, and has always felt that the more political interpretation of the convention of ministerial responsibility used by most scholars, involving the resignation of ministers, is simply inadequate.

Having been awarded three 'A' levels, the next stage in Richard Chapman's life was to apply to the three universities to which he was eligible: Hull, Leicester and London. He obtained leave of absence from the Ministry of Pensions and National Insurance and in October 1958 went up to the University of Leicester to read Politics. Thus began an illustrious academic career, which has been influenced by many people. Notable amongst the people at Leicester who had such an influence were Professor Bruce Miller, the distinguished Australian scholar, who was Head of the Department of

Politics, and Mr Maurice Hookham, who later became Chapman's Ph.D. supervisor.

Apart from a brief sojourn in Canada, where he was awarded an M.A. in Public Administration from Carleton University, and where he acquired an abiding affection for things Canadian, Richard Chapman's early academic career centred on Leicester. He obtained an upper second class degree, and went on to take his Ph.D. (which he read for part-time and which he completed in three years). The University of Leicester took him on as an Assistant Lecturer in 1962, and he became a Tutor in Beaumont Hall, one of the Halls of Residence of the University of Leicester. There he became a very close and lifelong friend of the Warden, Richard Bishop, a leading war-time conscientious objector, who also had a great influence on Professor Chapman's religious outlook. In 1963 he moved to Liverpool to be the Leverhulme Lecturer in Public Administration in Professor Wilfrid Harrison's department, and then to be Senior Lecturer at INLOGOV in the University of Birmingham, at the tender age of 31. He became Reader in Politics at the University of Durham three years later, where he remained until his retirement in 1996, being awarded a Personal Chair in 1986.

Professor Chapman's career at the University of Durham is fascinating because it reveals so much about his attitude to his work. First, it is clear that he was a devoted teacher. Teaching gave him enormous pleasure; more importantly, his teaching gave his students enormous pleasure. The pleasure was enhanced, both for Professor Chapman and for the students, because Dame Enid Russell-Smith, who had played a very significant role in the creation of the NHS, shared some of the teaching with him. His talent as a teacher was testified to by the consistently excellent ratings his students returned in the questionnaires which the University of Durham has employed since the early 1980s. More importantly, it is testified to by the number of former students whom Richard Chapman counts as friends. A simple anecdote will indicate the affection in which he is held by students. The undergraduate seminar on 'Public Administration' took place every Friday afternoon, usually between 2.15 and 4.15 (without a tea-break) for twenty five years – except for periods of sabbatical leave, and never cancelled because of illness. On one of these Fridays in 1985 the rumour started that Richard Chapman had been promoted to Professor. The students circuitously verified the rumour, and then engaged one of their number to delay the new Professor from turning up at his class at the normal hour. This was to allow the others time to buy some cakes and champagne, so that the seminar could be turned into a celebration – though, it must be noted, a working celebration!

Secondly, while at the University of Durham, Richard Chapman took a leading part in the administration of the University. He was Head of the Department of Politics twice and served as Dean of the Faculty of Social

Sciences. He was an elected member of Senate for innumerable years, and was twice a member of the Council of the University. He has served on the governing bodies of three of the Durham Colleges, and acted as Honorary Treasurer of St Chad's and as President of the Senior Common Room of that college. He has chaired the University's Library Committee and been a member of the most important standing and ad hoc committees of the University (including the Committee to Review the Structure and Government of the University of Durham and the Committee to appoint the Vice Chancellor). He was the founding Executive Vice-President of the University's Society of Fellows, – a cross-University body responsible for enhancing the research profile of the University and which, according to the University *Gazette*, he served with great distinction. He was also President of the Durham Branch of the AUT (a term of office which covered the miners' strike in the 1980s). And for seventeen years he was the convenor of the Public Policy Studies Group of the University which promoted and encouraged cross-disciplinary work in those disciplines concerned with public policy. He carried out all of this work efficiently, vigorously and with good humour. He was, indeed, a devoted servant of the University of Durham.

Thirdly, Professor Chapman's administrative skills were not confined to the domestic arrangements of the University of Durham. He has been a loyal and diligent servant of the academic community more widely, and in particular of the Public Administration community. For example, he has been Honorary Treasurer of the Political Studies Association, member of the Review of Activities Committee of the now defunct Royal Institute of Public Administration, Editor of *PAC Bulletin* (now *Public Policy and Administration*), Chairman of the PAC's Education and Training Sub-Committee and of its International Sub-Committee, Chairman of the PAC, Chairman of the JUC, and member of innumerable editorial boards. In addition, he has performed wider public service, for example, as a long serving member of the Final Selection Board for fast-stream entry to the Civil Service, as a member of the Lord Chancellor's Advisory Council on Public Records and as adviser to the House of Lords Select Committee on the Public Service. Moreover, he has been external examiner for numerous higher degrees and for undergraduate and taught Masters' degrees in thirteen institutions, including two in foreign countries. However, it is his service for the PAC and the JUC which has given him most pleasure, and for which he is held in the highest regard. He has sometimes been rather a difficult colleague in this context, and he would be the first to admit that he sometimes failed in what he set out to achieve, but nobody can deny that he has been an outstanding servant of and contributor to the work of both the JUC and the PAC. He richly deserved the Honorary Fellowship the JUC bestowed on him in 1997. He was touched by the award of that Fellowship, and by the invitation which the PAC extended to him to deliver the Frank Stacey Memorial Lecture at the 1996 PAC annual conference. Those who heard that lecture were not disappointed.

Fourthly, at the same time as giving enormous energy and talent to his teaching and his administrative duties, Richard Chapman has made a very significant contribution to the literature of politics and public administration. His canon consists of some fifteen books, seven single authored, one jointly authored and seven either edited or jointly edited, and, at the latest count over ninety articles and shorter pieces. This is a remarkable achievement, and one which led to the award in 1989 of the first D.Litt in the social sciences awarded by the University of Leicester. It is a record to which this chapter shall shortly return.

Richard Chapman's is a remarkable career. It has been marked by incredible industry, scholarship of the highest calibre and an integrity which puts most of us to shame. Much of the attitude of mind which has led to this success derives from his non-conformist religious convictions which originate from his time in the Scouting movement. Despite being President of the (evangelical) Christian Union at Leicester, he has never adopted a dogmatic approach. Instead, his convictions have sustained a personal work ethic and a Greenian view of morality as the 'disinterested performance of self-imposed duties'. Nevertheless, he has clearly enjoyed his work, though it is also clear that his industry has put an enormous strain on his health. Long a sufferer of migraine and latterly of severe sciatica, the strain landed him in hospital to undergo major back-surgery, from which he is only just recovering. Those health problems, combined with an increasing distaste for the lack of integrity which he believes pervades much of academic life now, have led Richard Chapman to take early retirement. Nevertheless, he is to continue to write, and we may yet look forward to more of the scholarship which has marked his illustrious and productive career.

If there were three words which would indicate directly the aspects of the study of public administration to which Richard Chapman has made his most important contributions, those three words would be 'reform', 'ethics' and 'leadership'. Indeed, it is fair to say that the entirety of his considerable output has been devoted to one or other of these topics. It would be more difficult, however, to decide which of his works falls into what category. There is a simple reason for this: it is extremely difficult when studying public affairs to define precisely what is meant by these words, and therefore which aspects of public administration fall within their ambit. The consequence is that where scholars write about one of these topics it is likely that they are also writing about one or other or both of the others. The tasks of this part of this chapter are: first, to extricate the three topics; secondly, to indicate Richard

Chapman's contribution to each individually; and thirdly, to provide an overall assessment, thus bringing the three topics back together.

The methodology to be used for the first of these tasks is one Chapman himself would approve of, and is as old as philosophy. It is simply to define the terms: what is 'reform'?; what do we mean by 'ethics'?; and what is 'leadership'? Naturally enough, given the purpose of this book, the place to look for answers to these questions is in the works with which this chapter is primarily concerned, those of Richard Chapman himself. First, what is 'reform'?

The answer to this question is to be found in the authoritative and characteristically scholarly book Chapman co-authored with J.R. Greenaway, *The Dynamics of Administrative Reform* (1980). Administrative reform, they suggest, is:

> the process of making changes in administrative structures or procedures within the public services, because they have become out of line with the expectations or values of the social and political environment. This means that the process is not a developmental one towards a clearly defined goal known in advance, but a complex matter of acceding to pressures, communicating ideas, stimulating comments from groups with potential interests, and making judgements within the administrative system about tactics and timing for the introduction of particular changes (p.183).

It is ironic, not to say confusing, that the most important reform which Chapman has considered at length is that of recruitment procedures for entrance to the civil service in the post-war years. The title he gave to that study was *Leadership in the British Civil Service* (1984), which examined in detail the creation of the Civil Service Selection Board (CSSB). He gave it the title *Leadership* because of the central role played by Sir Percival Waterfield, then the First Civil Service Commissioner, in bringing about the establishment of CSSB. However, in the context of discussing administrative reform this study is an ideal example because it fits in almost exactly with the definition quoted above. For example, Chapman makes it quite clear that the methods of selecting people who would eventually become senior civil servants had become out of line with the expectations or values of the social and political environment. Furthermore, he catalogues with forensic precision the ways in which Waterfield and others acceded to pressures, communicated ideas, stimulated comments and, in particular, made judgements about tactics and timing for the introduction of the changes documented. Thus, while this study was about leadership – in the sense of examining the contributions of a particular 'leader', of dealing with the recruitment of potential 'leaders' of the civil service, and of analysing the qualities of 'leadership' – it is clearly

7

also about a significant administrative reform, as defined in Chapman and Greenaway.

It is not so clear, however, that he is writing about administrative reform in his other contributions on the recruitment of civil servants. The most important of these have been in the form of editorials for *Public Policy and Administration* (1991, 1993a, 1996a and 1997), though, of course, he has also dealt with it elsewhere including in his magisterial inaugural lecture (1988b). The editorial format gave him the opportunity of direct criticism of numerous decisions made about recruitment procedures. These decisions were made without wide consultation, and generally on the basis of 'efficiency' considerations, not because the methods or institutions concerned had 'become out of line with the expectations or values of the social and political environment'. Professor Chapman was particularly unhappy about the decisions to abolish the Civil Service Commission and to privatise the Recruitment and Assessment Services Agency (RAS), both of which, in his view, have contributed to 'The End of the Civil Service' (1992; 1996b).

Richard Chapman has been of the opinion that the civil service as it came to be recognised – as a unified body with coherent structures, common standards of personnel conditions and a set of core values – was undermined by recent 'reforms', particularly those which followed the publication of the Next Steps report in 1988. The introduction of changes consequent upon that report, and other, more radical changes, have, in his view, contributed to the demise of a public service oriented civil service. When the Next Steps report was published he wrote a sceptical review which raised all sorts of questions about the role of ministers and civil servants in the new arrangements and, in particular, about accountability (1988c). This was followed by an even more considered series of comments made during his inaugural lecture, in which he noted that:

> Anxieties arise when the pressures for change and the emphasis on financial economies do not recognise the democratic context within which public services are administered. As already stated, one of the fundamental principles of British central government is the doctrine of ministerial responsibility. It is a doctrine which has been consistently and gravely weakened in the past thirty-five years and it may well be weakened further if the recommendations in *The Next Steps* are implemented without further careful thought about the consequences .... The tendency seems to be for the consistent growth of both private interests and group interests in public sector management ....These developments seem to represent such a significant change of emphasis and ultimately of direction, that even if welcomed on the grounds of cost-cutting and rolling back the frontiers of the state, they seem out of

8

character with the highly regarded traditions, standards and expectations of public sector management in this country. It may be premature to issue dire warnings of the dangers of corruption, but if the sorts of safeguards that worked so well in the past are removed – safeguards involving the regular posting of staff, recruitment on the basis of open competition with the objective assessment of applicants, and socialisation which encourages the highest standards of integrity and public service as the most desirable qualities in public sector management – if these safeguards no longer exist, then it may be necessary to ask if alternative measures should be introduced to ensure that high standards of public sector management are still achievable .... Quite simply, to move at great speed in the apparent direction of improved value for money, while disregarding other values, may not be what citizens would wish to experience if they were better educated about the British system of government and better informed about the probable and possible consequences of fashionable new management techniques (1988b, pp. 16-17).

Naturally enough, the leaders of the civil service have consistently denied all of the suggestions raised by Professor Chapman, particularly in relation to corruption, accountability and the values of public service. However, there are those who previously welcomed wholeheartedly the changes heralded by Next Steps who have themselves become sceptics, and, in the light of events and tendencies in public sector management since, the comments quoted here seem to have been particularly prescient. In particular, the debacles relating to accountability and other problems in the prison service and the Child Support Agency, the 1995 report of the Committee of Public Accounts which suggested that there had been an increase in financial corruption consequent upon the Next Steps and other reforms, and the recent promulgation of a 'Civil Service Code' all seem apt reminders of the dangers to which Richard Chapman pointed at the outset.

It may be that those dangers ensued because of the application of what Floyd Hunter called 'the principle of unanimity' (1963, referred to in Chapman, 1968, p.111), by which he meant that when policy is finally formulated by the leaders in a community, there is an immediate demand on their part for strict conformity of opinion. Chapman is a little less rigid in his theoretical studies of decision making, and it may be that his view of one of the factors in decision making is also appropriate as a tool of analysis in relation to Next Steps. In his first book, *Decision Making*, he made a significant contribution to the study of public administration which is now little referred to. The book, which was the first British contribution to the genre of analysing the factors involved in making decisions or the *method* of decision making, is about the 1957 decision to raise the Bank Rate to its highest level for thirty seven years and to raise it by the largest increase in peace time since 1847. In the analysis Chapman refers to an activity which had not been noted before, in shorthand 'inverse consensus'. In the book, Chapman says:

> Usually, when we speak of consensus, we refer to the general attitude or will on a particular matter, a form of pressure which may influence the government. The characteristic procedure associated with this notion is to look for a consensus among the relevant interest groups and then to translate the consensus into policy and action. The significance of consensus may be increased if the procedure is inverted ... instead of looking for a consensus, the decision makers, recognising its significance for their authority, set out to create it by consulting and informing as many people as possible .... [T]here are two aspects of this procedure which seem important from the standpoint of the accumulation of authority. The first aspect concerns the role of the decision makers, and the second concerns pluralism.
> As far as the decision makers are concerned, it may be that they [seek] to create a consensus to add to their authority ... they [want] to maximise their *real* [as opposed to their formal] authority by creating a consensus of support. In this way the importance of consensus may be to confer on the decisions of the administrators a higher degree of authority than they would otherwise have.
> As far as the pluralistic aspect is concerned, ... those involved [in decision making seek] to draw into the consensus as many interests as possible; they [are] not concerned with *why* people [support] them, they [are] concerned that they [have] the maximum possible support (1968, pp.109-10).

There is a *prima facie* case that the decision to implement the recommendations of *The Next Steps* report was an example both of 'inverse consensus' and of 'the principle of unanimity'. We are informed by Hennessy (1988a, pp.619-22) that the *Next Steps* report caused a great deal of consternation within the Whitehall machine, both at political and administrative levels. We know that the publication of the report was delayed until after the 1987 General Election. We know, too, that the response to the report *appeared* to be enthusiastic, both inside and outside the Whitehall machine. This apparent enthusiasm continued for some considerable time, and was reflected in cross-party support and in the numerous reports of the Treasury and Civil Service Committee of the House of Commons. There were those, of course, who objected, not least the (by then) unfashionable civil service trade unions and one or two 'maverick' Labour MPs. However, the sceptics were always confined to the sidelines, and there was never a full-scale House of Commons debate on the Next Steps or on the later management changes. Consequently,

10

these changes never became a matter for public concern. Of course, as Chapman has pointed out elsewhere, most notably in his article on 'The rise and fall of the CSD' (1983), the unwritten nature of the British constitution and the extensive prerogative powers of the Crown facilitate administrative changes or 'reforms'. It may be that, had Parliamentary and public opinion been alerted earlier than it was to the problems which Richard Chapman noted at the outset, we might not have witnessed the administrative revolution which has undoubtedly taken place in the British civil service, nor the consequent abandonment of important public service values.

Many of the issues which Professor Chapman dealt with in the works referred to here are, on the face of it, ethical issues. This raises the second of the questions referred to earlier, namely 'what do we mean by ethics?'. Again we can turn to Richard Chapman to provide us with a definition. He says:

> Ethics in the British civil service is about the application of moral standards in the course of official work. The practical dimension of the topic is that area of official conduct and actions where civil servants are not simply carrying out specific instructions or orders from higher authority but are making value judgements that have implications for their professional standing ... ethics in the British civil service therefore refers to moral standards in official work within the context of a specific political environment (1988a, p294).

In a later work, Chapman takes this definition further. Ethics in government:

> is not concerned simply with what the structure of government ought to be, nor with the nature and quality of measurable services carried out to meet the requirements or obligations of statutes, although these are most certainly relevant. It is, of course, concerned with those elements of structure and organisation that determine their quality and the acceptability of their standards, but it also extends more generally to the quality of government and its administration ....
> At a theoretical level ethics ... may encompass what government ought or ought not to do in given circumstances. It therefore reflects the standards and values of society: but what is acceptable in one place or at one time may differ from what is acceptable in another place or a different time. Ordinary citizens in western style democracies expect governments to abide by the rules and values of society in much the same ways as they are expected to abide by them themselves. In this context the subject may consequently be concerned with the implications for governmental structure and organisation of concepts like justice, fairness and equality ....
> From the perspective of liberal democracy, ethical behaviour in

11

government should reinforce the democratic process by ensuring that representatives and officials respect the rights of citizens and uphold those values which have been agreed as essential to a particular democracy (1993b, pp.1-2).

This is, indeed, a complex and wide-ranging definition. It covers many of the reform issues referred to earlier in this chapter, in so far as reform too is concerned with attempting to solve problems which arise where 'structures and procedures within the public services ... have become out of line with the expectations and values of the social and political environment'. It is also true that those changes referred to above which Chapman himself would not regard as 'reforms', according to the Chapman and Greenaway criteria, in particular those associated with Next Steps and other management changes in government, have ethical implications. This is mainly because the changes have affected the manifestation of concepts like justice, fairness and equality. However, it is also because those changes have affected the quality of services and the acceptability of their standards *and* the quality of government and its administration.

These questions and others are dealt with by Chapman on a wider scale than his particular concerns with Next Steps and the associated changes in recruitment procedures. Ethics, for him, covers an extremely broad range of issues, including 'efficiency' (1982, in Caiden and Siedentopf (eds)), open government (Chapman and Hunt, 1987), the relationships between ministers and civil servants (1987, 1993c), accountability (O'Toole and Chapman, 1995), and leadership (1984; Chapman and O'Toole, 1994). However, there is one branch of the study of ethics in government which has particularly engaged his attention: the values and standards which underpin the work of senior officials in British central government. His scholarship in that area resulted in his most important single contribution to the study of public administration, a contribution which ranks as one of the outstanding works of British administrative history: *Ethics in the British Civil Service* (1988a).

The book is about the work of Sir Edward Bridges as Head of the Civil Service from 1945 until his retirement in 1956 and about the profound effect his work and views had on the attitudes and ethics of British public adminis- tration. It is not a straightforward biography, although there is a biographical chapter; it is, rather, a thematic interpretation of numerous aspects of the activities of one of this century's most important public officials. Amongst other matters, it deals with the machinery of government, personnel management, the political activities of civil servants and the relationship of the civil servant to the constitution. These are issues that lie at the heart of the question of ethics both in the civil service and in government more widely. Chapman clearly illustrates that, while civil servants are non-party political, they nevertheless behave in an extremely political way – to such an extent that they sometimes become the real source of authority for decisions that are normally thought of as the province of politicians. Bridges himself seems to have been regarded as almost the oracle when questions of constitutional propriety were considered, for politicians as well as for other civil servants.

At a superficial level it may be argued that since this book is primarily about Bridges it ought not to have been entitled *Ethics in the British Civil Service*. This would be a misinterpretation. The book is, indeed, about Bridges and his personal ethics. However, it is much more than that because it is *primarily* about the influence which Bridges had on other civil servants and on public affairs, both directly and indirectly. In some ways Bridges was the personification of the public service ethic: 'A good civil servant has to be more anonymous and unselfish in his work than those in other walks of life ... the traditional outlook of the modern civil service is one that recognises that the interests and welfare of the whole country come first ...' (quoted at p.64). He communicated that view by example and by exhortation. As Chapman says, 'Bridges clearly had unambiguous standards for himself and he expected ... them to exist in others' (p.xix).

In addition, Bridges was the personification of generalist administration, and his career was an admirable example of the generalist administrator in action. Chapman cites Anthony Seldon's *Churchill's Indian Summer* and the extensive interviews used as research material for that work as evidence that Bridges 'excelled' in this context (1988a, p.33; Seldon, 1981, p.545). Nevertheless, generalist administration, as exemplified by Bridges, has often been criticised as being 'not sufficiently professional and inadequate in terms of training and expertise in economics' (Chapman, 1988a, p.33). Chapman's work on this aspect of Bridges' contribution illustrates the views Bridges himself had on the role of civil servants and provides a counterbalance to what Chapman refers to as the 'one-sided' debate about generalist administration (p.36) – a debate dominated by the fulminations of Thomas Balogh, the Fulton Committee, and Lord Crowther-Hunt. This debate, too, is an ethical one since it is about how best civil servants should go about their work. It is a debate about what qualifications, training and outlook civil servants 'ought' to have.

In some ways Chapman himself is not entirely at ease with some of the characteristics which Bridges epitomised and which seem to remain the hallmarks of the higher reaches of the civil service. In relation to Bridges he notes that 'there is not much evidence that he had any acquaintance with, or understanding of, people from different backgrounds or different age groups'. Indeed,

> in some respects Bridges typifies and epitomises the concept of a narrow, self-contained elite to which terms like 'Mandarins' and 'the Establishment' are conventionally applied. Questions may be asked not

13

only about his conception of 'the national interest' but also about the real ends (conscious or unconscious) for many of his activities. Furthermore ... in effect, he helped perpetrate the concentration of real power in the hands of an elite by controlling, or at least strongly influencing, recruitment to key positions in the public services, and by surrounding 'the administration' in an aura of mystery and secrecy which no outsider could penetrate (p.xviii).

These are problems which Chapman was concerned about long before his work on Bridges. They originate from the pioneering study he undertook for the Fulton Committee in the late 1960s, which resulted in his book *The Higher Civil Service in Britain* (1970). It was pioneering because this was the first time that a research study had been carried out on the higher civil service which relied on questionnaires and *structured* interviews. Kelsall (1955) relied almost entirely on documentary sources. In essence, Chapman found evidence of the elitism referred to above.

He also found, however, that the people who became senior civil servants were extremely able and hard working (pp.53-60; 60-83) and, as with Bridges, had a considerable sense of 'public duty' (pp.130-53). It is what he perceives to be the demise of this last aspect of public service which has come increasingly to dominate the way in which he now views the civil service. This demise he believes to be the natural consequence of introducing business-like methods into government administration and the replacement of social and public values with those of self-interestedness.

These issues have been explored by Professor Chapman in some notable works of critical scholarship, in particular his widely known essays on 'The End of the Civil Service' (1992; 1996b) and the amusing, scholarly and thought provoking lecture 'From Croquet Mallets to Flamingos' (1996c), delivered in honour of Frank Stacey at the 1996 annual conference of the PAC. In essence he considers that the organisational changes in the civil service mean that there is now no longer a unified civil service in the sense that has existed for most of the present century. These changes have both been underpinned by and encouraged the development of new sets of more materialistic values, at the expense of now old-fashioned ideas about public service and public duty. Together, these changes, which Professor Chapman considers to be ill-thought through and badly delivered, have altered, in his opinion forever, the nature of public administration and public service in the United Kingdom. While there have been some questionable improvements in some areas of work to which measurable criteria can be applied, the question Professor Chapman keeps asking in various forms is 'at what price?'. It is a question to which there have been no convincing answers.

One form of that question is about the relationship between 'democracy' and 'efficiency' – a topic which he first explored in 1982 in his essay

14

'Strategies for Reducing Government Activities' (in Caiden and Siedentopf).
In his 1988 review of *The Next Steps* report, Professor Chapman made the
following observations:

> Democratic government is not usually cheap government. It often
> involves processes of consultation and agreement; and management
> functions become involved with accountability to elected representa-
> tives. Nevertheless, it may be efficient and convenient government if it
> is what the people want and they are satisfied. However, the best value
> for money in terms of the delivery of services may be achieved in
> political systems that have few of the superficial inefficiencies or
> expense of democracies; but, perhaps surprisingly, this may not be what
> people want. Sometimes people actually prefer to do things in ways that
> are more expensive, require more consultation, and encounter more
> political interference in matters of day to day management. This is what
> some people cherish as one of the luxuries of living in democracies and
> the term efficiency does not to them seem appropriate.
> One important task of the government in Britain is to achieve an
> acceptable balance between, on the one hand, ... democracy and, on
> the other hand ... efficiency .... The balance may be different from time
> to time but it is a balance that has to be consciously considered .... It is
> in this context that *The Next Steps* is a very significant report, with
> potential implications that go far beyond what might have been
> expected from its terms of reference (1988c, pp.9-10).

For Chapman, one of the aspects of Next Steps which from the outset
threatened that balance was the injunction that senior managers must be
prepared 'to show real qualities of leadership, ... to back their judgement and
to take and defend unpopular decisions' (Efficiency Unit, 1988, para.35;
quoted in Chapman 1988c, p.4). Professor Chapman notes that:

> At a superficial level this statement may be unquestionable, but it is by
> no means clear what, exactly, is meant by these 'skills' as the scrutiny
> team calls them. For example, are 'the real qualities of leadership' in this
> context so unquestionably agreed that there is no need to spell them
> out? Might the scrutiny team be asked to say more precisely what may be
> expected from individual officials, and also to elaborate on how those
> leadership qualities are to be assessed when staff are recruited, and how
> they are to be developed after staff are appointed? (1988c, p.4).

He goes on to formulate questions which have been at the heart of the
debate about Next Steps and subsequent changes since. In retrospect, some
of his comments seem almost prophetic. He says:

to some people the recommended attributes in officials may appear alien in the British political system. In theory – or if not in theory then at least in public presentation – the convention of ministerial responsibility has required that it is ministers, not officials, who should demonstrate leadership and defend unpopular decisions in public. It may, of course, now be more acceptable for public sector managers to adopt a more public profile than in the past, and being largely unwritten the British constitution could easily accommodate such a further change of emphasis but, if it is, there might now be a need to reformulate the convention ... and even to enshrine it in an official statement. As seen from the perspective of *The Next Steps*, ministers could become largely superfluous as far as the delivery of many public services is concerned, and any change in their status could have widespread implications. Citizens expect ministers to be responsible for public services that affect them personally ... (1988c, p.4).

It is thus that this chapter turns briefly to the question of 'leadership'.

Professor Chapman's most significant work on leadership is not, as might be expected, his *Leadership in the British Civil Service* (1984). Rather it is *Ethics in the British Civil Service* (1988a). While the former work is more explicit and deals with theoretical considerations (for example at pp.149-50 and pp. 182-94), the latter work is a sustained account of somebody who was unquestionably *the* leader of the British civil service. It is an empirical study of leadership in action. While Sir Edward Bridges would have demurred, it is clear that he occupied an important position in British society, he made important national decisions, he was in a management position of supreme importance, he was accountable for large sums of public money, and he suffered, as a senior civil servant, from allegations that senior civil servants were largely responsible for Britain's declining role in the world because their 'amateur' approach was not suited to the tasks of modern government, an 'amateurism' which Bridges fostered. These are all empirical criteria suggested by Professor Chapman in his 1984 work on 'leadership' (pp.182-3). This empirical approach is appropriate since, as he notes, 'There is no complete and universally applicable explanation of leadership'. There are rather different 'approaches which can be recognised in the literature', three of the most important of which are the qualities or traits approach, the situation approach and the group approach (1984, p.182). Essentially these mean that people are either born with leadership qualities (though the literature is imprecise and scholars are divided about what these might be) or they develop such qualities depending upon the situations they may encounter (a variation on the contingency approach) or they share the leadership 'function' with others in a particular work situation. As Richard Chapman notes 'Each of these makes an important contribution to

16

understanding the problems associated with the selection and training of senior management [and] each may ... contribute to the analysis of particular management incidents or developments and to understanding particular management environments' (1984, p.182). None of these theories, however, is a substitute for empirical evidence about what leaders do, and this is Professor Chapman's major contribution to the literature on leadership, especially since, as he noted, 'little research [had] been undertaken into leadership in bureaucracies and there [had] been no significant work published on leadership in the British civil service' (1984, p.182).

'The reason why no such studies have been made is, of course, the veil of secrecy associated with most government work' (1984, p.183). This is an important aspect of the political environment or the administrative culture in which public officials in the United Kingdom operate. Again, this is an aspect of the study of public administration to which Richard Chapman has made a significant contribution. Administrative culture:

> consists of a set of patterns and guidelines for behaviour that are distinctive from, but not inconsistent with, patterns and guidelines more generally applicable in Britain ... [it] is an aggregation of the values and beliefs of the individuals who make up the higher civil service ... [it] can be observed in the attitudes and standards, values, beliefs and assumptions of individual civil servants. It has a variety of sources: some are developed from the structures and processes of the civil service; some come from precedents and have evolved into traditions and into working philosophies of administration .... The administrative culture of the higher civil service is an integral part of the wider culture of British society. It reflects various of the qualities and values of British society or parts of it, some with accuracy, some with exaggeration. Conversely, it makes its own contribution to that wider culture. It is, however, distinctive because it is so specialised in its area of operation: it relates to a very small minority of people, an elite within the system of government, an elite also within the civil service itself (1984, pp.167-68).

Leadership takes place within this administrative culture. To some extent it also moulds it. Both Waterfield and Bridges are examples in both cases, although Bridges may be regarded as making the greater contribution. He would not, of course, accept these observations. It is clear from Chapman's study, however, that Bridges exercised leadership throughout his career, especially as Head of the Civil Service. In particular, it is clear that through his actions, attitudes and standards he was extremely important in the development of the administrative culture of the British civil service in the second half of the twentieth century.

It is inevitable that society changes, as do the values and standards which guide it. So too, then, will the administrative culture change. This, clearly, is what has happened. Despite the oft-quoted words of Sir Robin Butler, the most recent holder of the position so illustriously held by Bridges, that the civil service remains 'unified but not uniform' and that the principles which underpin its work are 'integrity, impartiality, objectivity, selection and promotion on merit and accountability through Ministers to Parliament' (quoted in Cabinet Office, 1994, para.2.7), the administrative culture is now one which encourages personal gain at the expense of public service. In some ways, of course, this is simply a reflection of changes in society. In other ways it might reflect exactly the opposite of what *The Next Steps* report calls for. To put it crudely, it may be that there has been a *lack* of leadership on the part of those who have inherited the Bridges traditions and the mantle of public service. Professor Chapman would not argue that change should be stifled and discouraged; he would rather argue that change should not be for the sake of change (1996c, pp.13-14). He would further argue that the role of leaders in the public service is to test and challenge those who wish to see change simply for its own sake.

Before concluding this review of the contribution Richard Chapman has made to the literature of public administration, something ought to be said about his methodology. Making such comments, however, is a more difficult task than it might at first appear since he himself would probably and modestly claim not to know much about such matters. Nevertheless, the record speaks for itself. As noted above, he was a pioneer of the case-study method in this country (1968) and of the use of structured questionnaires in research on the civil service (1970). Perhaps more importantly he has created what Michael Lee refers to as 'a new genre – "bureau-biography"' (1989), a genre which the distinguished American scholar John Rohr refers to as a 'fresh and most welcome approach', 'a trail that Chapman has blazed' which 'American scholars would do well to follow' (1989). The works concerned are, of course *Leadership in the British Civil Service* and, most importantly, *Ethics in the British Civil Service*. Chapman himself has made only one contribution to the *theoretical* discussion of methodology (Chapman and O'Toole, 1994), and would probably say that his methodology is quite simple – he reads files in the Public Record Office and other publicly available documentation (including private archives), he talks to relevant people in a relatively structured way (having briefed himself fully), he thinks about what he has learned, and he writes in what the armchair theorists would probably call a 'descriptive-critical' fashion. His work is primarily empirical.

One consequence of this approach is that, without exception, Professor Chapman's works are written in an elegant and readable style, devoid of the jargon and illiterate gobbledegook which mars much modern academic writing. Some quotations from reviewers illustrate the point. For example,

Lee Brown, writing in the *Municipal Review* thought *Decision Making* 'as enthralling as the most popular thriller' (1969), and *The Times* reviewer regarded it as 'an exciting reconstruction of how decisions are taken' (1969). Peter Self judged it 'an elegantly written account' (1969). Dame Enid Russell-Smith, before she became a close friend and colleague, thought *The Higher Civil Service in Britain* 'a joy to read', written in 'clear, effortless English and spiced with humour' (1970), while the anonymous reviewer of *The Press* in New Zealand described it as a 'lucid book ... astonishingly informative' (1971). D.J. Murray said the book 'prompts a wish for more ... a most readable and informative book' (1971).

The reviewers of *Leadership in the British Civil Service* were no less flattering. For example, David Ennals, a former Secretary of State for Health, noted that Chapman had 'produced a well-written and elegant book' which was 'essential reading' and in some parts 'excruciatingly funny' (1985). Lord Crowther-Hunt wrote of a 'splendid study' (1984) while Geoffrey Fry thought it 'an admirable contribution to the study of British administrative history' (1985). Paul Cousins described it as 'an important book to be referred to by all interested in administrative history' (1985).

As noted above, however, Richard Chapman's most important contribution to administrative history is *Ethics in the British Civil Service*. This received universal laudatory approval amongst reviewers, indicating both the depth of its scholarship and the simple elegance of the style of writing. R.A.W. Rhodes called it 'an enjoyable book' (1989). Kevin Theakston thought that 'Professor Chapman is to be congratulated for the impressive skill with which he has assembled his story ... [he] writes with authority and insight ... a stimulating account' (1989). Peter Hennessy judged *Ethics* 'an admirable study' 'crafted by the careful hands of Professor Richard Chapman' (1988b). Sir Douglas Wass noted that 'Chapman perceptively illuminates' by his writing skills (1989). And Colin Fuller summarised Richard Chapman's career by commenting that 'This book is typical of the high standards of scholarship which we have come to expect from [him]' (1989).

The intention of this chapter has been to indicate the areas in which Richard Chapman has made his most significant contributions to the study of public administration. At the beginning, those contributions were summarised by the three words 'reform', 'ethics' and 'leadership'. It was also indicated that it is very difficult to separate out which of Professor Chapman's works fall into what category, since there is a considerable overlap between the three areas. Perhaps, then, one word should be used to summarise his contribution. That word would probably be 'Leadership'. Richard Chapman's main scholarly interest has been to examine the role of individuals in shaping administrative reform, in contributing to the 'administrative culture' and in setting the ethical standards which have, until recently, played such a significant role in British public administration.

The rest of this book is devoted to essays specially commissioned by the Editors in honour of Richard Chapman. However, the usual pattern of *festschriften* has not been followed. Instead, the contributors were each asked to write a chapter on one of the three themes outlined here. Thus, there are three sections to the book: Reform, Ethics and Leadership. The intention is to honour a most distinguished scholar by making contributions which reflect both his academic interests and the academic excellence with which he explored those interests. Each essay is an individual contribution in its own right. Nevertheless, the book should be judged as a whole. This is not because it is intellectually coherent in the sense of itself being the work of a single author. It is rather that it takes the themes developed by one author and brings to bear the scholarship of nine other authors in the hope that more light can be cast upon them. Professor Chapman, we hope and think, would approve. It is with respect, admiration and affection that the contributors dedicate this book to him.

References to works by Richard Chapman

(1968), *Decision Making*, Routledge and Kegan Paul.

(1970), *The Higher Civil Service in Britain*, Constable.

(1982), 'Strategies for Reducing Government Activities' in G.E. Caiden and H. Siedentopf (eds), *Administrative Reform Strategies*, Massachusetts, Lexington Books.

(1983), 'The Rise and Fall of the CSD', *Policy and Politics*, Vol. 11, pp.41-61.

(1984), *Leadership in the British Civil Service*, Croom Helm.

(1987), 'Minister-Civil Servant Relations', in Richard A. Chapman and Michael Hunt (eds), *Open Government*, Croom Helm, pp.49-66.

(1988a), *Ethics in the British Civil Service*, Routledge.

(1988b), *The Art of Darkness*, University of Durham.

(1988c), '"The Next Steps": A Review', *Public Policy and Administration*, Vol. 3, No. 3, pp.3-10.

(1991), 'New arrangements for recruitment to the British Civil Service: cause for concern', *Public Policy and Administration*, Vol. 6, No. 3, pp.1-6.

(1992), 'The End of the British Civil Service?', *Teaching Public Administration*, Vol. 22, No. 1, pp.1-5.

(1993a), 'Civil Service recruitment: fairness or preferential advantage', *Public Policy and Administration*, Vol. 7, No. 2, pp.68-73.

(1993b), (ed) *Ethics in Public Service*, Edinburgh University Press.

(1993c), 'Reasons of State and the Public Interest: a British variation on the Problem of Dirty Hands' in Richard A. Chapman (ed), *Ethics in Public Service*, Edinburgh University Press, pp.93-110.

(1996a), 'Tragedy and Farce: the decision to privatise the RAS agency', *Public Policy and Administration*, Vol. 11, No. 3, pp.1-7.

(1996b), 'The End of the British Civil Service', in Peter Barberis (ed), *The Civil Service in an Era of Change*, Dartmouth, pp.23-37.

(1996c), 'From Croquet Mallets to Flamingos: perspectives on change', *Public Policy and Administration*, Vol. 11, No. 4, pp.1-17.

(1997), 'Civil Service Recruitment: the Civil Service Commissioners Annual Report 1996-7', *Public Policy and Administration*, Vol. 12, No. 3, pp.1-5.

with J.R. Greenaway (1980), *The Dynamics of Administration Reform*, Croom Helm.

with Michael Hunt (eds) (1987), *Open Government*, Croom Helm.

with Barry J. O'Toole (1994), 'The Heroic Approach in the Historiography of public administration in the United Kingdom', *Yearbook of European Administrative History*, Vol. 6, pp.65-77.

with Barry J. O'Toole (1995), 'Parliamentary Accountability', in Barry J. O'Toole and Grant Jordan (eds), *Next Steps: Improving Management in Government?*, Dartmouth, pp.118-141.

Other References

Barberis, P. (1996), *The Civil Service in an Era of Change*, Dartmouth.

Brown, Lee (1969), 'Decision Making', *Municipal Review*, May.

Cabinet Office (1994), *The Civil Service: Continuity and Change*, Cm.2627, HMSO.

Caiden, G.E. and H. Siedentopf (eds) (1982), *Administrative Reform Strategies*, California: Lexington Books.

Cousins, Paul (1985), 'Leadership in the British Civil Service', *London Review of Public Administration*.

Crowther-Hunt, Lord (1984), 'Selected for the Elite', *The Times Higher Education Supplement*, 16 November.

Efficiency Unit (1988), *Improving Management in Government: The Next Steps*, HMSO.

Ennals, Lord (1985), 'For those civil servants at the top of the tree', *Health and Social Service Journal*.

Fry, Geoffrey K. (1985), 'The ethos of British public administration', *Parliamentary Affairs*, Vol. 38, pp.119-21.

Fuller, Colin (1989), 'Ethics in the British Civil Service', *Teaching Public Administration*, Vol. VIII, pp.51-53.

Hennessy, Peter (1988a), *Whitehall*, Secker and Warburg.

Hennessy, Peter (1988b), 'Whitehall Watch: Ethics of a formidable Maiden Aunt', *The Independent*, 9 May.

Hunter, Floyd (1963), *Community Power Structure – A Study of Decision Makers*, Chapel Hill: North Carolina University Press.

Kelsall, R.K. (1955), *Higher Civil Servants in Britain*, Routledge and Kegan Paul.

Lee, J.M. (1989), 'Ethics in the British Civil Service', *Public Administration*, Vol. 67, pp.110-11.

Murray, D.J. (1971), 'The Higher Civil Service in Britain', *Journal of Administration Overseas*, pp.150-51.

O'Toole, Barry J. and Grant Jordan (eds) (1995), *The Next Steps: Improving Management in Government?*, Dartmouth.

The Press (1971), 'The Higher Civil Service in Britain', 23 March (New Zealand).

Rhodes, R.A.W. (1989), 'The Changing Civil Service', *Parliamentary Affairs*, Vol. 42, pp.271-72.

Rohr, John (1989), 'British and American Approaches to Public Sector Ethics', *Public Administration Review*, July/August, pp.387-90.

Russell-Smith, Dame Enid (1970), 'The Higher Civil Service in Britain', *The Durham University Journal*, pp.268-69.

Self, Peter (1969), 'Decision Making', *Social and Economic Administration*, Vol. 3, pp.208-9.

Seldon, Anthony (1981), *Churchill's Indian Summer: the Conservative Government 1951-1955*, Hodder and Stoughton.

Theakston, Kevin (1989), 'Ethics in the British Civil Service', *The Service Industries Journal*, Vol. 9, No. 4, pp.179-181.

The Times (1969), 'New light on Bank rate rise', 24 February.

Wass, Sir Douglas (1989), 'Ethics in the British Civil Service', *Political Studies*, Vol. XXXVII, pp.290-91.

Part One

REFORM IN PUBLIC SERVICE

2 Who Benefits from Administrative Reform?

John Greenaway

Clive Priestley declared in 1984 that the 'Civil Service is a great rock on the tide-line. The political wave, Labour or Conservative, rolls in, washes over it and ebbs. The rock is exposed to the air again usually virtually unchanged. But Mrs Thatcher has been applying sticks of dynamite to that rock' (quoted in Hennessy, 1989, p.623). A decade later it might be argued that the whole of Whitehall had suffered a demolition job at the hands of a brash firm of New Right contractors. Almost everyone agrees that since 1979 the Civil Service and Whitehall have experienced the most intense change since early this century and possibly since the time of Northcote/Trevelyan. Here consensus ends. There is little agreement among commentators about either the significance or the desirability of the 'reforms'. Some argue it marks the end of the Civil Service or the Whitehall tradition as we know it (Chapman, 1992; Chapman & O'Toole, 1995); others, from the New Right, see the reforms as halfhearted or falling short of influencing the core of the mandarin elite (Kemp, 1993). Some see the values of 'Can Do' entrepreneurialism as incompatible with the ethos of public service; while others have argued that the best of the old Whitehall virtues have been reinforced with the merits of New Public Management. In this chapter I do not wish to enter into these debates or attempt an assessment of the changes of these years. Instead I want to raise some general reflections about the implementation of recent administrative reforms in the light of historical parallels. I will argue that the pattern of administrative reform is more complex than is usually allowed, and that the whole process can only be understood by examining the forces and interests at any time who actually *benefit* in the long and complex process of implementation.

There is a natural tendency to write the history of Whitehall since 1979 primarily in terms of the assault of the Thatcherites upon existing structures, values and behaviour. There is a great deal of sense in this. For the first time since the liberal ambitions of Gladstone and his allies in the 1850s, administrative reform was intimately linked to the broader political and economic objectives of a government. The Rayner Efficiency Scrutinies and the Citizen's Charter received the closest possible encouragement and patronage from the Prime Minister of the day; the FMI and Market Testing were closely associated with the economic policies of the Conservatives. The intellectual ideas of the New Right, as exemplified in the teachings of the public choice theorists, when combined with the temperamental aversion of Mrs Thatcher and her close associates to the mandarin values and style, proved a powerful combination. Furthermore, the intellectual climate saw a paradigm shift, as the values of the New Public Management challenged the assumptions of traditional Public Administration. Reform in Whitehall, therefore, chimes in with the broader developments in such areas as the public utilities, health care and local government. The most straightforward way of interpreting administrative reform is therefore to see it in terms of the implementation of a New Right programme. Its successful implementation can then be explained by such factors as the intellectual coherence of the programme, the political determination of the government, the skill of the reformers within the administration and the favourable social and intellectual environment. This successful pattern can be contrasted with, for example, the attempted reforms of the Fulton era when such features were largely lacking.

Another perspective, however, stresses the extent to which all administrative reform has origins deep in the administrative process itself. The long gestation of all administrative reforms does not fit a simple pattern of reform being implemented. A plethora of forces work together to shape the ensuing pattern. According to this perspective, the Thatcher reforms had their origin in many of the ideas of the Fulton era. Additionally, the development of the New Right agenda should be seen in incremental terms. One reform built upon another. Moreover, at times there were important shifts of objectives. Thus the idea that ministers should take on board management responsibilities was a feature of the FMI, but was contradicted by the creation of Next Steps Agencies; similarly the autonomy of these Agencies was undermined by Market Testing. This interpretation stresses the complex bureaucratic interplays within Whitehall, the plethora of policy objectives at any one time, the ability of administrators to steer the reform process and the extent to which events, sudden crises or scandals can shape the pattern of change – for example the Civil Service strike of 1981. As Peter Barberis has pointed out, both perspectives are valuable, but neither on its own is satisfactory: a concentration on 'grand strategy' distorts a complex process, while incrementalist perspectives can be criticised for being narrow and for screening out broader ideological and political factors (Barberis, 1995).

The intensity of political interest shown in the civil service and the organisation of Whitehall by politicians in recent years is certainly not typical of

26

administrative developments in Britain. There have been long periods when changes in the civil service have proceeded away from overtly political scrutiny. Richard Chapman has shown in his detailed studies of Percival Waterfield and Edward Bridges how important developments in British administration can be fostered and developed by creative administrators themselves without much in the way of political input (Chapman, 1984, 1988). The recent change in tempo, content and context of administrative reform therefore must caution us against attempting to produce any general model of administrative reform, which, given the vastness of the subject matter and the variation of historical circumstances, must vary so much. However, it may be possible to illuminate some of the recent shifts by examining two other periods of radical change when innovation in Whitehall was related to political aspirations and ideologies. These are the Northcote/Trevelyan years and the period around the First World War.

The Northcote/Trevelyan Reforms

The Northcote/Trevelyan reforms were essentially the product of three major concerns which fused together. First Charles Trevelyan at the Treasury wished to effect economies and efficiencies in government administration: this he sought to do by introducing systematic division of labour in government offices and instituting appropriate recruitment tests of fitness. Secondly Jowett and other educational reformers saw the opportunity of using the reform of the civil service to further the interests of reforming the University of Oxford and other educational establishments. Finally, came the political anxieties and aspirations of Gladstone and his associates. The 1850s were widely perceived by contemporaries to be a time of crisis in the British state. Continental Europe had been in turmoil and Chartism had presented a revolutionary challenge in the 1840s. The Administrative Reform Association was mounting an assault upon aristocratic government of which the call for the introduction of commercial men into the civil service was one part. Meanwhile the Benthamite reformers, like Edwin Chadwick were seeking to circumvent Parliamentary ministerial government by fostering the establishment of *ad hoc* independent boards and commissions like the Public Health Board (Greenaway, 1996).

Gladstone, Trevelyan, Delane and others saw the political aspects of their reforms as crucially important. Their plan was to encourage the emergence of an intellectual super-elite of liberal minded public officials. The era of corruption and patronage would be supplanted to the simultaneous benefit of the efficient conduct of government offices and the purification of Parliament. The new Civil Service Commission, Trevelyan believed, would act as a stream to purify administration. But more than this was at stake. The abolition of patronage was the means to revitalise Parliament: Gladstone described the Northcote/Trevelyan Report as his 'contribution to the picnic of parliamentary reform'. Reform of the civil service was one means by which the politics of influence would be supplanted and a new era would dawn based upon the enlightened debate of policy issues. Nonetheless, if the reformers wanted radical change, at the same time they wished to avoid the excesses of either a democratic polity or a Benthamite state. They wanted to avoid class conflict. They wished to purify the old order of its excesses and shortcomings. Gladstone argued to Russell the Prime Minister that the reforms would tend to 'strengthen and multiply the ties between the higher classes and the possession of administrative power' (Morley, 1903, I, p.649). One aspect of this was the way in which the civil service would, in Delane's words, act as 'school' for 'such as were really anxious to study the duties of a legislator'. Former civil servants would become 'among the most useful and respected members of the House of Commons' (*The Times*, 24 February, 1854; Trevelyan, quoted in Hughes, 1949).

The complex story of the implementation of the Northcote/Trevelyan reforms need not detain us here (Wright, 1969). It is generally recognised by modern historians that the introduction of competitive examinations and the division of labour took many years to bring to fruition. What is not so commonly stressed is the degree of public and political hostility which the Report met in 1854 and which Trevelyan faced within the civil service. The reformers received enthusiastic support and lobbying from Jowett and other university leaders as well as Delane and *The Times* and the backing of John Stuart Mill. But beyond that there was little enthusiasm. The Prime Minister, Russell, was horrified at the political implications of the loss of patronage, a sentiment shared by most Cabinet ministers at this time. Equally, most Radical politicians ridiculed its accent on academic qualifications and the failure to attack 'bureaucracy'. Of the Benthamites, Chadwick attacked the idea that the examiners would give precedence to classical scholars rather than experts in public administration. Most of Trevelyan's colleagues among permanent secretaries were distinctly cool about the idea of a division of labour and of the recruitment of academic high-fliers to the civil service (Greenaway, 1992). The scandals of the Crimean War ensured some limited reform was undertaken; however, the subsequent popularity of the Northcote/Trevelyan principles needs more careful explanation than it is usually granted. Certainly, there were social, economic and ideological factors which assisted the acceptance of the principles. Among these were educational developments which ensured that the English and Scottish education levels broadly corresponded to the social strata of British society. Another was the nurturing of an ideology of a public service ethos, fostered at the universities by T.H. Green and others (O'Toole, 1990; Gowan, 1987). On the other hand, it could equally be argued that the Northcote/Trevelyan ambitions actually contradicted other developments. The recruitment of liberally-educated generalists hardly seems an appropriate response to meet the sharply increased specialisation of government work after 1870; and at the political level the rapid development of adversarial political parties undermined the rationale of young men entering the higher civil service as an apprenticeship for an independent Parliamentary career, which Trevelyan and Gladstone had set such store by.

Why then did the reforms have such a successful history? In explaining this paradox, we should look at the question 'who benefitted?' from the reform agenda. Here we find a variety of groups and interests which found the Northcote/Trevelyan agenda to their liking. Some of these were instrumental in the formative stage of the proposals. Here the most obvious group was the academics, especially the Oxford reformers, who did so much to influence Trevelyan in favour of opening up the Service for the benefit of their graduates, and who continued to influence Gladstone and Lowe during the reforms of 1870 (Wright, 1969, pp.74-85; Gowan, 1987). Secondly, the Treasury saw the opportunity to strengthen its position and become, in Trevelyan's words, something of 'a Superintending Department' over the other financial offices such as the Inland Revenue. The development of the Civil Service Commission helped give some kind of a unity to the 'public establishments', as they had been hitherto called, and made possible the conception of a single service, which redounded to the prestige of the Treasury. On the other hand, from the 1860s Trevelyan's successors showed little inclination to press ahead with any systematic division of labour or schemes to unify the civil service departments further, preferring the short-term expedients of getting work done at the cheapest possible rate through *ad hoc* arrangements (Chapman & Greenaway, 1980, pp.27-36).

During the process of implementation and development of reforms other groups came into play and here we find some surprising participants. One such group was formed of those lower down the social scale who saw the opportunity for bettering their families. Gladstone from the start was conscious that 'the middle class people and the majority of public officers look with great jealousy upon our Cambridge and Oxford men to whom they cannot attain' and it was therefore necessary to make clear that the vast majority of the 'second class examinations' would be well within the range of the 'middle class'. Trevelyan later recalled how large numbers of retired army officers and clergymen 'wrote in shoals' to their M.P.s when his scheme was in jeopardy, which accounted for the majority for the 1855 Order in Council (Playfair Commission, 1875, app. F). Another group which rapidly acquired an interest in the reforms was M.P.s themselves. Already by 1855 the demands for patronage were far outrunning the supply. The limited competition, which prevailed from 1855 to 1870, was actually very convenient for politicians because it meant they could nominate more supplicants than before for the examinations, while passing on to the Civil Service Commissioners the responsibility for those who failed or were rejected. After the extension of the franchise in 1867 to householders and rent-payers, M.P.s, and especially ministers, became even more alarmed at the implications. They would be subject to enormous electoral pressures from their lower class constituents and from organisations and associations of civil servants themselves (Shefter, 1977). This was undoubtedly a factor which made the reforms of 1870, which finally removed to the Commissioners complete responsibility for recruitment, more palatable. Moreover, after 1870, with the rise of adversarial party battles, it became convenient for politicians to insulate the top levels of central administration from party politics, while enthusiastically dispensing patronage in other areas, notably the distribution or even sale of honours.

Another force which encouraged the Northcote/Trevelyan ideas was that of the civil service associations among the middling and junior ranks. These grew in strength after 1870 and had every interest in securing uniform conditions and grades of service. As they were an electoral force to be reckoned with, they enjoyed the support of a large body of backbench M.P.s who were prepared to back their claims. They played an important part in preventing departmentalism or wildly idiosyncratic methods of administration.

Whitehall in Ferment 1906-1926

The ideological imperatives of reform at this time were much less clearly focused than in the 1850s and the 1980s; but Whitehall was nonetheless in a state of confusion and fluidity during these years and there was a lively debate about the nature of the British state. The background here was the ideological challenge to the liberal parliamentary establishment by the idea of 'national efficiency' in Edwardian Britain. This had its roots in the period of the Boer War: the perceived failings of the British army's high command; revelations about the poor social conditions of the urban working classes; and anxieties concerning the supposed physical decline of the race. National efficiency ideas called for technocratic and militaristic organisation of both the state and of administration. The core idea was that, along the lines of the pre-war German General Staff, policy-formulation and long term planning could be separated from routine administration. As Geoffrey Searle has pointed out, national efficiency was a 'cohering ideology' which had a broad appeal (Searle, 1990, p.xx). Campaigns for reform took various forms, ranging from Lord Milner's ideas for streamlining central administration to the more populist and strident demands of those who wanted to replace the existing civil service elite with businessmen. The ideas also appealed to many on the left including the Fabians such as the Webbs and Haldane and all who saw themselves as heirs of the Benthamite/Chadwick tradition of professional administration by experts. National efficiency, partly because of the breadth of its appeal was somewhat incoherent, in contrast to the liberalism of Gladstone's day or the New Right of the 1980s. But it did present a challenge to conventional parliamentary politics and to the position of the academically-recruited liberal civil service elite.

Alongside this ideological attack upon Whitehall came several political pressures which pointed to radical changes. The great expansion in government, beginning with the social reforms of the Liberals after 1906, required creative thinking and new initiatives. The establishment of labour exchanges and insurance schemes led to such things as the direct recruitment of outsiders and interdepartmental transfers. During the First World War, under the Lloyd George regime, a chaotic proliferation of independent boards and agencies mushroomed as the state was faced with the unprecedented demands of intervening and controlling in vast areas of economic and social life, ranging from control of alcohol, to food production, to regulating shipping. All these pressures required *ad hoc* solutions and the recruitment of specialist outsiders. The pressures of war required new forms of co-ordination within central government.

Another force at this time consisted of increasingly well-organised and assertive Trade unions. The MacDonnell Royal Commission had been appointed in 1911 largely to take the wind out of the sails of the agitation from the clerical associations. Almost 400 M.P.s had supported their demands for a wholesale inquiry into the anomalies of grading. The various civil service associations called for some sort of parliamentary oversight or independent commission to control the civil service, independent of the Treasury. These demands grew during the War (Parris, 1973).

The period of the First World War and immediately after was therefore one of great fluidity. There were rapid developments in central administration, particularly at the level of the Cabinet. It was not clear whether a personalised prime ministerial network of offices would develop along presidential lines. Nor was it obvious that Whitehall would evolve into a unified entity rather than fragment into a series of more specialist agencies and departments. Although the pressures during the height of the war had been for *ad hoc* expansion, after 1918 there was a backlash and strident press campaigns were mounted against 'squandermania' in government offices. The Geddes axe was wielded within government; meanwhile from the outside various temporary war-time civil servants launched attacks on the lack of business expertise in Whitehall.

Between 1918 and 1930 very important developments took place in Whitehall and British central government. It is striking that radical ideas of Milnerite national efficiency were adapted and used to benefit some of the traditional patterns. The change was essentially evolutionary rather than revolutionary. Key figures here were Warren Fisher at the Treasury and Maurice Hankey at the Cabinet Office. Although the logic of national efficiency seemed to suggest specialist expertise and possible fragmentation, a concatenation of circumstances in 1918-19 helped consolidate civil service structure. Between 1916 and 1918 a series of internal committees pointed to the need for more unity of the civil service and the strengthening of Treasury control. Hence there was an unusual community of interest between those interested in improving the civil service and those wanting to cut the costs of government (O'Halpin, 1989, p.25). A reorganisation of the Treasury took place along functional lines with a strong Establishments division.

After 1919 Fisher and other associates in the Treasury were able to build upon the reorganisation of 1919 to pursue the following objectives: (1) establishing the principle that the permanent secretary of every department was responsible for public expenditure; (2) strengthening the connections between Treasury and spending departments, especially by recruiting Treasury civil servants from other departments; (3) transforming the previously departmentalised structures of Whitehall by encouraging interde-partmental transfers; (4) bringing about a comprehensive reorganisation of grading in the civil service as a whole; (5) developing the Whitley councils as a means of settling industrial disputes 'within the family' (O'Halpin, 1989; Greenaway, 1983). At the same time the Cabinet Office survived moves, in the reaction against Lloyd George, to abolish it. Under Hankey its position became regularised as, along with the Treasury, the co-ordinating force in British government. A well-structured pattern of committees emerged and it became accepted that career civil servants, rather than personal party political or outside appointees, were to have the major say in servicing the Prime Minister and Cabinet. It is interesting to note that Lord Milner played a role in the 1919 reorganisation and that Milnerite ideas had been to the fore in the creation of the War Cabinet and of such bodies as the Committee for Imperial Defence. Both Fisher and Hankey, moreover, held Lord Haldane's ideas in high esteem; and the Haldane Report on the Machinery of Government, even though its precise recommendations were not followed, encouraged the idea that the machinery of government should be viewed as an entity.

The above thumbnail sketch obviously gives a truncated account of a complex process. What is interesting, however, is the dynamic nature of the reform pattern and the way in which creative administrators were able to mould the inputs, both political and bureaucratic, into ways which suited their interest. Who benefitted from the reshaping of Whitehall during these years? The first beneficiary was the Treasury itself. Fisher saw this as the 'general staff' of the service. During the inter-war period it became a truly supervisory department for the whole of Whitehall. A second group was, ironically, the liberally-educated mandarin elite which had been the main target for attacks by national efficiency propagandists in the pre-1914 years who had urged the application of militaristic discipline and scientific methods to administration. Fisher argued that the civil service was, after the armed services, the fourth service of the Crown and did all he could to develop its *esprit de corps*. But the service he and his associates cultivated was a non-specialist one dominated by an officer caste of generalist all-rounders, who learnt their craft on the job, and whose plaudits were so fulsomely sung by Edward Bridges, a generation later. Fisher and his successors had little time for the professional study of public administration or outside expertise on the subject. Whitehall was to become remarkably insulated from other areas of public administration such as local government during this period.

Moreover, the culture of seclusion and secrecy, which was undoubtedly encouraged by the developments in Whitehall, was one which was beneficial to both civil servants and their political masters. The depoliticisation (in party terms) of the Cabinet secretariat and the highest levels of ministerial advice was mutually convenient for the dominant politicians of the 1920s: Baldwin and Ramsay Macdonald and their followers. These both had an interest in seeing the back of the supra-party Lloyd George who had showed every inclination to develop a highly personalised regime at the centre of government. Equally suspect were other political loose cannons of the period such as F.E.Smith and Churchill. Finally the trade union leaders themselves benefitted from the process. Although originally they had seen the Whitley procedures as a means of shortcircuiting narrow Treasury control, they (as well as Treasury officials) came to see the advantages of a formal negotiating procedure away from the vagaries of the political climate, which was so often dictated by financial crises and short-term expediency. The process legitimated the associations, turning them in the words of one leader 'from somewhat vituperative and protesting bodies into committees of negotiation and experiment.' Agreements could be made to stick which was not always the case in previous periods (Chapman & Greenaway, 1980, pp.97-98).

What broad conclusions may be drawn from these historical episodes? In the first place the context of reform is crucially important. The development of the nineteenth century career civil service, non-political in character and recruited by examinations, was only made possible by the developments in education and in social classes. Similarly, the growth of the interventionist state, the rise of trade unions and the development of professional codes of conduct and organisation was the background against which Fisher and others could develop the cohesion and unity of modern Whitehall. Secondly, although it was political factors and aspirations which played a crucial role in motivating leading reformers at these two critical periods, the inputs into the reform process were both complex and varied. In both periods a variety of pressures and problems presented themselves. Thirdly, and crucially, the implementation of reforms was a lengthy and complex affair with all sorts of factors coming into play, including the impetus of events. But a crucial component in explaining the course of reform was the issue of who benefitted? Sometimes those who benefitted from radical changes had been pressing for them from the outset; but equally other groups and interests began to spin them along in their own direction and for their own interests.

The New Right Reforms and Who Benefits?

This perspective can shed light on the rapid changes of recent years. As in the 1850s and the pre-1914 periods, the context of the reforms was a profound anxiety about a perceived crisis in the British state. The doom-laden prophesies of overload, ungovernability and fiscal crisis of the welfare state provided the context against which reform of Whitehall came to be seen (as in the earlier periods) as far more than a mere detail of civil service organisation but rather as part of the reconstruction of the British state. However, as in the previous periods, the ideology which underpinned reform was not totally coherent. The New Right itself constituted various elements. Even within the narrow ambit of New Public Management can be found a variety of values and principles which are not always in harmony: e.g. market forces, efficiency, devolution of management responsibility and consumer accountability (Hood, 1991).

As we saw when discussing the incrementalist interpretation of the reforms, the whole process of the changes from Rayner onwards also owed much to forces and interests from within the bureaucracy. Partly these stemmed from the working through of some of the Fulton era's ideas of accountable management and managerial training. They were also linked to problems posed by social and economic changes. Amongst these we can find: changes in the labour market which encouraged more part-time working and flexible career patterns; the rapid development of information technology which was having profound implications for conventional models of office management and accountability; changes in economic activity (such as the rise of service industries and so-called 'post-Fordist' production) which erode the distinctions between the public and the private sectors; the decline of trade unions and the rise of a socially more heterogenous population requiring more flexible patterns of public service. More specific problems related to the Treasury's difficulties with control of public expenditure and the PESC process.

The detailed story of Whitehall reforms from the Rayner scrutinies in the early 1980s to Next Steps and Market Testing in the mid-1990s need not detain us here. Instead it is important to analyse the beneficiaries of the radical changes which have resulted. As in the case of Northcote/Trevelyan there are some obvious candidates and others which may be more surprising. The first category comprises the large numbers of advisers, consultants lawyers and marketing individuals. Very large sums of money have been made in advising successive New Right administrations in their restructuring of the state. This has, of course, been most evident in the privatisation process, culminating in the railway sell-off which has been a lawyers' and consultants' paradise. This phenomenon affected the civil service directly at a relatively late stage in the process of reform. The top management programme of the mid-1980s was an early indication. By the early 1990s the proliferation of semi-autonomous agencies and the hiving off of functions of government to contracted bodies had provided rich pickings for consultants of one kind or another. It would be interesting to know how much has been spent on the production of logos in those areas which were once part of the civil service. Private firms, purporting to specialise in management training, have an enormous market in servicing the plethora of government agencies. Very large sums of money, for example, are being made by a new breed of firms organising conferences and courses for civil servants. Elizabeth Symons, when General Secretary of the FDA, pointed out that many conferences were organised by firms in which government departments were being asked to pay £800 or £900 per head to send their civil servants to events to be lectured by other public servants (*FDA News,* May 1996, p.6).

A second group to benefit from the reforms of the 1980s has been M.P.s. It is fair to say that for the long period from the 1920s to the 1980s M.P.s were largely excluded from civil service questions, with the exception of the influential Select Committee on Public Expenditure of 1942. The two Royal Commissions and the Fulton Report were almost deliberately engineered to take discussion away from the parliamentary level. However, the Rayner efficiency drives struck a rich seam of parliamentary interest. The elimination of waste and improving accountability in government was after all one of the classic functions of the House of Commons and the new initiatives offered scope for some active participation in this area. The emphasis on outside accountability and monitoring of service delivery was one which was tailor-made to suit the enthusiasms of the relatively small number of frustrated backbenchers who had an interest in administration and government. The last fifteen years have seen a whole spate of parliamentary enquiries into civil service matters with an interesting element of bipartisanship up until the issues of Market Testing and the Citizen's Charter. There is, however, a much less savoury aspect of M.P.s' interests being served. The shift away from hierarchically-organised civil service departments towards a plethora of agencies and appointed bodies, along with the erosion of corporatist-style links between pressure groups and civil servants, has encouraged the rapid growth of lobbying firms. As more patronage returns to ministers, so the role of the individual M.P. as a facilitator has grown, often with large pecuniary benefits. Political parties also stand to gain from the process. The growth in public relations and advertising in the new era of media-based electioneering has made politics more expensive at the very moment when grass roots activities in political parties is on the decline. Political leaders are therefore forced back on dealing out patronage by using the new powers of appointment (Foster & Plowden, 1996, pp.39-40).

The New Right programme has also served to further the interests of ministers themselves. On the broader front of privatisation ministers have been able, with some success, to discard responsibilities to independent operators. Thus it is individual water companies or train operators which can be held up as failing the public when things go wrong, rather than the government of the day. This arms-length relationship has been much easier to sustain than in the days of the nationalised industries and has shifted attention away from issues such as the resources provided for the provision of services. Similarly, the creation of the Next Steps Agencies and other moves towards decentralised management have also helped muddy the waters as far as the vexed question of ministerial responsibility is concerned. The dispute between Michael Howard and Derek Lewis is the most obvious example; but the difficulty of drawing a firm distinction between policy and administration, when the theory of Agencies is based upon such a distinction, enables politicians to gain the credit for successes while avoiding the blame for policy failures. All this has become more convenient at a time when party discipline has become more rigid in the House of Commons so that all issues of accountability have come to be seen through the spectacles of party conflict, as the fate of the Scott Report testifies. All these developments are likely to be welcomed by ministers of any party and possess a dynamic beyond the New Right agenda. Given the enormous discretionary powers which ministers enjoy, the weakening of both the structures and cultures of the old Whitehall model of a unified civil service may encourage the use of power in an arbitrary way: the problem here is that most ministers are more interested in short term advantage than strategic considerations of a long-term nature.

Another beneficiary of the Thatcher/Major years has been some departmental forces within Whitehall. Bureaucratic battles and clashes of interest are always important in Whitehall, and control and direction of civil service matters had long been an issue under dispute. For the Treasury, furthermore, the whole issue was related to the restoration of controls over public expenditure. The disbandment of the Civil Service Department in 1981 and subsequent reorganisations meant the restoration to the Treasury fold of management sections which had been lost in the post-Fulton era. However, the changes in the 1990s were to have even more profound implications. Initially the Treasury had been at least sceptical, if not hostile, to the idea of the creation of Next Steps Agencies, since the decentralisation of central government administration seemed to spell loss of control and accountability (Hennessy, 1989, pp.618-21). With the introduction of Market Testing, however, the devolution of responsibilities came to be seen as a positive advantage. The old pattern allowed hierarchically-organised conventional departments an opportunity to control within measure the flow of information and to protect, where necessary, vital interests and programmes. The Market Testing mechanisms, however, have allowed the Treasury to dig deep down into the grass roots of the Agencies. At the same time the review of the Treasury in 1994 envisaged strengthening the strategic and agenda-setting role of the Department. The other beneficiary of the post-CSD Whitehall has been the Cabinet Office. A feature of changes at the 'Centre' has been the increasing significance of the Cabinet Office as a focus of coordination in government. This has much to do with other factors notably the development of the European Union and the increasing need to coordinate work for the Council of Ministers; but the New Right reforms have encouraged the transformation of the Cabinet Office from the small post-War unit which serviced the Cabinet to something much more approaching an office superintending the reform of the British state. Thus within the Cabinet Office are to be found different sections superintending the various programmes such as Market Testing, the Citizen's Charter and the Next Steps programme.

New Right political theory is sharply critical of the conventional values of bureaucracy and public administration. One might therefore expect the reforming impetus to be circumvented or even obstructed by Whitehall mandarins. However, it would be wrong to see the reforms as always inherently inimical to the interests of this group. It is only possible here to touch generally upon this aspect, but there are several ways in which this is true. Let us take, for example, the employment of outside management consultants from the private sector. Superficially this could be seen as a challenge to Whitehall. In fact it has had various positive advantages in different areas of Whitehall. For ministers, this device had many political objectives: sometimes to help shift a policy direction by providing alternative advice, at other times to divert pressure for action, at others to legitimate a desired action. For senior civil servants, too, there were advantages. Consultants themselves, being in a competitive market, had to tailor their advice to keep in with their 'clients' and presented no permanent institutional threat to the department. Moreover, the use of consultants can strengthen a central department's policy prescriptions against the influence of internal interests lower down in the administration, which can often have a stultifying effect upon initiatives (Henkel, 1991, pp.128-29)

Another area is the transfer of risk to the private sector. This has been particularly marked in such issues as the development of computerised systems and other similar high-tech ventures. Civil servants at the centre in Whitehall departments are not skilled in these sorts of areas and it is every bit more satisfactory to farm out the process with its potential risks, as well as rewards, to independent contractors. Risks of policy failure, too, can be jettisoned since in many areas of service delivery the risk of going over budget is now passed over to agencies or contracted operators. This has been marked in an area like railway policy where the Department of Transport can lay down the details of investment judged necessary through contracts with train operating companies, and effectively wash its hands of responsibility for going over budget. But similar patterns are developing in the relationships of core Whitehall departments and the agencies which deliver benefits and other services to the citizen. There are in fact a whole series of advantages to the senior civil servant in the pattern of recent years. The troublesome aspects of controlling militant trade unionists and conflict-ridden field services is shifted into the hands of the private sector. Political attention of M.P.s and pressure groups is diverted away from the core of Whitehall to the new agencies and those contracted bodies who are delivering services at the sharp end. The central administration is able to specialise on the production of contracts while retaining strategic control. As Dunleavy has pointed out, the losers will be the lower paid, less skilled civil servants at the clerical level along with the consumers of services, whereas the interests of senior officials will be largely unaffected (Dunleavy, 1986). Indeed, the current fluidity of career patterns, with interchange with the business world, stands materially to enhance the status and salaries of top officials. A loss of job security may be a price worth paying for enhanced career prospects in the private sector on early retirement.

In the past, New Right public choice theorists made much of the skill and vested interest of bureaucrats in maximising their budgets to the detriment of the public interest. Since the 1970s, however, the political climate has been one of cut-backs in government expenditure and we have seen everywhere an emphasis on finite resources. Civil servants have adapted to the new policy paradigm. Growth no longer comes solely from the bargaining process with the Treasury, but rather from the pursuit of efficiencies through such devices as contracts and Market Testing. The delicate processes within the Whitehall village which Heclo and Wildavsky wrote about so eloquently a generation ago are effectively no more. There is a combination of interests here with Treasury and the managerially-minded ACEs who are concerned to use the new flexibilities to cut down costs and meet performance indicators. The new recruitment and work patterns, alongside developments in IT have made possible the casualisation of much work, increasing deployment of part time employees, the shifting of work to provincial centres and the search for the lowest rates of pay possible. The whole process, in short, can hardly be seen as impinging on the autonomy or initiative of the central policy-making core, rather the reverse.

Conclusion

Major administrative reform should not be seen as stemming from a simple manifesto programme. Equally, it is wrong to screen out the ideological and political forces and regard, as some writers have done, the British pattern of administrative reform as essentially pragmatic with no ideological motive (e.g. Caiden, 1969, p.95). In each of the three periods examined here the process of reform has gained momentum and has fitted the requirements of social and political change. The process is a dynamic one as certain devices or processes which work are developed while others are discarded. Critically important in shaping the pattern is the cluster of interests which benefit. Certainly in the last two decades the pace and scope of change in Whitehall has been phenomenal. In contrast with the past periods the discontinuities with the past are now marked. Changes have taken place simultaneously in institutions, personnel and values. Many interests stand to benefit, but there are losers as well. Among these may rank the public interest, as standards of probity in politics and administration no longer enjoy the protection of an administrative tradition which has been undermined.

References

Barberis, P. (1995), 'The Civil Service from Fulton to Next Steps and Beyond – Two Interpretations, Two Epistemologies', *Public Policy and Administration*, Vol. 10, No. 2, pp.34-51.

Caiden, G.E. (1969), *Administrative Reform*, Chicago: Aldine.

Chapman, Richard A. (1984), *Leadership in the British Civil Service*, Croom Helm.

Chapman, Richard A. (1988), *Ethics in the British Civil Service*, Routledge.

Chapman, Richard A. (1992), 'The End of the Civil Service?', *Teaching Public Administration*, Vol. 12, No. 2, pp.1-5.

Chapman, Richard A. and Greenaway, J.R. (1980), *The Dynamics of Administrative Reform*, Croom Helm.

Chapman, Richard A. and Barry J. O'Toole (1995), 'The Role of the Civil Service: A Traditional View in a Period of Change', *Public Policy and Administration*, Vol. 10, No. 2, pp.3-20.

Dunleavy, P. (1986), 'Explaining the Privatization Boom: Public Choice Versus Radical Approaches', *Public Administration*, Vol. 64, No. 1, pp.13-34.

Foster, C.D. and F.J. Plowden (1996), *The State under Stress: Can the Hollow State be Good Government?* Open University Press.

Gowan, P. (1987), 'The Origins of the Administrative Elite', *New Left Review*, No. 162, pp.4-34.

Greenaway, J.R. (1983), 'Warren Fisher and the Transformation of the British Treasury, 1919-1939', *The Journal of British Studies*, Vol. 23, No. 1, pp.125-42.

Greenaway, J.R. (1992), 'British Conservatism and Bureaucracy', *History of Political Thought*, Vol. 13, No. 1, pp.129-60.

Greenaway, J.R. (1996), 'Politicians, Civil Servants and the Liberal State in Britain', *Jahrbuch für Europäische Verwaltungsgeschichte*, Vol. 8, pp.213-31.

Henkel, M. (1991), 'The New "Evaluative State"', *Public Administration*, Vol. 69, No. 1, pp.121-136.

Hennessy, P. (1989), *Whitehall*, Secker and Warburg.

Hood, C. (1991), 'A Public Management for all Seasons?', *Public Administration*, Vol. 69, No. 1, pp.3-19.

Hughes, E. (1949), 'Sir Charles Trevelyan and Civil Service Reform, 1853-55', *English Historical Review*, Vol. 64, Nos. 250-51, pp.53-88, 206-34.

Kemp, Sir Peter (1994), 'The Civil Service White Paper: A Job Half Finished', *Public Administration*, Vol. 72, No. 4, pp.591-98.

O'Halpin, E. (1989), *Head of the Civil Service: A Study of Sir Warren Fisher*, Routledge.

O'Toole, Barry J. (1990), 'T.H.Green and the Ethics of Senior Officials in British Central Government', *Public Administration*, Vol. 68, No. 3, pp.337-53.

Morley, J. (1903), *The Life of William Ewart Gladstone*, 3 Volumes, Macmillan.

Parris, H. (1973), *Staff Relations in the Civil Service: Fifty Years of Whitleyism*, Allen and Unwin.

Playfair Commission (1875), *Reports of the Civil Service Inquiry Commission*, P.P., 1875, [C.1113].

Searle, G.R. (1971, 1990 edition), *The Quest for National Efficiency: A Study in British Politics and Political Thought, 1899-1914*, Ashfield Press.

Shefter, M. (1977), 'Party and Patronage: Germany, England and Italy', *Politics and Society*, Vol. 7, No. 4, pp.403-51.

Wright, M. (1969), *Treasury Control of the Civil Service*, Oxford University Press.

3 Citizenship and Freedom of Information

Michael Hunt

The numerous attempts to encourage a more open style of government in Britain have been spread over a substantial period of time, and the achievements to date seem to have been gained against determined opposition that has only grudgingly given ground on what, in other western countries, would seem to be a fundamental feature of democracy. It is eleven years since, in the introduction to his book on open government, Richard Chapman quoted the 1946 UN Resolution that 'Freedom of Information is a fundamental human right and is the touchstone for all the freedoms to which the United Nations is consecrated' as part of the background to a discussion of the practical problems of introducing open government in Britain (Chapman, 1987, p.12). Although some progress has been made since then, particularly in the proposals of the 1994 Code of Practice on Access to Government Information and in the greater access by individuals to files about themselves kept by various (but not all) state organisations, successive administrations have remained reluctant to recognise the fundamental importance of access to information both as part of the mechanism for holding the government to account and as a way of encouraging citizens to play their full part in the functioning of the state. The Labour Government's proposals of December 1997, although promising, have yet to be tested in practice.

Comparisons with other countries inevitably seem invidious because of their different structures and political cultures. Nevertheless, three examples might be selected in order to provide some understanding of the reasons why FOI legislation has been introduced elsewhere and the effect this has had on relationships between citizens and the government. In Sweden, the right of access to information has been enshrined in Freedom of the Press Acts since 1776 and originated in the wish by Parliament and its committees to see documents produced by administrative agencies; wider citizen rights of access have developed from this (Elder, 1973, p.25). In other words, the separation of powers in the state was a powerful reason for establishing some form of access to information. In America, the granting of access to Federal documents came much later (1967) and followed the example of a number of States who had begun to introduce legislation from the early 1950s (Rowat, 1979. p.310). But the real issue was, again, the separation of powers which meant that the legislature had to be informed about the activities of government if it was to do its job at all. Furthermore as Robertson (1982, p.92) notes 'the dominant ethos is one, and was one, of suspicion of government'. This resulted in 'the placement of the individual, his liberty and his rationality, at the centre of the political process'. In Australia, it is acknowledged that 'Information is an essential feature of democratic government. Without adequate information, choices cannot be made and government cannot be properly scrutinised and held accountable' (Western Australian Commission on Government, 1995, p.40). As further justification, the Commission notes that government information should be available to the people because, ultimately, 'it belongs to the people'. All three countries therefore acknowledge the fundamental right of citizens to hold the state to account and the importance of access to information to enable them to do this.

A number of reasons may be suggested for the (comparative) failure of British attempts to secure access to information. It is often claimed that a fundamental problem is the absence of a written constitution establishing the individual rights of citizens; and it is certainly true that the three countries mentioned above enjoy both the benefits that a written constitution can offer as well as legislation allowing a right of access to information held by the government. As the Labour Party's Green Paper of 1979 noted in relation to the USA, 'the introduction of a statutory right of access to official documents derived from basic constitutional principles as well as contemporary political sentiment' (Lord Privy Seal, 1979, p.10). However, the Green Paper does not make clear which of these two factors was the more important, and the sceptic might wonder at the value of 'basic constitutional principles' which took nearly two hundred years to be enshrined in legislation on freedom of information.

The absence of a written constitution in Britain does not prevent legislation for access to information any more than it has made it inevitable in the countries cited above. However, the lack of such a constitution, and the associated lack of agreement about the basic components of citizenship in contemporary British society, coupled with the ambiguity of the relationship between the citizen and the Crown (even the Crown mediated through the government of the day), means that demands for greater access to information have to be expressed through concepts such as 'accountability' and 'democracy' rather than by reference to fundamental rights. In practice, these two concepts are so elastic that they can be reformulated by any government that wishes to demonstrate that the essential requirements of accountability and democracy are being met. Governments are invariably able to cite traditions, precedents and conventions in support of their particular interpretation of these terms and such interpretations are unlikely to indicate a need to define the requirements of citizenship in order to protect the interests of the citizen against the actions of the state. Stewart, for example, has suggested that 'some of the (recent) changes introduced were probably intended more to secure central policy aims than to introduce new forms of accountability as such' (Stewart, 1984, p.23).

In Britain, notions of citizenship exist alongside notions of being a 'subject' of the monarch and, traditionally, have only had significance to the extent that they represent the people's right to be independent of the wishes of the Crown. They are thus intimately linked to the struggle between the Crown and its subjects which is associated with the development of parliamentary government. This struggle was not, initially, concerned with notions of citizenship. Ronald Butt notes that 'Parliament arose from the *need* (emphasis added) of early English rulers to consult with their more influential subjects' (1969, p.31), thus drawing attention to the fundamental significance of power in the relationship between the government and the people that they rule. He goes on to make clear that this is not a static relationship but (in the long term) one that is continuously changing. Although he also argues that consultation, as a long established feature of early medieval life, formed a tradition that was built on as Parliament developed; he also makes clear that this consultation was only with the barons and did not represent the fundamental civic rights of the ordinary people. Thus, although a gradual ceding of power continued through the industrial revolution and the passage of the Reform Acts of the nineteenth century, at no time was there any suggestion that Parliament, as an institution, should relate its powers to any conception of citizenship. Parliament, indeed, has been more concerned with protecting its own rights than those of the individual citizen. Such a focus has led to a linkage between Parliament and democracy which frequently confuses Parliamentary rights with democratic (citizen) rights to the benefit of neither.

Whilst Parliament may have been successful in establishing its rights against the Crown, it has been less effective in its battles with the political executive, not least in its attempts to gain access to information held by the government. A second fundamental problem, therefore, is the dominant political culture that recognises Parliament as being supreme but does not fully recognise the limitations of Parliament in terms of its ability to hold the executive to account or its ability to represent the views of the people. As Miliband points out, Parliament acts as a buffer between the government and the people (Miliband, 1982, p.38). The people's rights to knowledge about the activities of government are upheld through the doctrine of ministerial accountability and through various Parliamentary devices (Question Time and the Select Committee system, for example) which provide the public with the opportunity to obtain information from the government via their M.P.s. The fact that these mechanisms are currently deficient in many respects is glossed over both by many of those who should know better and also by those who have a vested interest in the *status quo*. Whilst Parliamentary reform may, therefore, seem desirable, some informed critics have argued that it is unlikely to enhance the power of the individual citizen against the state unless accompanied by more fundamental reform of the electoral system which will reduce the likelihood of any one party having an overall majority (see, for example, Walkland, 1976). Whatever the desirability of such a change, it seems reasonable to argue that it should be made in the context of a wider understanding of the rights and the duties of citizenship.

A further problem is that, although the terms 'citizen' and 'citizenship' are in common use in Britain, there is no common agreement about what they mean in practice, or how they might be used as a reference point for the effective operation of democracy. By and large they are used synonymously with 'elector' or 'member of the public'. In so doing, the rights and duties that might be associated with 'citizenship' are ignored. The Citizen's Charter provides a relevant illustration of the sorts of issue raised here. A number of commentators have noted that its proposals are directed more at the consumer than the citizen, and the nature of the 'charter' between the supplier of goods and the (citizen) is determined strictly by the supplier (see, for example, Elcock, 1996). There has been little public participation in the construction of individual charters and, in spite of the rhetoric of the original charter proposals, little expectation that there should be. This is more than a reflection of the ideology of the government of the day (it is reasonable to assume that Mr Major hoped there would be some benefits for the public in his proposals, not to mention some political capital). The proposals reflect British assumptions about the term 'citizenship', not only in the sense of regarding it as a self-evident concept which does not need to be defined with any precision but also in the related perception that any 'rights' associated with the concept are not fundamental rights but simply additions that might offer some benefits in some circumstances. The failure to link these rights to other rights decreases the chances of them being taken seriously by either service providers or their customers

The 'rights' offered by the Citizen's Charter White Paper in relation to openness provide a good example of the inherent weakness of its proposals. They amount to little more than the cosmetic requirement that officials should wear name badges and that the performance of organisations, judged by carefully chosen indicators, should be made available to the public. These may be helpful to individual customers but, since many of the services provided are monopolies in all but name, customers are rarely able to take effective action in response to the information provided. There is, therefore, little expectation that the accountability of managers of services will be significantly enhanced by the Charter. Stewart has noted that 'the relationship of accountability can be analysed as a bond linking the one who accounts to the one who holds to account'. Further, 'for accountability to be clear and enforceable the bond must be clear. The relationship expressed in the bond is a relationship of power...'. (Stewart, 1984, p.16). But the Citizen's Charter proposals give only limited power to the consumer and none to the citizen. Redress for an error results in compensation rather than the acknowledgement of any fundamental fault, still less a recognition that the citizen might reasonably expect a change in processes to prevent the error happening again.

The lack of any serious consideration of fundamental citizen rights is a serious matter. The redress available under the Citizen's Charter is little more than the redress one might expect from any commercial organisation; repayment, under some circumstances, of the costs of a service that was not delivered. There is no recognition of the need to review those systems or processes that have caused the problem – reflecting the Thatcherite (and evidently incorrect) assumption that a dissatisfied customer always has the right to take his custom elsewhere. The tone of the available redress is similar to the tone that informs the workings of the Parliamentary Commissioner for Administration. Whatever the (undoubted) diligence of the individuals who have filled this post in representing the interests of individual citizens, and whatever their successes, it is a feature of their work that they are unable to do anything other than represent the interests of individual citizens, and are unable either to ensure redress for a wrong, or require that processes leading to this wrong are examined, or take action on their own initiative without a referral from an individual member of the public. They are thus unable to represent the collective rights of citizens as opposed to individual consumers. They are, therefore, vastly more constrained in their activities than the Scandinavian officials with whose name and functions they are frequently and casually linked. The reasons for this are not hard to find. It is evident from the report by *Justice* in 1961, and from the Parliamentary debate of 1967 which established the PCA, that MPs did not want to appoint an official who, in some way, would detract from their own traditional function of seeking redress for the grievances of their constituents. However, by imposing such constraints on this office they inevitably ensured that it would be no more capable than Parliament of ensuring redress, when Parliament itself is subject to limitations in ensuring the accountability of public servants.

It is perhaps no surprise that the general reaction to the Citizen's Charter proposals seems to be one of benign acceptance of an interesting but limited idea rather than any feeling of empowerment. If British governments are serious about citizenship – as they should be – then there is an overwhelming requirement that they make citizenship worthwhile. This means that there must be some tangible reward for the effort involved in the exercise of citizenship and, for many people, this must be a reward that does not require Herculean efforts for its achievement. In the case of the Citizen's Charter, the failure to recognise the essential requirements of citizenship means that, yet again, a real opportunity to enhance the rights of ordinary citizens has been missed.

The same vague language about citizenship was used in the Conservative Government's 1993 White Paper on Open Government. The White Paper, which set out the initial proposals for a Code of Practice, stated quite clearly that 'Citizens must have access to the information and analysis on which government information is based' (Cabinet Office, 1993, p.1). But no attempt was made to indicate what the rights of citizens might be and it is clear that the word was used simply as a synonym for other words, such as 'elector'. A concern for the way in which language is used may seem pedantic to many people; indeed, many will simply be grateful that the government had, at last, recognised the need for (some degree of) openness. However, language is important, and the absence of any understanding of what it means to be a citizen not only leaves the government free to choose the level of openness that it is prepared to concede, but also provides it with a continuing opportunity to imply that it has complied with (universal) understandings of political rights that are freely available in other advanced democracies. Even worse, it may encourage feelings of cynicism amongst those who feel that their legitimate expectations have not been fulfilled.

Citizenship

Plant (1990) suggests that the reason why 'citizenship' has become an issue of concern for many people in Britain is, in part, a reaction to the dominant market approaches of the 1980s. Contrary to the expectations of some advocates, such approaches have not led to the empowerment of ordinary citizens, either by delivering promised freedoms of choice over goods and services (and the associated improvements in service delivery) or by increasing the opportunities to participate in policy making. Indeed, the declining economic and political status of many people has reduced their freedoms in this regard. Held finds that interest has also been stimulated by demands for regional autonomy in Britain and also by the development of the European Community. In both of these examples, the need for an explicit statement of rights based on citizenship reflects the need to protect individuals from the arbitrary use of state power (Held, 1991, p.19). To some extent this is reinforced by those who have argued the case for a written constitution in this country and the replacement of many (unsatisfactory) constitutional conventions by a formal and agreed system of 'higher' laws (see, for example, IPPR, 1993). Other writers have focused on the need to protect the rights and dignity of those who risk being marginalised by dominant interests in society. Dummett and Nicol (1990), for example, refer particularly to those from ethnic minorities but the arguments can be equally well related to those who are unemployed. In both cases the expression of rights associated with citizenship may be a way of ensuring that minorities do not suffer from social, economic or political arrangements that are designed (implicitly or explicitly) to protect the interests of the majority. Both of these reasons may also be linked to the demands for 'public participation' in policy making that were particularly evident in the 1960s and 1970s and which, in different guises, have re-emerged in the 1990s.

Definitions of 'citizenship' abound: Barbalet (1988, p.2) suggests that citizenship can 'readily be described as participation in, or membership of, a community'; Wright develops this by suggesting that 'citizenship ... is a matter of defining in a more general way what membership of a political community entails in terms of both state and civil society' (Wright, 1994, p.129). Marshall's familiar differentiation suggests that the term comprises three aspects:

1. the civil rights that are necessary for individual freedom.
2. political rights: that is, the right to participate in the exercise of political power either as a member of a duly elected legislature (Parliament or a local council, for example) or as a member of a relevant electorate.
3. social rights which include the right to economic welfare and security (Marshall, 1992, p.8).

Oldfield has taken this further by identifying two conceptions of citizenship; first, a liberal or liberal-individualist conception which emphasises status and rights and which may involve a private relationship to the state and, secondly, a civic republican conception which emphasises duties and which therefore involves a community focused relationship to the state (Oldfield, 1990, p.178). The former reflects the liberty and freedom of the individual from encroachment by the state whilst the latter refers to the social and economic rights an individual might seek in order to maintain or improve his position in society. The crucial difference between the two, suggests Oldfield, is 'the toleration that liberal individualism has for abdication from politics...'. This is quite different from the civic republican tradition which 'holds out the possibility of ... a form of human consciousness, being, and living, that is simply not catered for in liberal individualism' (Oldfield, 1990, p.185). In Britain this is reflected in a culture that, by and large, does not value the activity of politics and accepts (with gratitude) the traditional (negative) freedoms (freedom from arbitrary arrest, freedom of speech) that already exist. Such traditions and culture ignore the existence of political arrangements and political forces which exclude the majority from rights they do not even feel they should possess. Further, as Tony Wright has noted, by tradition British subjects have not been expected to exert themselves in strenuous political activity (Wright, 1994, p.106). Thus a combination of abstinence from political activity (together with a failure to understand the distinction between 'political' and 'party political') and an overconcentration on traditional rights inhibits any real consideration of the proper role of the British citizen in the modern state.

Marquand has suggested that 'an active state needs active citizenship, willing and able to accept their share of the obligations (of citizenship)', (Marquand, 1988). Such obligations are unlikely to be accepted without a wider appreciation of political processes and without opportunities to exercise effective power and influence in those processes – the tangible rewards referred to earlier. Oldfield refers to the need to inculcate 'an attitude of mind, an attitude which prompts individuals not just to recognise what their duties are as citizens, but to perform them as well' (Oldfield, 1990, p.184). This requires a confidence that involvement will lead to desired (personal and group) outcomes which will not be hampered by the work of others with more power and influence. One of the ways of encouraging such involvement would be to recognise the right of the electorate to be fully informed about the activities of government by allowing them access to the information that they need to make an effective contribution to the policy making process. This has clearly worked in other countries. Although the balance of requests for information in Australia and in Canada is overwhelmingly tilted towards issues of personal concern (Hazell, 1989, p.199) there have been some notable instances where information on matters of corporate concern has proved immensely valuable. In any case, the possibility of obtaining information about particular issues is a valuable weapon for the citizen. There is no reason to doubt, therefore, that such active citizenship would be political in the civic republican tradition described by Oldfield, or indeed, that educating people for this purpose would, in itself, be a political act. There can equally be little doubt that without access to information effective citizenship will be impossible.

Freedom of Information

Robertson (1982, p.42) argues that official secrecy in Britain developed as part of the attempt by elected representatives to control bureaucrats and Ponting has noted that early secrecy laws were intended, in part, to prevent civil servants passing information to the press (Ponting, 1985, p.7). The attitudes behind this were less concerned with the reservation for the government of (private) material than with a desire to prevent sensitive information reaching the hands of other governments: to that extent, the focus of government action was more concerned with treason than with the suppression of official information. But it is easy (and instructive) to see how the two were related. As Robertson notes, by 1832 domination of the Crown over office holding was lost, to be replaced (by the 1870s) by parliamentary control of office holders. Fairly rapidly, given the rise of mass parties and the development of the doctrine of ministerial responsibility, civil service loyalty to Parliament came to mean, in effect, loyalty to the government of the day – a view reinforced (but not established) by Sir Robert Armstrong's memorandum of guidance of 1985 (Armstrong, 1985). The expansion of government activities in the nineteenth century (and the consequential increase in the number of public servants involved in supervising those activities) raised inevitable questions about the privacy of government activities. Engelfeld (1985, p.96) draws attention to the rise of 'the large anonymous government department', where the traditions of small intimate departments staffed by administrators with similar values and assumptions to politicians, no longer applied. In such circumstances it was increasingly difficult to maintain control over the amount of information available to departments and ensure that it was not used in ways that were inimical to the interests of individual departments.

Although an Official Secrets Act was passed as early as 1889 it is the Act of 1911 which has been the principal focus for criticisms of secrecy, for reasons developed in a number of polemical works on the subject. Nonetheless, as Trevor Barnes has noted, the movement against government secrecy is essentially a post war activity (Barnes, 1980, p.1) and the debate about openness developed primarily in response to criticisms of the Official Secrets Acts, particularly Section 2 of the 1911 Act. Such complaints had little to do with citizenship and much more to do with the 'blunderbuss' nature of the Act and the failure of several, well publicised, attempts to prosecute individuals under the terms of the Act. These included the trial of Jonathan Aitken and the *Sunday Telegraph* in 1972 over the publication of details about the Nigerian civil war (which led the trial judge, Mr Justice Caulfield, to comment that it was time Section 2 was 'pensioned off'); the trial of Crispin Aubrey, John Berry and Duncan Campbell in 1978 in relation to the publication of details of the government's communications network; the trial of Clive Ponting in 1984 for revealing details of government attempts to mislead the House of Commons; and the *furore* which followed Peter Wright's publication of his book *Spycatcher*. This combined criticism contributed to the repeal of Section 2 in 1989 and its replacement by an Act that was (allegedly) more liberal but, in practice, intended to tighten the law of secrecy in certain specific areas. These were notably those of prior disclosure (thus preventing someone importing into Britain information that was covered by UK secrecy laws but obtainable under the American FOI legislation), and the issue of 'public interest' defences against prosecution.

Nevertheless, the apparent relaxation of the risk of prosecution has not, in itself, increased the amount of information being made public. More important perhaps (though less tangible) has been the gradual loss of deference towards senior public figures in Britain, occasioned *inter alia* by more widespread educational opportunities and increased wealth; the advent of a more permissive culture in the 1960s; increasing demands for public participation in determining service provision; and *cause celebres*, such as the publication of the Crossman diaries (after the failure of the attempt to prosecute his executors for publishing the diaries and a growing realisation that the government's reasons for discouraging publication had more to do with preventing embarrassment to individuals than with the protection of state secrets). In addition, between 1979 and 1993 a number of MPs introduced Private Member's Bills in an attempt to reform the Act. All of these were important contributions to the climate of opinion developing in the 1980s that demanded some sort of commitment by the government to freedom of information and which led to the White Paper on Open Government of 1993.

The Code of Practice on Access to Government Information

The Code of Practice, which was originally set out in the White Paper of 1993, clearly marks a significant advance in open government and, taken with those Acts which allow greater access to information (for example, in local government), the Data Protection Act, and the reform of the 1911 Official Secrets Act, might be regarded as contributing to a shift in the balance of power between the State and the citizen. It begins in promising vein by outlining its aims which are to 'improve policy making and the democratic process by extending access to the facts and analyses which provide the basis for the consideration of proposed policy' (Cabinet Office, 1994). This seems to imply a greater willingness to involve an informed public in the process of government decision making. However, it is not difficult to find constraints in the Code of Practice which are clearly designed to leave ultimate power in the hands of the government. Warning signs appear in the first paragraph of page one where the Code announces that its proposals are intended to support 'the Government's policy under the Citizen's Charter for extending access to official information' (Cabinet Office, 1994). Not only is this a reminder of the very limited amount of information available under the provisions of the Charter but it also ignores the issue of *who* owns 'official' information. In a state where the rights of citizenship are accepted it is difficult to see how the government has a 'right' to own information which challenges the rights associated with citizenship. 'Rights' of ownership at the moment are based on the premise that ministers and civil servants owe their principal loyalty to the Crown. In a practical sense this may be a convenient fiction but it is, nevertheless, a fiction (and one that does not seem to cause too many FOI difficulties in, for example, Australia). Citizenship rights must surely mean that governments exist to serve the people and do not have responsibilities outside that (although they must balance collegiate interests with individual needs, they need to be very careful when using the former as an excuse for refusing requests for information). All information collected by a government, therefore, should (potentially) be available to the public.

The opening paragraph goes on to refer to 'reasonable' requests for information, implying that this is a neutral term rather than the fulcrum of the debate about openness (Cabinet Office, 1994, p.1). The fact that interpretations of what is 'reasonable' may be challenged through the Parliamentary Commissioner for Administration is helpful in its own way, but does not fundamentally address the rights of individual citizens. Nor does the subsequent statement that the government will 'publish facts and analyses of facts which the government considers relevant in framing major policy proposals...'. This is, in effect, yet another assertion of the 'rights' of government against those of citizens. The essential feature of any FOI proposals must be that (apart from clearly agreed exceptions) the people have access to any information, not simply the information that the government considers relevant to a particular policy. A similar issue arises over the actual information provided, with the government arguing that information, rather than documents, will be provided (Cabinet Office, 1994, p.2); not only will this cause more delay whilst the information is provided in a suitable form but it fuels the suspicion that the government has only a limited interest in allowing access to information. The issue of delay was raised by Mr Ronnie Campbell in a debate in the House of Commons when he drew attention to one department that had taken over eight months to produce a particular item of information (Hansard, 1996). Whilst there may be some attempts to conform to shorter periods, it is not entirely clear what sanctions may be taken against departments who fail to comply. Finally, in a neat irony not lost on those who have long favoured increased access, the provisions of the Code of Practice only refer to those departments and public sector bodies which lie within the jurisdiction of the Parliamentary Commissioner; the scope of access is thus limited by the scope of the mechanism for enforcing the Code's proposals. It hardly need be added that the framers of the legislation establishing the ambit of the PCA could have had little idea of the use to which their creation might subsequently be put.

Citizenship and Rights

In his book *Citizenship and Social Class,* Marshall argues that as capitalism evolves in a social system, and as the class structure develops with it, so modern citizenship changes from a system of rights which arise out of, and support, market conditions to being a system of rights which exist in an antagonistic relationship with the market in the class system (Marshall, 1992, p.5). Similarly, Lister has noted that our understanding of citizenship rights and obligations cannot be divorced from their wider social and economic context and the inequalities of power resources and status that permeate it (Lister, 1990, p.31). The Commission on Citizenship, established by the Speaker of the House of Commons, noted that 'the lack of clarity about entitlements, duties and obligations of public institutions are key impediments for British citizens today' (Report of the Commission on Citizenship, 1990, p.22) and went on to argue that education is necessary, involving both the theory and the practice of community involvement (p.36). This is welcome, but hardly sufficient. The activity of citizenship requires more than education about the structure of government. It requires engendering both the will to exercise citizenship and also the means to do so. The task before those who wish to improve the accountability of governments, or improve the level of interaction between government and the people in the development of policy, is to encourage a wider understanding of the rights and duties of citizenship. This means moving beyond the liberal-individualistic understanding of the term as identified by Oldfield, to an understanding that acknowledges that the proper functioning of democracy requires much more than quinquennial exercises in public involvement. Much of the responsibility for this falls on government. Fundamentally, it involves a recognition that the existing structures of power do not allow the exercise of 'full citizenship' and that the latter can only be possible if the government recognises the need to relinquish some of its weapons for controlling both Parliament and the electorate. Miliband has argued that one of the concerns of those who run the state is to reduce popular pressure. This is done partially by deliberate management and also by encouraging habits, traditions and constraints which make for inertia and acceptance rather than pressure and conflict (Miliband, 1982, p.2). In recent years this has been particularly reflected in the failure by the government to act clearly and decisively over moral issues in which it has had some involvement – whether in the casuistry which typified its reaction to the report of the enquiry by Sir Richard Scott into the sale of Arms to Iraq or in the way in which it has dealt with members of the Commons over issues of 'sleaze'. It is unsurprising that such a cynical response to public concern is met in turn by a cynical (and unhealthy) public perception of the processes of government themselves. This is the exact opposite of what is necessary to promote an appreciation of the responsibilities of citizenship.

Public trust in the processes of government is the responsibility of the government of the day and something which cannot be taken for granted. A Freedom of Information Act could be a powerful means for securing and enhancing that trust since it would be a recognition by the government of the public's right to be informed about its activities for the purpose of ensuring accountability. It would therefore be a contributory factor to establishing a sense of ownership of the state's activities which is the foundation of citizenship. By itself it would not produce a sense of civic duty of the sort implied by Oldfield's civic republican conception although it would provide an opportunity for people to gather information for corporate rather than individual purposes. It would be, in short, a necessary but insufficient condition for citizenship in a mature democracy.

References

Armstrong, Sir Robert (1985), 'Note by the Head of the Home Civil Service', *The Duties and Responsibilities of Civil Servants in Relation to Ministers*, Cabinet Office.

Barbalet, J.M. (1988), *Citizenship: rights, struggle and class inequality*, Open University Press.

Barnes, T. (1980), *Open Up!* (Fabian Tract 467), Fabian Society.

Butt, R. (1969), *The Power of Parliament*, Constable & Co.

Cabinet Office (1991), *The Citizen's Charter, Raising the Standard*, Cm.1599, HMSO.

Cabinet Office (1993), *Open Government*, Cm.2290, HMSO.

Cabinet Office, Citizens Charter Unit (1994), *Code of Practice on Access to Government Information*, HMSO.

Chapman, Richard A. (1987), 'Introduction' in Richard A. Chapman and Michael Hunt (Eds), *Open Government*, Croom Helm, pp.11-29.

Dummett, Ann & Andrew Nicol (1990), *Subjects, Citizens, Aliens and Others*, Weidenfeld and Nicolson.

Elcock, H. (1996), 'What Price Citizenship? Public Management and the Citizen's Charter', in J. Chandler (Ed), *The Citizen's Charter*, Dartmouth, pp.24-39.

Elder, N. (1973), *Regionalism and the Publicity Principle in Sweden*, Research Paper 3, Commission on the Constitution, HMSO.

Engelfeld, D. (1985), *Whitehall and Westminster: Government informs Parliament: the changing scene*, Longmans.

Hansard (1996), 6th series, Vol. 287, No. 33, Col. 164, (10 December).

Hazell, R. (1989), 'Freedom of Information in Australia, Canada and New Zealand', *Public Administration*, Vol. 67, No. 2, pp.189-210.

Held, D. (1991), 'Between State and Civil Society: Citizenship' in G. Andrews (Ed), *Citizenship*, Lawrence and Wishart, pp.19-25.

IPPR (1993), *A Written Constitution for the UK,* Mansell.

Lister, R. (1990), *The Exclusive Society: Citizenship and the Poor,* Child Poverty Action Group.

Lord Privy Seal (1979), *Open Government,* Cmnd. 7520, HMSO.

Marquand, D. (1988), 'The Old Politics is Over', *The Observer,* 31 January.

Marshall, T.H. & Tom Bottomore (1992), *Citizenship and Social Class,* Pluto Press.

Miliband, R. (1982), *Capitalist Democracy in Britain,* Oxford University Press.

Oldfield, A. (1990), 'Citizenship: An Unnatural Practice?' *Political Quarterly,* April/June, pp.177-187.

Plant, R. (1990), 'Citizenship and Rights' in R. Plant and N. Barry, *Citizenship and Rights in Thatcher's Britain: Two Views,* IEA Health and Welfare Unit, pp.2-32.

Ponting, C. (1985), *The Right to Know. The inside story of the Belgrano affair,* Sphere Books.

Report of the Commission on Citizenship (1990), *Encouraging Citizenship,* HMSO.

Report of the Western Australian Commission on Government (1995), Vol. 1, Perth, W.A.: The Commission.

Robertson, K.G. (1982), *Public Secrets: A study in the Development of Government Secrecy,* Macmillan.

Rowat, D.C. (Ed), (1979), *Administrative Secrecy in Developed Countries,* Macmillan.

Select Committee on the Parliamentary Commissioner for Administration, Session 1995/96, Second Report, *Open Government,* HC 84, HMSO.

Stewart, John (1984), 'The role of information in public accountability' in A. Hopwood and C. Tompkins (Eds.), *Issues in Public Sector Accounting,* Philip Allan, pp.13-34.

Walkland, S.A. (1976),'The Politics of Parliamentary Reform', *Parliamentary Affairs,* Vol. 29, No. 2, pp.190-200.

Wright, Tony (1994), *Citizens and Subjects,* Routledge.

4 Moving from Public Administration to Public Management

David S. Morris

As an undergraduate student in the 1960s, the tenets of Weber's *Verstehen* sociology were drilled into me by my teachers. Generalisations were treated with a healthy modicum of scepticism which, on occasions, bordered on the cynical. Nonetheless, generalisations were accepted as feasible and viable if (and the word 'if' is worthy of emphasis) they could be substantiated. In that context, I intend to examine the movement from public administration to public sector management and the forces which have been formative in that transformation. In undertaking such a task I am acutely aware that I am engaging in an exercise which Richard Chapman would possibly have considered, and probably decided against, on the grounds of frivolity. My defence is simple; I have merely stolen a little freedom to pay, in my own way, a modest and assuredly flawed tribute to a man who I hold in the highest regard, primarily as a friend but also as a fellow academic. All researchers in the field of public administration owe him a profound debt for his contribution to the way in which the subject should be studied.

It was Alexander Pope who observed that,

> For forms of government let fools contest
> What'ere is best administered is best (Pope, 1966, 1.303).

Such a citation should not be taken to mean that Pope was the founder of what we have to come to recognise as public administration. Instead, his words provide a counterbalance to the over dominance of investigations into forms of government; these began in ancient Greece and seem to have pre-occupied academic minds ever since.

Perhaps the first writer to draw a welcome distinction between the state and civil society was Hegel, who portrayed the former as representing the general interest and the latter as comprising particular interests. Under Hegel's schema it fell to the state administration to transform, in some largely mystical fashion, sectional interests into the will of all – the general interest. Marx, whilst readily accepting the Hegelian distinction between the state and civil society, offered a markedly different interpretation of the nature and role of each. For Marx, the state represented nothing more than the interests of the dominant class in society and the state administration was the vehicle through which that class exercised its domination over all of the other particular interests of civil society. Weber's concern with the differences which distinguished power from authority directed attention towards the form of state administration and, by so doing, opened the door to the study of the machinery of government. It may be argued that Weber has a realistic claim to being the founding father of public administration (although I would be prepared to countenance a counter-claim from advocates of Machiavelli's credentials).

In order to chart the nature and the magnitude of the changes which have resulted in the study of public administration being transformed into the study of public sector management, as well as the forces which have shaped that movement, it is necessary to begin by delineating a starting point. Here, I may upset some of those who have devoted themselves to describing, analysing and specifying the domain of public administration by arguing that its students have failed to divorce their chosen area of study from the wider area of political science. Whilst many have been aware of the need to do this, it may be argued that their attempts foundered because of the way in which the policy process was generally conceived.

In essence, policy making was seen as a process, as a set of interrelated activities which accorded to a simple systems model (Fig.1). Based upon the biological analogy of the human body, the systems approach initially found favour among social anthropologists before its efficacy was more widely proclaimed in other areas of the social sciences:

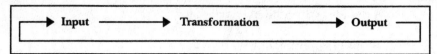

Figure 1

Sociologists and political scientists, particularly those of structuralist and functionalist persuasions, lost little time in adopting the tenets of systems theory. Political scientists quickly sought to apply a systems approach to the policy making process. Although the model employed was relatively simple, it may be argued that it played a significant part in determining the domain of public administration when applied to the policy making process.

This assertion may be supported by offering a more generalised model of the policy making process (Fig 2). Such a model leads to both the specification of actors and factors in the policy making process, whilst also

56

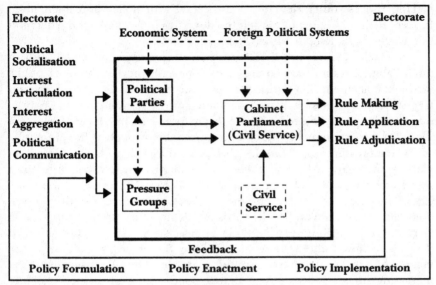

Electorate		Electorate
Political Socialisation	Economic System Foreign Political Systems	
Interest Articulation	Political Parties	Cabinet Parliament (Civil Service)
Interest Aggregation		Rule Making
Political Communication		Rule Application
	Pressure Groups Civil Service	Rule Adjudication
	Feedback	
Policy Formulation	Policy Enactment	Policy Implementation

Figure 2

permitting linkages to be drawn to the three stages of that process, namely: policy formulation, policy enactment and policy implementation; each of which may be respectively matched with inputs, transformation and outputs of the simple systems model. Public administration became inextricably associated with policy implementation; the structures and means through which policies were delivered. Of course, the study of policy implementation, the essential focus of public administration, could not be comprehensively analysed and explained without recourse to policy formulation and policy enactment, but it may be argued that such necessary recourse presented difficulties to those who sought to discern a unique field of study which was both separate and distinct from political science, because of their dependence upon the broader policy making framework that was demanded by a systems approach. This difficulty was further compounded by the depiction of the policy making process as a lateral process. A feedback loop, linking outputs back to inputs and suggesting that imperfections or unintended effects in policy delivery provided a fresh source of inputs or demands into the policy making process, appeared in many systems models of policy making. However, I would hold that, had the policy making process been depicted as cyclical, the subject matter of public administration would not have been as artificially constrained as it subsequently came to be. Again, in holding that such constraints were experienced by students of public administration, I am aware that many sought to break these fetters and provided significant contributions and insights into areas of the policy

57

making process other than those associated with policy implementation. Indeed, Richard Chapman himself has done this in his book on the decision to raise the Bank Rate in 1957 (Chapman, 1968).

Nevertheless, it was not these constraints which gave a seminal push to public administration and forced it to appear in the new guise of public sector management. Forces far greater than those of academic nicety and terminological precision played a much more important formative role; forces which may be seen to have been forged at the time of the first Thatcher Government and which have continued through to the present.

For the greater part of two decades, profound changes have been taking place in the character of the public sectors of Western Europe, largely as a result of changes in governmental attitudes toward the role of the state. These include the recent ending of the Conservative Party's political dominance in Britain and of the Christian Democratic Party's dominance in Germany, the collapse of socialism in France, the search for alternatives to the all-encompassing welfare state in the Scandinavian countries, the entrenchment of democratic regimes in the Iberian Peninsular, the increasing integration of governmental policies as a consequence of the development of the European Union and the growing awareness of the threat posed to the European economies by the seemingly limitless and inexorable rise of Japan and the countries of the Pacific Rim, at least until recently. All of these changes have collectively led to consequential changes in the role of the public sectors of Western Europe, the ways in which those sectors are viewed by governments and the ways in which their responsibilities are discharged. It is these profound and far-reaching changes which have come to constitute the movement of the study of public administration to public sector management, even though they have fallen short of expanding the domain of such study, which has remained primarily focused upon policy implementation.

So, what of these profound changes? At the most general level they may be accounted for by a consideration of government policy. With the notable exception of the United States, the end of the Second World War saw both victors and vanquished sharing a similar fate: impoverishment. Whilst conceding that such a fate did not result in equal misery, it has to be recognised that it did result in an equal need, namely, the rebuilding of the war damaged European economies. A general consensus existed among European governments that, for this necessary rebuilding to take place, the joint efforts of governmental and private capital would be required since the task which confronted their respective societies was beyond the capability and capacity of either sector operating in isolation. Hence, mixed economies became the norm and the vehicle became collectivist efforts in pursuit of the attainment of a common, collective goal. Later, this was to be increasingly transformed into the pursuit of trans-national, European goals through the partial surrender of national sovereignty to the supra-national institutions of the European Union.

Initially, however, a panacea for the ills of the separate European nations was thought to reside in three main elements which were to serve as the focus for governmental policy, namely, the role of the state in economic affairs, the state provision of welfare, and corporatism (Savage and Robins, 1990). The character of those three elements, and the forms which they assumed, will each be considered in turn.

The Role of the State in Economic Affairs

Here the contention is that, for certainly the first two and a half decades after the restoration of peace to Europe, there was a widespread acceptance that the central role of government was to manage the economy, and the favoured form of economy was a "mixed economy" incorporating both private and public sector organisations. Over time, this perception entailed the further acceptance of a number of differing forms of amalgamation of those two types of enterprise and permitted state ownership of particular parts of the economy, as well as the granting of subsidies to discrete industries along with specific measures such as control over prices, incomes and credits. The rationale underpinning all of these measures was the expressed intention of governments to maintain full employment. This latter objective had arisen because of the manifest acceptance by governments of Keynesian economic theory which advocated that government play the role of partner to the private sector in the national economy. That partnership entailed the public sector not in seeking to do that which the private sector already did, but rather to supplementing the role of the private sector by undertaking those necessary functions which, because of commercial and other considerations, the private sector did not, or was unwilling to, perform. Hence, the role of the state became twofold; on the one hand, that of changing or amending the part played by the dominant economic forces in society whilst, on the other, that of protecting that role and ensuring its continuation.

The Role of the State in Welfare Provision

There was a common agreement amongst the majority of Western European governments that not only should welfare provision be made, but that government should play an active role in that provision. Differences lay in the extent to which state provision was countenanced, and not in state provision *per se*. As a generalisation, governments came to accept that the state should assume a central role in the provision of welfare. They

59

concurred that health care, income support, personal social services, care for the elderly, for children, the disabled and the homeless was provision that the government of any democratic and humane society should accord its citizens. Such a consensus led to policies which gave the state a formative part to play in the spheres of education, housing, health, pensions and social security. Even so, the state did not have an exclusive role, for state provision co-existed alongside that provided by other agencies which offered services compatible with, and parallel to, state provision in all of those policy areas. Additionally, voluntary organisations contributed their efforts to the totality of provision. What distinguished one nation from another was the degree of contribution made by the state and the private sector respectively and not the question of whether or not it was proper and appropriate for the state to perform and fulfil a wider function in response to societal needs.

Corporatism

Throughout the immediate post-war years, the need to rebuild and rejuvenate the economies of Western Europe led governments to adopt a consultative approach to decision making over a broad spectrum of policy areas, ranging from economic policy through to the more specific elements of health provision and industrial policy. This meant that, at the formulation stage of policy, governments sought the views and opinions of interest groups who might possess specialist knowledge of the relevant policy area and, not infrequently, the active support of those interest groups in the implementation of policy. The rationale underpinning this approach was the belief that efficiency and effectiveness could best be achieved through policies which enjoyed the widest possible level of support from those most intimately involved in the area on which the policy was intended to impact. In the field of industrial policy, for example, this corporatist approach led to the development of "tripartism"; the creation of a forum in which the government and the two sides of industry, management and labour, sat down together to negotiate, with the intention of producing policy proposals which were acceptable to all three parties. The compromises which were the inevitable outcome of the corporatist approach were regarded as preferable to the potential conflict which might otherwise have arisen; confrontation was perceived as a hindrance to the attainment of the desired goals of efficiency, effectiveness and economy.

Such a scenario, which held sway throughout most of Western Europe for the greater part of three decades after the end of the Second World War, was subject to radical revision in the late 1970s. A number of factors can be said to have contributed to that transformation, among which would be included the effect of the first "oil shock" of 1973, the ever-increasing cost of state provision, the challenge presented to the European economies (and particularly to their manufacturing bases) by the rapid emergence and growth of Japan and the "Five Tigers" of the Pacific Rim, and the growing acceptance, especially in governmental circles, that Keynesian economics could no longer provide a solution to the problem of stagflation. A new economic doctrine was therefore needed to break out of the spiral of incipient economic decline.

The response which emerged in the late 1970s, developed in the 1980s, and which is still in evidence today (although now being expressed with less conviction than previously) challenged earlier thinking by questioning, from a neo-liberal perspective, the role to be played by the state in the affairs of the nation. Three new elements came to replace those which had formerly characterised the policy making process; the primacy of the market, individualism, and strong, if minimalist, government.

The Primacy of the Market

The virtues of the market were to reign supreme in economic affairs, the views of its advocates typified by Prime Minister Thatcher's often repeated assertion that "you cannot buck the market". The state's role in the management of a mixed economy was now regarded as an encouragement to the inefficient, ineffective and uneconomic distribution of finite resources. The supremacy of the market over state run or state directed processes in all sectors of the economy was proclaimed, with the former being viewed as the means through which economic rejuvenation could best be facilitated and secured. The acceptance of neo-liberal principles provided the ideological justification for the strategy employed by many Western European governments to "roll back the frontiers of the state" in the economic life of their nations, and for the active measures taken in many parts of their respective public sectors to encourage competition. For example, in Britain, compulsory competitive tendering of previously publicly managed services, market testing, hiving-off and privatisation of wholly state owned assets became the norm. Interestingly, especially given the opposition of Britain's "reforming governments" to anything even remotely left of centre, the former Soviet Union and other states of the former Eastern Bloc appear to have embarked upon the same journey and with similar consequences. The point, however, is that such actions were incompatible with the Keynesian economic theory which had long provided an accepted basis for the management of the Western European economies. It was abandoned in favour of the more avowedly micro-economic and monetarist views of Hayek and Friedman.

Increasing Individualism

Neo-liberalism led to the elevation of the market to a position of primacy over the role of the state as a provider and distributor of finite resources. It also led to the championing of the self-reliant, self-directing and responsible individual as opposed to the dependent and complacent individual seen as the product of the state assuming a too wide, too deep and too paternalistic a concern with an individual's welfare. This, it was claimed, had given rise to a "dependency culture" incompatible with the goal of ever-increasing national prosperity and international competitiveness. The solution again entailed "rolling back the frontiers of the state" and obliging the populace to rely on its own efforts to secure its own well-being, to make provision for the future and to cease to be dependent upon the state for welfare provision. Moves in that direction are clearly discernible in Britain, France and Sweden.

Strong Government

At first glance this may appear to stand in marked contradiction to a reduced role for the state, but closer examination reveals that, at least in the short term, strong government is a pre-requisite for ensuring a departure from former patterns. Only strong government, it was argued, could free the economy from the constricting web of state regulation which was seen to impose unwanted and unwarranted limitations upon the development of an enterprise culture. Only strong government could cut through the constraints imposed upon private enterprise by trade unions who (it was suggested) had become too powerful. Only strong government could oblige the citizenry to recapture their former initiative, self-respect and self-reliance and ensure national prosperity. Only strong government could ensure the ending of wasteful practices in the remaining organisations of the public sector. In the case of Britain, only strong government could offer the prospect that its efforts on each of those fronts would not be undermined by increasing European integration, by the threat that was seen to be posed to British national interests by those arguing for a federal Europe and by the creeping socialism associated (by his opponents) with Jacques Delors.

Whilst these environmental forces were fundamental to the movement from an emphasis upon public administration to an emphasis upon public management, it is also possible to chart the transformation by examining the changes which have occurred within public sector organisations. Lawton and Rose differentiate between characteristics supportive of a continuing focus upon public administration and characteristics which may be taken to encourage the re-directing of attention toward public management. The traditional character and characteristics of the public sector, they suggest, may be delineated as follows:

- public sector organisations are not exposed to the competitive world of the market and hence have no incentive to reduce costs or operate efficiently.
- objectives are usually ill-defined and expressed in vague terms; such as serving the public, maintaining law and order, reducing inequality, removing poverty or improving health.
- strategic planning is more difficult because of the short term considerations of politicians.
- the public sector is susceptible to greater and more open accountability with politicians, pressure groups, taxpayers and voters all having an interest in the performance of the public sector.
- the functions of the public sector are limited by statute.
- the public sector is funded by taxation and not by charging the market price for its services.
- certain services have to be provided by the state. Defence, law and order, and street lighting are enjoyed collectively and are, in theory, equally available to all. The provision of such "public" goods cannot be left to the vagaries of the market (Lawton and Rose, 1991, pp.5-6).

Such a scenario stands in opposition to those who contend that a convergence is already well established between practice in the public and private sectors of Western European economies; a convergence which Lawton and Rose delineate as follows:

- increasingly, the public sector charges for some of its services, for example, through increased prescription charges or charges for leisure services.
- the private sector also operates within a political environment as decisions made by politicians to – for example – keep interest rates high will have a profound effect upon the very existence of some firms charged with high borrowing costs and reduced sales.
- the activities of the private sector are also constrained by statute as firms are regulated over unfair trading practices, health and safety at work or environmental pollution.
- joint public and private schemes have developed over urban redevelopment where groups such as *Business in the Community* have promoted private sector involvement at local levels (1991, p.6).

This convergence has been essentially uni-directional, with the organisations of the public sector adopting practices which have already become established in organisations in the private sector. As an example, one might cite the increasing emphasis on user needs typified by approaches such as Quality Management; the Citizen's Charter serves as an example of this. Yet such approaches have rarely been adopted in the public sector with the rigour that has characterised their introduction in the private sector. For example, in the case of the Citizen's Charter the standards for the quality of service delivery are determined not by the end user, the client or customer, but by the supplier; a pattern not countenanced in the literature of quality management where the tenet that "the customer is king" is a *sine qua non* of quality, and customer needs and expectations determine the standard of service that is offered and the means by which it is delivered (Chandler, 1996).

The profound macro and contextual changes which have moved the focus of policy making and which have resulted in an orientation toward the primacy of the market, increasing individualism, and strong government, have resulted in the convergence so aptly delineated by Lawton and Rose but they have not resulted in the comprehensive adoption by public sector organisations of the managerial practices of private sector organisations. Those changes have, however, given rise to a movement within public sector organisations from an administrative to a managerial ethos. Such a transformation was noted, but went almost unnoticed, as long ago as 1972 when Keeling contrasted the two styles (see Fig 3).

No student of, for example, the National Health Service over the last twenty years, would have any difficulty in finding a plethora of empirical data to support the argument that the NHS has moved from an administered to a managed organisational culture. It is not my intention to provide such supportive evidence but merely to draw attention to the introduction of the general management concept (largely as a replacement for the former consensus management), and to the policy of *Patients First*, as being indicative of these changes manifested in the NHS. Similarly, comparable evidence could be found elsewhere in the public sector in response to the introduction of compulsory competitive tendering and hiving-off.

It may be argued that these changes have altered the way in which organisations in the public sector should be studied and analysed. Such study can no longer be focused upon structures which perform functions but upon the processes by which services responsive to the needs of users are designed and managed, and upon the outcomes that are delivered. This is not to suggest that there is, or indeed should be, any change in the locus of study. Such study should still focus upon the implementation of public policy and a comprehensive and coherent picture of the implementation of public policy must necessarily be informed by a consideration of the contextual elements of policy formulation and policy enactment. However, because of the changes which I have outlined above, policy implementation must now be

	Administration	**Management**
Goals	In general terms, infrequently reviewed or changed.	Broad strategic aims supported by more detailed short term goals and targets. Reviewed frequently.
Attainment criteria	Mistake avoiding.	Success seeking.
Resource use	Secondary task.	Primary task.
Organisational structure	Roles defined in terms of responsibility. Long hierarchies: Limited delegation.	Roles defined in terms of tasks. Shorter hierarchies: Maximum delegation.
Management role	Arbitrator.	Protagonist.
Perceptions	Passive: workload determined outside system. Best people used to solve problems. Time insensitive. Risk avoiding. Emphasis upon procedure. Conformity: national standards.	Active: seeking to influence environment. Best people used to find and exploit opportunities. Time sensitive. Risk accepting but minimising. Emphasis upon results. Local experiments: need for conformity to be proved.
Skills	Legal or quasi-legal. Literacy.	Economic or socio-economic. Numeracy.

Figure 3
Source: Keeling, 1972, pp.91-92

studied through the employment of analytical tools and techniques of management. These would include the inter-related concepts of planning, controlling, organising and leadership (itself also the subject of a study by Professor Chapman in 1984).

The large scale, macro changes to which the public sector has been subjected in the last twenty years, and the responses to those changes, makes it imperative that the techniques of analysis employed today to the further understanding of policy implementation must be techniques which recognise and take into account the responses made to those changes by public sector organisations; changes which have seen the introduction of a managed rather than an administered culture. New processes of policy implementation demand to be studied through the use of complementary means and this makes it incumbent upon all who study that area, and those who teach it, that they become familiar with current managerial approaches and their associated analytical techniques. The means and methods by which policy is implemented by public sector organisations have changed in response to governmentally inspired demands for change. In response, we must change; not in terms of the area which provides the focus for study but in our way of analysing policy implementation. We must move from the study of public administration, with its tried and tested forms of analysis, to the study of public sector management and, in doing so, acquire a new language and a new set of techniques to aid us in that task. Failure to do so will otherwise leave us forever confronted by '... a riddle wrapped in a mystery inside an enigma...' (Churchill, 1939).

References

Chandler, J.A. (Ed) (1996), *The Citizen's Charter*, Dartmouth.

Chapman, Richard A. (1968), *Decision Making*, Routledge and Kegan Paul.

Chapman, Richard A. (1984), *Leadership in the British Civil Service: a study of Sir Percival Waterfield and the creation of the Civil Service Selection Board*, Croom Helm.

Churchill, Winston S. (1939), Speech in London, October 1.

Department of Health and Social Security (1979), *Patients First: consultative paper on the structure and management of the national health service in England and Wales*, HMSO.

Keeling, Desmond (1972), *Management in Government*, Allen and Unwin.

Lawton, Allan and Aidan Rose (1991), *Organisation and Management in the Public Sector*, Pitman.

Pope, Alexander (1966), 'An Essay on Man. Epistle lll', *Poetical Works*, Herbert Davis (Ed). Oxford University Press.

Savage, S. and L. Robins (Eds) (1990), *Public Policy Under Thatcher*, Macmillan.

Part Two

ETHICS IN PUBLIC SERVICE

5 Revisiting the Art of Darkness

Malcolm Jack

Richard Chapman has never been one to read politics narrowly. In the background of much of what he has written (and, at times in the foreground) lies his keen awareness of the human condition, with all its quirks and oddities. Reading politics, including public administration, has to involve defining human nature and understanding the behaviour of men involved in public life. In particular it must deal with one specific human proclivity – the instinct that directs men to moral behaviour, to behaviour acted out according to precepts and norms – which vitally affects the structure of society and also provides grounds for the legitimacy of government. Now this does not mean that the Chapmanesque analysis ignores those more measurable aspects of human behaviour so beloved of contemporary social scientists; rather it means that no serious student of the body politic should dare to cut the umbilical cord that links his subject to political theory, after all, Aristotle's master science.

Such an approach to political studies should not come as a surprise to us from a devotee of T.H. Green, a neo-Hegelian idealist who was himself in revolt against the fashionable calculable, utilitarianism of his time, but it has led to interesting and at times surprising slants to Chapman's study of public administration (see Chapman, 1962). Let me consider two examples. The first is in those case studies that Richard Chapman made of the culture of the higher civil service (Chapman, 1984; Chapman, 1988a). His decision in those works was to approach the subject of 'administrative culture' in the United Kingdom by way of biography, admittedly biography of senior public servants and therefore by way of a kind of institutionalised biography. In his book on Bridges, Richard Chapman makes it clear that he is concerned with the idiosyncrasies of an individual who is both heir of, and contributor to, a particular professional life, with its own peculiar values and codes of behaviour. However, that professional life is no isolated bourgeois activity, although it may have its own charm: it is also at the centre of national decision making; it is part of the politics and administration of its age, with its own ethical and Greenian target of self-fulfilment. We need to understand it every bit as much as we need to analyse particular historical events for our analysis of public administration to be penetrating. Thus individuals, like the highly placed Bridges, giving ministers political as well as constitutional advice, 'simply because in the British system of government it is impossible to make a clear division between the two' (Chapman, 1988a, p.284), must be understood within their milieu, in the clubs and corridors of power as much as in the most formal of briefing sessions if governance is to be properly understood.

My second example is connected to the first but arises in another context – namely on the occasion of Richard Chapman's inaugural lecture at Durham University in 1988 (Chapman, 1988b). Here talking to an assembly gathered to hear his reflections on the 'state of the art', Professor Chapman decided to give a lecture on the connection of his subject to grand political theory, calling forth the sonorous voices of Plato and Rousseau (hardly heroes of quantitatively-minded social scientists) to his aid. His concern was once again with the 'higher culture' of administrators whom both Plato and Rousseau believed needed to be shielded from pursuit of private interests if the common good was to be protected. Paradoxically, for public administration to work properly, leaders need to behave 'unnaturally' (i.e. they have to set aside their personal interest in the interests of the common good) and it follows from this premise that 'the best social institutions were those most fitted to make a man unnatural, so that he no longer regarded himself as an individual but as part of the whole' (Chapman, 1988, p.11). Once more we hear echoes of T.H. Green. Nevertheless, it is Rousseau's observation about the 'guardians' that most grips Professor Chapman in his lecture. For according to Rousseau, the guardians need to remain detached, even ascetic, if they are to pursue the common good rather than their own interest. Without a core of dedicated, disinterested leaders, society would only survive by the exercise of dark, Machiavellian arts, what Mandeville so blithely called 'dextrous management', the political pyrotechnics of his wisemen or legislators (Mandeville, 1924, 1, pp.411-12). But practising these dark arts, according to Rousseau, was a corrupting business; in itself it would lead to social fragmentation and, eventually, to decay. Here, in the middle of the inaugural lecture is the theme that I want to seize upon, corruption and decay, and beneath that much discussed eighteenth-century paradox, the ancient connection observed since the time of Plato, between private morality and public welfare.

Corruption and Decay

Although I have found my entrée into the great debate about private interest and public good through Chapman's references to Plato and Rousseau, I want to begin my remarks on corruption by considering Machiavelli, particularly his observations in his *Discourses on the First Ten Books of Livy*.

In that work Machiavelli had traced the collapse of the state to the gradual lessening of the commitment of the rulers to actually carrying out their public responsibilities. The collapse in civic spirit, or Machiavellian *virtù*, could be closely identified with an increase in the material standard of life of the leaders. Imperial Rome provided greatly increased opportunity for personal aggrandisement: individuals channelled their energies into the pursuit of wealth and luxury at the expense of public service. The old republican virtues of dedication to the city-state were thrown aside as the nation lost the services of its most able and well-placed citizens. In proportion to the increase in luxury, a malaise invaded Roman society which rendered individuals corrupt and incapable of managing the onerous burden of government. The moral decadence of individual citizens was thus closely reflected in the public life of society.

Although Machiavelli had offered no simple solution to the problems of a nation in decline, he had insisted that the moral integrity of its rulers was a prerequisite for political stability. All the efforts of the nation had to be directed toward maintaining a class of public-minded leaders. That necessarily entailed attention to political education and to the psychological need for recognition on the part of statesmen. It also meant that political life had to be organised so as to obtain maximum benefit from *Fortuna,* which Machiavelli believed swayed the affairs of men. An efficient legal system, a national religion and a loyal civic militia were some of the institutional requirements for a successful polity. The proper harnessing of men's energies to the national purpose through these means would be enhanced by the establishment of a mixed form of government, reflecting the various interests of different groups in the nation.

Machiavelli's political theory was transmitted to Augustan England through the works of James Harrington (see Pocock, 1968). In *The Commonwealth of Oceana* (1656) Harrington sought protection against the collapse of *virtù,* by providing a constitution impregnable against corruption. It balanced aristocracy and popular sovereignty which he believed might rectify the imbalance that had followed the collapse of the ancient 'Gothic' harmony created by King, Lords and Commons. Harrington's political prescriptions were republican: he envisaged a nation free from kingship and supported, in the Machiavellian way, by a militia of citizens voluntarily banded together to protect the commonwealth.

If Harrington's approach to public corruption was republican, the restoration of Machiavellian *virtù* by a rebalancing of the constitution without the monarch, then another great tradition of English political theory saw the strengthening of monarchy as the device to prevent the decline of the nation. This school of thought might be traced back to Sir Robert Filmer, although its Augustan expression was found in Bolingbroke's *The Idea of a Patriot King* (1738) (see Kramnick, 1968).

Bolingbroke voiced the Tory hope for a return to the moral life of pre-Revolutionary England, based on a hierarchical society which was headed by a patriotic, landed aristocracy. The role of the monarch in such a society was that of supreme magistrate, who, by his own lofty personal example of disinterested service to the nation, would turn his people's energies away from the sordid pursuit of private gain toward public virtue. The Patriot King would personify the leader as a man of high *virtù* whose influence would save the nation from the threat posed by the enormous growth of material wealth in the hands of a ruling minority. Bolingbroke's ideas were supported by the literary circle of Swift, Pope and Gay who ridiculed the Mandevillean notion that luxury would promote national greatness. Instead they employed various satiric weapons to make the point that moneyed wealth was incompatible with public spiritedness (see Pope, 1966 – Pope incorporated Mandeville in his *Dunciad*).

However, the influence of Machiavelli was not confined to English ideologists. In seventeenth and early eighteenth century France we find features of the Machiavellian approach intermingled with the Augustinian, *moraliste* tradition so ingrained in French sceptical literature. Both Bayle and Fontenelle advanced conspiratorial theories of government, especially insofar as the clergy were involved. They accepted without hesitation the Machiavellian idea of politics which Richard Tuck has described as 'the public arena of the passions' (1979, p.141) since their own view of human nature was that of a man as a fallen creature, motivated more by instinct than by reason. Political technique, according to their almost purely Machiavellian view, consisted of the clever manipulation (what Mandeville called 'dextrous management') of the correctly understood passions.

Later, Montesquieu may be seen as an exponent of what Duncan Forbes has described as the Machiavellian 'science of national manners' (1966, p.xxviii). That 'science' consisted of contrasting the virtue and the achievement of classical society with the corruption of contemporary society, largely attributable to the growth of luxury. Its assumption was that there were certain patterns of behaviour constant in the great flux of human history, the actual manifestations of which varied from one culture to another. The moralist had to locate the 'relations which derive from the nature of things' so that he could understand the workings of human nature and provide prescriptions for the diseased body politic. One of the most important body of such relations for Montesquieu was the law, a complex and changing set of rules which varied from one society to another. He set out to locate the pattern of different sets of laws or constitutions – the spirit that prevailed in different political cultures. Like Machiavelli, his analysis was directed to understanding how different societies, whether free or despotic, might be kept stable in the interests of their citizens. He searched out that quality of *virtù* so highly prized by his Florentine teacher (Forbes, 1966, p.xxviii).

These various political theories of virtue thus aimed at finding the good life for both the citizen and the state. Often, as in the case of political theorists like Rousseau and Adam Ferguson, there was an identification with a classical, republican model like Sparta. In that ancient city, it was postulated that the 'lawgivers and other wise men' ruled disinterestedly in the cause of the national good. Modern political theorists of virtue, inspired by a patriotism no less than the Spartan, sought to re-establish or maintain that politically ideal way of life. They insisted that the most important way to do so was by restoring moral rectitude among citizens. However, their civic humanist pleading did not go unchallenged: Bernard Mandeville, a Dutchman who made London his home, proved to be one of their most effective critics (Mandeville, 1924).

Mandeville's attack upon the ancient notion of a connection between private morality and public good centred upon those pious citizens of early Augustan England who formed the cadres of the Societies for the Reformation of Manners to combat public corruption which they saw everywhere, from the extent of blasphemy in common language to the debauchery of the court aristocracy. From the 1690s onward, the organized effort against crime and immorality reached a new level of sophistication: societies, whose sole purpose was to 'improve' public morals, sprang into being. These Societies for the Reformation of Manners were dedicated to the eradication of every kind of vice; their members made it their business to spy upon their fellow citizens, and when necessary, to inform the magistrates of breaches of the law and codes of public morality. Thus for example, action against brothels – bawdy houses – often originated on the basis of information supplied by the Societies to the public authorities.

If the Societies had been concerned only with the reformation of private morality, no doubt they would have been less prominent in the affairs of the realm. As it was, they increased in strength during the period of Protestant reaction against what were seen as the arbitrary intentions of the Catholic King, James II. They thus became politically identified with the Glorious Revolution and benefited from this association with a deeply patriotic movement. The morality which the Societies defended was the morality of the free Englishman; it was a defence of the constitutional liberties gained against the arbitrary kingship of the Stuarts. When constitutional monarchy was accepted and established, the Societies even gained royal recognition.

Yet their establishment as recognised public bodies was not the end of their influence upon national life. It was the firm belief of the reformers that there was a direct connection between private morality and public welfare. The members of the Societies wanted to reform individuals because they believed that it was only by this means that the state itself could be saved from decline. They were convinced that unless such reform was undertaken, then the very fabric of society was threatened. This message, thoroughly patriotic in sentiment, was bound to gain them widespread support.

During the period when the Societies were growing, considerable changes in the organisation of public finance were taking place in England. Joint stock companies came into being and, in 1694, the Bank of England was established. With the growth and importance of the City of London, a new political interest based upon the trading wealth of the bourgeoisie was forming (see Plumb, 1969; Longford, 1989). While the aristocracy took some part in the growth of commercial enterprise, the Bolingbroke Tories and others saw the commitment to money as no substitute for the possession of land as the true bond between the individual and the nation. Defoe may have exaggerated the social reformation that money could bring, but there is no doubt that the financial revolution implied a complete change in the values of a traditionally land-based society (see Novak, 1962).

By 1700 the new source of civic corruption was identified as commerce. The debate about public corruption was not always conducted at the lofty level of political theory. Pamphleteers, like Ned Ward, flourished in the atmosphere of public moralising. Journals, such as the *Tatler* and the *Spectator* came into being to improve manners. Moralists and polemicists joined in identifying the increase of wealth as the main threat to social cohesion; in their minds commerce was associated with the ancient vice of avarice and it directly encouraged the substitution of love of money for love of country.

Moralists also worried about the growth of luxury that invariably accompanied successful commerce. As society became richer, the taste for luxury would be cultivated to a greater and greater degree. The aristocracy, instead of attending to their public duties, would become obsessed with indulging their comfort. Addicted to luxurious modes of living, they would become effeminate; the hard, clear virtues of leadership would diminish and eventually disappear entirely. While the effect on leaders was bad enough, a more general economic effect would be felt by the whole society, for labour would be diverted from the production of essential goods and services to the provision of superfluity which is what the puritans perceived luxury to be.

It was in such a climate that the Bolingbroke Tories sought to return to a pre-revolutionary England in which land was the basis for social hierarchy and in which the Patriot King represented the supreme Machiavellian prince of *virtù*. If the reformers did not look to the monarch alone to restore moral values, they certainly believed that by preaching against private indulgence they would create the right moral climate for a group of Machiavellian lawgivers to emerge in their own society. Whether the reformers were mere practical zealots or whether they aimed in some way to turn men toward a purer, moral order, they intended a revolution in private morality which

74

would lead men away from the corruption of public life in newly established commercial society.

The thrust of Mandeville's spirited attack was that the reformers were either hypocrites who at one and the same time enjoyed the benefits of good living while decrying them, or that they were fools, insisting on the material benefits of commercial society while asking inconsistently that life be made more simple, less pampered. In *The Grumbling Hive* (1924,1, p.17), Mandeville compares Britain with

> A spacious Hive well stockt with Bees
> That lived in Luxury and Ease.

The hive is prosperous, bustling and populous. It is a society where a large population of individuals, acting mainly at the prompting of their passions, manage not only to survive but to maintain a high standard of living. We are told that:

> Vast numbers throng'd the fruitful hive
> Yet those vast numbers made 'em thrive
> Millions endeavouring to supply
> Each other's Lust and Vanity.

Mandeville is suggesting that society, like the hive, benefits from having its vast numbers but that this is the case only because the individuals who compose those throngs pursue different interests and provide different services, services which turn out, incidentally, to be of most benefit to the professional bourgeoisie – physicians, clergymen and lawyers (1924, 1, p.18). It is this recognition of distinct functions – a proto-theory of the division of labour – which makes the Mandevillean account so modern in tone. The reciprocal services that men provide one another are the economic forces that drive society: Adam Smith has his cue.

But layered over the more sophisticated psychological and economic theory that Mandeville developed at greater length in the two volumes of *The Fable of the Bees* is the satirical, fun-poking that he will have against the reformers. If their wishes for a return to the simple life were to be granted (and they are, in the traditional manner, by Jove in the *Grumbling Hive*) then prosperity declines; commercial England is in ruins (1924, 1, pp.34-5)

> As Pride and Luxury decrease
> So by degrees they leave the Seas
> Not merchants now but Companies
> Remove whole manufactories.
> All arts and crafts neglected lie

Content, the Bane of Industry
Makes 'em admire their homely Store
And neither seek nor covet more.

Mandeville's emphasis on the self-interested behaviour of man is of course an echo of Hobbes but his particular way of linking an egoistic theory to economic structures is novel. It was that aspect of his polemic – the subtitle of *The Fable of the Bees* was *private vices, public benefits* – that attracted the attention of serious philosophers, among them, the most eminent names of the eighteenth century. Joseph Butler, in his impressively argued *Sermons*, attempted to show that Mandeville was twisting language beyond permissible usage – that in fact his 'pride' encompassed actions of an other-regarding sort. Hume tackled his notion of luxury, redefining Mandeville's premises, and Adam Smith, careful to disassociate himself from someone as notorious as the licentious doctor from Rotterdam in this *Theory of Moral Sentiments*, sets about applying much Mandevillean argument in his better known and less elegant work, the *Wealth of Nations*. But to guide the reader back to the art of darkness, I would like to consider the reaction of Rousseau, highlighted in Richard Chapman's inaugural lecture, to the Mandevillean paradox.

Rousseau and the Mandevillean Paradox

The central paradox of the corruption debate – that material progress entailed moral decline – was a matter that perplexed Rousseau profoundly. Indeed, it is possible to interpret his entire social philosophy as a response, at two levels, to the dilemma. The first of these responses, which can be called the critical, involved his early attack upon what he saw as the corruption of contemporary society; the second, the redemptive or regenerative, consisted of a plea for the reconstruction of society along new, ideal lines.

In his earlier writing Rousseau first identified the malaise or corruption of public life which he saw threatening the very fabric of modern states. He believed that the materialism and refinement of polite societies were symptoms of a rottenness which contemporary moralists had entirely failed to identify. His first efforts were therefore directed at awakening his fellow citizens to the decadence of modern life. In his *Discours sur les sciences at les arts* (1750) he vigorously attacked the codes of honour and polished style of modern, European man. He described the enervating effects of luxury, insisting on a correlation between the rise of material standards and debauchery. Rousseau intended to show his contemporaries that their lives were a form of existence as contemptible as slavery. The traditional moral criticisms of excess which had been voiced throughout the early

Enlightenment, found an advocate of immense eloquence and rhetorical power in the young Genevan polemicist.

The frontal attack upon social order was carried further in this next important work, the *Discours sur l'origine et les fondements de l'inégalité parmi les hommes* (1775). In that work, Rousseau set out to instil in others the discontent that he had already expressed in the *Discours* of 1750. He revived that ancient philosophy of history in which progress was seen as a secular falling from grace, a descent from, if not a golden age, then an age in which man was very much more in charge of his individual destiny than was his enfeebled, modern, descendant. He depicted the course of human history as a gradual process of decay: man's life in the modern state was little more than a form of slavery, a subjugation that was not worthy of the citizen. The process of decline was exactly matched by an increase in the material wealth of society. Private property introduced the idea of individual acquisitiveness, of man serving his own interest instead of that of the state. From this beginning, the serfdom of modern life could be traced.

As part of his demonstration of the poverty of progress, Rousseau idealized the conditions of the state of nature in the *Discours* of 1755. Although he did not seek a return to nature, a charge which many contemporaries, like Voltaire, made against him, he did use the device of the natural state to show up the deficiencies which he found in modern society. In the ancient way, he harked back to a golden age when a certain freedom and equality, lost to modern man, still persisted. Natural man could lead a simple existence uncluttered by the refinements of polished life. Rousseau believed that something of its pure quality of life in a state of nature could be imported into a regenerated society.

This political motivation – the crusade to regenerate Fallen Man – finds mature expression in Rousseau's *La Nouvelle Héloise* (1761), in the *Contrat Social* (1762) and in *Émile* (1762). In those works, Rousseau began the enormous task of the reconstruction of society along lines that he believed to be good and just.

In *La Nouvelle Héloise*, a novel in the sentimental genre, he depicts a society of ordered, rational beings whose life is a microcosm of the good life that he wishes to create in this ideal polity. The characters of the novel enjoy the benefits of a way of living that is both moral and natural because they behave sincerely and according to their instincts. But the natural environment in which they operate has an ordered pattern which ensures that reason interlinks each individual's separate but instinctive pursuit of the good life.

This moral concern reaches its apogee in *Émile* where Rousseau is concerned with describing the education of the ideal citizen. He begins by asserting the inherent goodness of the natural order which has only been disturbed by the meddlesomeness of man. In order to restore this pristine goodness, he outlines a programme of education based upon natural values.

The solitariness and simplicity of Émile's life is not only a direct indictment of the polished life of man in European society but it is also a plan for moral reform. I shall return, shortly, to consider the educational programme in greater detail since it vitally affects Rousseau's view of good, moral citizenship.

Finally in the *Contrat Social*, Rousseau tackled headlong the question of the political organisation of the ideal state. He begins with his famous assertion that man is born free but is found everywhere in chains. He then turns to the ancient question of political theory: what makes the state legitimate? But it is not until some way further on in the treatise that the reader realises that he is being taken on a grand, utopian journey that will end with the earthly reconstruction of the heavenly city of the philosophers (see Becker, 1967).

All three of these later works form the core of the second, redemptive phase of Rousseau's reaction to the corruption debate. They show that he had left the critical, deconstructive exercise of his early *Discours* and was now embarked upon the great task of describing the conditions of the good life. The *status quo* had been exposed as an impossible anachronism; the new order had to be presented as a feasible, theoretical project.

Rousseau launched into the corruption debate in a controversial and deliberately polemical manner. His observation of man-in-society though close and detailed, was not undertaken in a detached, academic spirit but rather as part of a teleological concern with man's status as a moral being. His analysis of history is intertwined inextricably with the moral recognition that society and its institutions reflect the ethical condition of man through the ages. Social theory, though vital for an understanding of the human predicament, is subservient to the moral purpose of reform.

Rousseau's Theory of Education

Let me now return to Rousseau's theory of education since it is, in essence, the answer to the dilemma of leadership in democratic society and of good citizenship in a Chapmanesque sense.

In his preface to *Émile*, Rousseau regrets the lack of attention given by philosophers to one of the most useful of the humane arts, namely the education of man (Rousseau, 1967, 3, p.16). Until the time of Locke, little progress had been made in constructing a sound educational theory; subsequently the subject was again neglected. Though Rousseau affects a modesty about his own contribution to it, he is direct enough in insisting on the need to revive the intellectual debate about learning. *Émile* is therefore a treatise on education; its author intends to begin by concentrating on the way in which children actually learn rather than on setting out what they should learn. By this method an education suited to the pupil's needs as well as one that guides him, will emerge. The hero of the story is an imaginary student, Émile, and we are asked to embark with him upon his intellectual journey through life in the company of his tutor, none other than Rousseau himself.

Though the overt intention to provide an educational programme for Émile is more than adequately set out in the five books that follow the preface, Rousseau has another, covert purpose, in guiding his reader through an imaginary upbringing. That purpose is the same examination of the moral conditions of man which we have seen was his preoccupation in the various *Discours* and which subsequently expressed itself in the political theory of the *Contrat Social*. The very first sentence in *Émile* attests to Rousseau's moralising intention for he says that everything that has been given by the 'author of nature' is good until it falls within man's grasp, where it degenerates. Mankind meddles in the divine order and produces evil. Society itself is a monument to his capacity for bad work. Nevertheless, all is not lost: evil can be remedied and primarily so by a sound education. The two subjects of the book, education and moral order, are thus inextricably fused.

Though many modern scholars have been concerned with the coherence of Rousseau's thought, few have understood his style as in any way part of it. Yet Rousseau himself worried about modes of expression continuously, pointing out such difficulties as using words consistently in a complicated text where the purpose of their employment varied. The reader of *Émile* finds the same, tense flowing rhetoric that he came upon in the *Discours*. Rousseau's early penchant for a polemical, and at times paradoxical, handling of his subject matter had not left him. Indeed, in *Émile* the seductive style so criticized by the first readers of the *Discours* of 1750 can still be found, though it is now more fully sublimated in the quest for a complete understanding of men and manners.

However, it is in the conceptual architecture of *Émile* that we most clearly recognise the world of the inhabitant of the *Discours*, natural man. In the new context, childhood is substituted for savagery: the infant and the child who has not attained the age of reason correspond to the savage who was left behind in the state of nature by the *Discours* of 1755. The two abstractions, childhood and savagery, emphasize man's isolation: both depict the conditions of life and human psychology outside the framework of civil society. Like the state of nature, the idea of childhood in *Émile* is a conceptual tool designed to heighten our awareness of how social intercourse affects mankind.

The early personal history of Émile is therefore the history of a savage, whom Rousseau says on several occasions, needs to be educated for life in society. Like natural man, Émile displays ignorance, simplicity, and a lack of guile. He is not a moral creature because he lives in isolation from other men. His physical strength is encouraged by a hearty upbringing which includes much vigorous outdoor activity in the country setting where he is being raised. Rousseau, ever an admirer of the Spartan model, insists that Émile's early education must inure him to hardship, thereby preparing him for the vicissitudes of adult life. In Émile's early days, the emphasis is therefore placed on developing manly, self-reliant qualities; physical fitness as an important part of his psychological and moral well-being. At this stage, there is little need for books or study; indeed, the only book Rousseau feels may be of use to Émile is *Robinson Crusoe* because of its emphasis on practical matters. Indeed, Rousseau refers to *Robinson Crusoe* as 'le plus heureux traité d'education naturelle' (1967, 3, p.129).

Émile's education, aimed at making him perfectly adjusted to a natural, non-urban environment, is not designed so that he must remain there. Childhood might be an amoral condition, but Émile must grow into manhood and assume the responsibilities of a moral agent. If his tutor failed to prepare him for that transformation, he would have failed in his most essential duty. Luckily his task is made easier by the instincts inherent in Émile's nature, instincts that he shares with the rest of mankind. Most significant are those passions that we have seen operate within the soul of natural man in the *Discours*, namely self-love and pity.

Self-love is that natural instinct for self-preservation that is implanted in all men to ensure their survival and that of the species. A child, like man in nature, will only be concerned with his own welfare. Nevertheless, Rousseau is anxious to identify self-love as the source of that inherent sociability which will manifest itself once the child is an adult or once savage man has left nature. In an interesting footnote in Book IV of *Émile*, after beginning by considering the true foundation of the precept 'Do unto others as you would have them do unto you' to be in the emotions rather than in the reasoning of men, he says:

> D'où je conclus qu'il n'est pas vrai que les préceptes de la loi naturelle soient fondés sur la raison seule, ils ont une base plus solide et plus sûre. L'amour des hommes dérivé de l'amour de soi est le principe de la justice humaine. Le sommaire de toute la morale est donné dans L'Évangile par celui de la loi (1967, 3, p.165).

The love of others thus derives from self-love and it is the source of human justice. Émile's education must therefore consist in a proper harnessing of this passion so that he can develop into a fully moral being. His tutor's principal method of teaching is to encourage Émile to think for himself and develop naturally. Rather than attempt to teach him by citing authority, this approach entails allowing Émile to learn his lessons directly from experience. He will be encouraged to satisfy himself that the steps to be taken and the conclusions to be reached in each particular case are valid. Much emphasis is put on practical, useful exercises, for it is in this domain that the most fruitful lessons will be learned. Though Émile is born to the ease of a wealthy life, Rousseau suggests that he should learn a trade in order to discipline himself and to understand the lot of ordinary men and women.

The moral development of Émile, his humanising, will be greatly aided by the other natural instinct that Rousseau identified, that is pity or compassion. In the context of *Émile*, pity is described in a Mandevillean way as arising from human weakness. It is the insecurity and defencelessness of both childhood and savagery that makes men realize their need for others. Association with others arises because individuals cannot fend for themselves: 'Tout attachment est un signe d'insuffisance: si chacun de nous n'avait nul besoin des autres, il ne songerait guére à s'unir à eux' (1967, 3, p.156).

However the need to depend on others may be counted a social virtue. In the *Discours* of 1755, Rousseau had identified the natural capacity of men to share the suffering of others by making it their own. Émile will pity men because he can recognise their suffering: his nascent sensibility must be nurtured and encouraged by proper instruction.

This maturing of our hero brings Rousseau close to what is the final object of his education, that of making him a moral citizen. Rousseau echoes the account of the origin of society that he had given in the *Discours* of 1755, reminding his reader of the singular importance he attaches to the acquisition of property and the division of labour that is characteristic of life in developed societies (1967, 3, p.137). Leaving the state of nature is a necessary act of self-preservation. For Émile the idea of being an active member of society is inculcated during his adolescence. Hitherto Émile, like the savage, needed only to practice the natural arts which are so profusely displayed in *Robinson Crusoe*, in order to survive. Now, in society, he must learn the industrial arts which call for the cooperation of many individuals, as opposed to the natural arts which can be formed by an individual alone (1967, 3, p.132).

The entire bent of Émile's education will make his adaptation to social living a natural and certain course. The emphasis on practical achievements will mean that he will put the right value on those arts that are useful, despite the opinion of the general public which tends to the opposite view of valuing what is useless. His reason, always trained to follow the just sentiment of his heart, will now serve him usefully in his exchanges with other men. He will have come to an understanding both of his own nature and of his environment. A harmony will characterise his actions and he will have gained that inner strength which Rousseau had identified as the object of his education at the beginning of the book. Because he will know how to distinguish between good and evil, indeed to be wise, Émile will be ready to benefit from social life without being corrupted by it. Society, for its part, will benefit from the dedication of a truly moral citizen.

The relationship between Émile as an individual and society as a collectivity, is vital. Rousseau says that society must be studied in the individual just as the individual in society must be examined. Whoever wants to treat politics and ethics apart will never understand either. But the study of this relationship begins in the state of nature because there we first see man stripped of his acquired, civilized attributes. We can do this by conjecturing on the course of history, as Rousseau did in the *Discours*, especially that of 1755, or we can do it by considering the process of growing up, which he had done in *Émile*. In either case the object of the analysis is the same: to identify the moral base upon which we can erect the social superstructure.

Just before the *'Profession de foi du vicaire savoyard'* in Book IV of *Émile*, Rousseau uses the striking phrase *'mort morale'* which threatens the young, so far only partially-educated *Émile*. It is the object of all his profession in the rest of *Émile* to prevent his hero, as a citizen, from being part of the moral death of society. Émile's education will ensure that he is in moral good health and that all the Émiles who form society share his good fortune. What remains to be done is to match their individual resilience with a firmness in social arrangements. The political reconstruction of institutions had now to be undertaken.

Revisiting the Art of Darkness

Rousseau's programme of education for Émile is the preparation of a citizen who will take part in the political life of a mature democracy where no one should abdicate responsibility to leaders. The idea that each citizen has a responsibility to participate is part of the concept of Greek civic democracy; it is also a sentiment often expressed by Richard Chapman and one he has closely linked to high standards in leadership. Surveying the first Nolan Report he concluded:

> A society which fails to demand high standards in public life and which sneers and denigrates those who are doing their best in difficult circumstances in public life, cannot expect that high standards will be achieved or maintained. This is not just the responsibility of a relatively few people in public life, but a social responsibility for everyone (Chapman, 1995).

Such an exhortation might easily have been expressed to Émile by his tutor fearing the consequences for the social fabric of any decline in civic participation. Without the ethic of engagement to rely upon, the only recourse left to political leaders would be to trick the masses into obeying them; at such a time we must expect to revisit the blackest art of darkness.

Note
Some of the material from this chapter was derived from M.R. Jack *Corruption and Progress: the Eighteenth Century Debate* (New York: AMS, 1989) and from a lecture delivered to the Johnson Club in November, 1996.

References
Becker, C. (1967), *The Heavenly City of the Eighteenth Century Philosophers*, New Haven: Yale University Press.
Chapman, Richard A. (1962), *An Examination of T.H. Green's Philosophy of the State, with particular reference to its applicability to some Theoretical Problems of the Twentieth Century Welfare State*, unpublished M.A. Thesis, Carlton University, Ottawa.
Chapman, Richard A. (1984), *Leadership in the British Civil Service*, Croom Helm.
Chapman, Richard A. (1988a), *Ethics in the British Civil Service*, Routledge.
Chapman, Richard A. (1988b), *The Art of Darkness*, University of Durham.
Chapman, Richard A. (1995), 'The First Nolan Report on Standards in Public Life', in *Teaching Public Administration* Vol. XV, No. 2, pp.1-14.
Forbes, D. (1966), 'Introduction' to Adam Ferguson's *An Essay on the History of Civil Society* (1767), Edinburgh University Press.
Kramnick, I. (1968), *Bolingbroke and His Circle: The Politics of Nostalgia in the Age of Walpole*, Clarendon Press.
Longford, P. (1989), *A Polite and Commercial People, England 1727-1783*, Oxford University Press.
Mandeville, B. (1924), *The Fable of the Bees*, Clarendon Press.
Novak, M.E. (1962), *Economics and Fiction of Daniel Defoe*, Los Angeles: University of California Press.
Plumb, J.G. (1969), *The Growth of Political Stability in England 1676-1725*, Peregrine.
Pocock, J.G.A. (Ed.) (1968), 'Introduction' in *The Political Works of James Harrington*, Cambridge University Press.
Pope, A. (1966), *Poetical Works*, Oxford University Press.
Rousseau, J.J. (1967), *Oevres Completes* (3 Volumes), Paris: Editions du Sevil.
Tuck, R. (1979), *Natural Right Theories*, Cambridge University Press.

6 'We Walk by Faith, Not by Sight': The Ethic of Public Service

Barry J. O'Toole

Thomas Hill Green is one of Richard Chapman's great intellectual heroes. There are a number of reasons for this, notable amongst them the fact that Green's idealism was firmly rooted in his religious convictions. Those convictions prevented his idealism from being merely sterile intellectual reflections. They encouraged the development of a strong and practical social conscience, a conscience which Green fostered in his students. As these students became leaders in British public service that conscience underpinned the emergence of a philosophy of administration, a philosophy which formed the basis of the ethic of public service throughout most of the present century (O'Toole, 1990; Richter, 1967). Thus, while the title for this chapter may seem, at first glance, somewhat unusual, students of English Idealism will recognise that it is, in fact, from the text which Green used for his lay sermon on *Faith* (Green, 1900).

Green was, of course, referring to faith in the religious sense, that is '... a consciousness of God, which is not a knowledge of him of a kind with our knowledge of matters of fact ...' (p.269). In the sermon he observed that the enemy which religion has to fear is not a passionate atheism. The danger, he argued, is rather from 'the slow sap of an undermining indifference which does not deny God and duty, but ignores them; which does not care to trouble itself about them, and finds in our acknowledged inability to know them, as we know matters of fact, a new excuse for putting them aside' (pp.270-71). The same observations seem to be true for the more mundane matters with which this chapter is concerned, namely those connected with the ethic of public service. The enemy of such an ethic, clearly, is not passionate antagonism on the part of deeply corrupt individuals, but an indifference, not professed (indeed largely denied) by both practitioners and observers of public life. Practitioners seem increasingly to pay lip service to such concepts as the public interest and public duty while at the same time promoting reforms which undermine the very basis of those concepts.

Observers, primarily academic observers, go further. They ignore such concepts because they are not susceptible to the fashionable techniques of measurement so beloved of modern social science. Those scholars who do raise their heads above the parapet in defence of the concepts are declared to be relying on anecdote, or sentimental feeling, or to be harking back to a non-existent golden age of British political and administrative history. Those cynics who make such accusations demand 'evidence' for the existence of an ethic of public service, much as with those who do not share religious faith in God require 'evidence' for His existence. However, simply because an ethic of public service cannot be easily and reliably measured and is not susceptible to the arguments of the pure rationalists, does not mean that it does not exist. It is rather that its existence does not depend on material manifestations of that existence. As with religious faith, it is a 'primary formative principle, which cannot be deduced or derived from anything else' (p.263).

This chapter seeks, first, to establish the characteristics of the public service ethic, secondly to indicate that recent changes have undermined some of those characteristics, and thirdly to consider the implications of these changes for the public service ethic.

Idealism and the Public Service Ethic

While perhaps not the most obvious place to look for a succinct statement of English Idealism, Green's sermon on *Faith* contains a passage which could easily be transposed into his more famous philosophical writings. It reads thus:

> The existence of specific duties and the recognition of them, the spirit of self-sacrifice, the moral law and the reverence for it in its most abstract and absolute form, all no doubt pre-suppose society; but society, of a kind to render them possible, is not the creature of appetite and fear, or of the most complicated and indirect result of these. It implies the action in man of a principle in virtue of which he projects himself into the future or into some other world as some more perfect being than he actually is, and thus seeks not merely to satisfy momentary wants but to become 'another man', to become more nearly as this perfect being. Under this influence wants and desires that have their root in the animal nature became an impulse of improvement, which forms, enlarges and recasts societies ... (p.269).

It is clear that, in this passage, Green is dealing with concepts which he refers to elsewhere as 'self-realisation' and 'the common good'. Man's nature is to be part of society, and it is only within society that self-realisation can be achieved – because the self-realisation of each individual is dependent upon the self-realisation of others. In other words, anything which contributes to the creation, well-being or harmony of society is to be encouraged: there is a 'common good' in social organisation without which the capacity for self-realisation could not be achieved. It is the duty of government to ensure that there are no impediments to achieving the common good. Indeed, the real function of government is to maintain the conditions of life in which morality shall be possible. Moreover, there is a special duty on those who are in positions of authority to behave in a 'moral' way, where morality is 'the disinterested performance of self-imposed duties', where to act morally is to set aside all personal interests, and where an act is moral insofar as it contributes to the 'common good' and has as its motive such a contribution (see Chapman, 1965; Green, 1931, pp.32-33 and 39-40; Green, 1969 pp.210-212; O'Toole, 1990).

It is a belief in the 'common good' which is the most important of the characteristics of the morality of public service. The problem, however, is that it is difficult to relate such a concept to the practical world of politics and administration. What does the phrase 'the common good' mean in the world as it actually is, rather than in the real world of English Idealism? In other words, how do ideas about morality and the relationship between morality and public service, translate into a public service ethic?

The conventional answer to this question is simply to assert that Green's 'common good' can be more easily understood in contemporary political terms as 'the public interest'. That in turn, however, begs the question, what is the public interest? Unfortunately, that is a question to which there is no simple answer. This is because it is a concept which can be understood at a number of different levels, and in a number of different contexts, legal, political and administrative. Even when confining the discussion to political and administrative aspects of the public interest, there are innumerable problems. These arise mainly from 'the complexity of government, the multiplicity of participants in government and the enormous pressure brought to bear on government from hundreds, possibly thousands of sources ....'. Furthermore, 'not only is government complex in the ways outlined, it is not a machine: it is made up of individuals who have their own ideas about what is right and wrong, about their duty in relation to official work, and ultimately about what the public interest is' (O'Toole, 1997a, p.131). In addition, these individuals, at whatever level, are primarily concerned with their own small area of public policy. It is very unusual for them to be able to take an objective view of the overall picture of government (O'Toole, 1997a, p.131). Thus, rather than trying to think about the public interest 'as if it were something concrete and comprehensible, against which all actions can be judged' it might be more feasible to think of the public interest 'in different circumstances, for different departments, for different

86

individuals and in relation to each decision' (O'Toole, 1997a, p.132). Perhaps there is both 'an overall public interest, which it is the duty of government as a whole to protect and promote, and a public interest as perceived by individuals and smaller collectivities, such as government departments or agencies, which it is their duty to protect and promote' (O'Toole, 1997a, p.132). All this leaves the question posed earlier unanswered. Perhaps a more fruitful line of inquiry would be to consider further how, indeed whether, public officials, politicians and administrators, think about, or themselves conceive of, the public interest. This brings the discussion to the second of the characteristics of the public service ethic: the increasingly unfashionable concept of public duty.

The concept of public duty is simply stated. It is that the public servant, politician or official, puts the interests of society above his or her personal interests and is a public servant out of an altruistic desire to serve the public. It is a concept as old as philosophy itself. Indeed, perhaps the most important statement on its practical meaning is contained in one of the noble classics of ancient thought, Plato's *Republic*. Essentially, the Guardians, the foremost of public servants, would lead a pure and simple life, without the temptations of private property, the intention being to remove the temptation to sacrifice the welfare of the wider community to personal interests (see Plato, 1941; O'Toole, 1993, p.1; O'Toole, 1997b, pp.83-85). Of course, in practice each individual will have great difficulty in setting aside personal interests, and of later political thinkers it was Rousseau who considered that to expect public officials to behave without personal ambition or the desire for personal gain is to expect the unnatural. Nevertheless, he too believed that officials should set aside their personal wishes, and act in this unnatural way: that is, to subordinate themselves to the general will (Rousseau, 1911, 1913, 1953; Chapman, 1988a, pp.10-13).

If T.H. Green had expressed a view *specifically* on this question, his thinking would almost certainly be more in line with Plato than with Rousseau. Richard Chapman, writing about this aspect of the public service ethic in relation to Green, suggested that 'it is possible to reason as he reasoned by taking as a basis the teaching in his work as a whole':

> In this way the official is seen as a person, with one morality, but with attributes of an administrator and an individual in society, who is himself concerned with his own development. ... Green would have stressed that his exercise of power must be temperate, and above all – and this is of supreme importance – he should always have before him a clear understanding of what the state is trying to do, that is, 'the end' of state action (to maintain conditions in which morality is possible ...), so that in making any decision he realises that the result of his decision is but a means to an end (Chapman, 1962, pp.149-150).

87

Of course, the views of political philosophers cannot be accepted absolutely as being the basis for practical action in government. Questions may be raised, for example, about the necessity, in a democracy, for appointed officials to pursue the settled will of the electorate as expressed through the ballot box. For example, Green's views about 'the end' of government (and, by implication, about how public officials should behave) need to be reconciled with the intentions of elected politicians. In other words, the necessity for accountability is also central to the notion of an ethic of public service, and this is a question which will be returned to in due course. However, the necessity for accountability in a formal, democratic sense, does not negate the requirement for moral accountability and for the public official to act in ways which accord with such requirements. Examples from history indicate that sometimes public officials ought to exercise independent moral judgement, and the inculcation of such an independent spirit has been central to the socialisation of British public servants for most of the past century and to the development of the public service ethic amongst officials. Three examples will illustrate the point. The first is that of Sir Stafford Northcote and Sir Charles Trevelyan, whose famous *Report on the Organisation of the Permanent Civil Service* of 1853 laid the foundations of the civil service until the vagaries of commercialisation set in. Their Report was inspired by the need to do something about the manifest and widespread corruption (in its narrowest sense) which bedevilled the great offices of state and which led to the national disasters of the Crimean War. The principles they laid down for the recruitment of civil servants led to the emergence of a famously incorrupt and meritorious civil service, a civil service which became the envy of the world.

Much of the credit for the later development of that civil service must go to Sir Warren Fisher, who was largely responsible for the creation of a unified civil service during the inter-war years (O'Halpin, 1989). In that service civil servants were recruited on merit, worked as part of the Whitehall team, were paid according to reasonably uniform scales, as befitted people working in a collegiate atmosphere, and could be posted to any department because of their generalist, but nonetheless professional, administrative skills. Their code of ethics was based on the pure concept of public duty. All this was exemplified by Fisher himself whose most famous statement on public duty remained at the heart of the ethos of public service for many decades: 'The first duty of a civil servant is to give his undivided allegiance to the State at all times and on all occasions when the State has a call on his services ... A civil servant is not to subordinate his duty to his personal interests' (Fisher et al., 1928, para 56).

The sentiments expressed by this formal statement were consistent with the 'concept of public duty' and its application in British public administration, and were personified in Sir Edward Bridges. Indeed, Fisher's most

88

distinguished successor as Head of the Civil Service was in some ways more assertive. As an exemplar he was more important, for he was the arch proponent of generalist administration and the whole ethos of public service which went with it. As Richard Chapman notes in his masterly study of Bridges, 'of those who joined the civil service Bridges thought it fair to say that nearly all had in common "a disposition to find public affairs of interest; no desire or intention to take part in political life; and a desire to work as a member of a team, rather than seek personal glory"' (Chapman, 1988b, p.38, quoting Bridges).

The subordination of 'personal glory' was central to Bridges' ethos of administration. He believed, for example, that 'A good civil servant has to be more anonymous and unselfish in his work than those in other walks of life ... the traditional outlook of the modern civil service is one that recognises that the interests and welfare of the whole country come first ...' (quoted in Chapman, 1988b, p.64). He thought that civil servants should be influenced 'by no thoughts of private advantage or advancement' and that they should have no end in view but that 'the work be carried out faithfully and well' (quoted in Chapman, 1988b, p.314).

These are truly platonic sentiments and Bridges believed in them passionately. Moreover, he apparently believed that others accepted and lived by them too. According to Chapman '... it seems to have been normal to assume in conversation with Bridges that people always had uppermost in their minds a general anxiety to do what was right or what was best in the public interest' (1988b, p.63).

Those who demand harder evidence than merely the example of leading members of the administrative élite tend to scoff at the idea that all civil servants would have the same set of principles. Of course they are right. However, such scepticism should not be allowed to detract from the influence people such as Fisher, Bridges, and other, more recent, exemplars of public service, such as Sir Ian Bancroft, had, both in relation to their immediate colleagues and more widely (Dalyell, 1996). Apart from direct professional relationships, this influence occurred through the process of socialisation, which is such an important element of the education and personal and professional development of British civil servants (Chapman, 1970). In Britain it has been probably the most important means of communicating values, standards and methods of administration. It is about the acquisition and development of certain characteristics and codes: it is, indeed, about the acquisition and development of an administrative ethos. It is about the administrative culture (for a fuller discussion of this see Chapman, 1984; Chapman and O'Toole, 1994; O'Toole, 1997b).

The question, of course, is: whose values and standards; whose ethos; whose culture? The answer is that the values by which the bureaucratic and governmental system operates must be in line with those of the society the bureaucracy and government serve. In a democracy, those values are communicated by the politicians, and it is the politicians who are both responsible and accountable for not just the work of the officials and of the government machine generally, but the values which inform that work. This brings the discussion to the third of the characteristics of the public service ethic: accountability.

The accountability of public servants is one of the cornerstones of liberal democracy. Simply stated it means that those who are entrusted with public affairs answer to the citizens for the conduct of those affairs. Free, fair and regular elections are the ultimate arenas in which this answerability takes place. However, elections are held only infrequently, and in between elections other mechanisms of accountability operate. In the United Kingdom these mechanisms revolve around the most basic of constitutional doctrines: the sovereignty of Parliament and the conventions of ministerial accountability (see O'Toole, 1995). The focus of this chapter therefore gives special attention to the accountability of ministers in Parliament for the actions of civil servants, and to the accountability of civil servants.

The most important of those conventions is that of individual ministerial responsibility: that each individual minister is answerable in Parliament for all of the actions which are carried out in his or her name. It is a convention which allows for both the party political impartiality and the anonymity of civil servants, whose advice is thus protected, allowing it to be clear, candid and comprehensive. It also means that civil servants are not constrained to give advice which is in line with 'public opinion', and are able to encourage ministers to act in ways which accord with the public interest. In other words the civil servant's advice can be framed with the independent moral spirit referred to above. The minister is at liberty to ignore such advice, but he is accountable and responsible for those acts. At the same time, however, he or she can have confidence that officials are loyal and their advice is honest.

It has been argued that such a system is a nonsense because ministers cannot reasonably know all that is being done in their name. The argument is that government is so complex, its activities so comprehensive, and its scope so wide that only those issues which are politically sensitive will ever reach the minister. It follows that the convention of individual ministerial responsibility is a sham. The convention may have been appropriate in the past, but government has grown too big for it to have any meaning any more. Is this a reasonable argument? After all, it has been the case throughout most of the present century that most decisions have been taken by officials. These officials have no constitutional personality of their own; they always act in the name of the minister. The point is that it is for the official to know what the minister's policy is, and, more importantly, for the minister to make known that policy to them. They will then be in a position to put that policy into effect. Where there are political problems for the policy, that is a matter for the minister. Where civil servants make mistakes they are subject to internal, hierarchical disciplinary procedures, and are accountable for their actions just as employees in private organisations are accountable. External accountability, however, is always to Parliament. If this were not the case, what would be the necessity for ministers, or indeed for Parliament itself? (O'Toole, 1995, pp.58-70).

This point can be illustrated by two examples which Richard Chapman refers to in one of his contributions to the book he edited with Michael Hunt on *Open Government* (Chapman and Hunt, 1987; Chapman, 1987, pp.50-52). The first example is that of Herbert Morrison who, when he was Home Secretary, had to explain to the House of Commons about 'an unfortunate blunder in connection with the creation of the National Fire Service', and to apologise for the blunder. Morrison later explained:

> Somebody must be held responsible to Parliament and the public. It has to be the Minister, for it is he, and neither Parliament nor the public, who has official control over his civil servants. One of the fundamentals of our system of government is that some Minister of the Crown is responsible to Parliament, and through Parliament to the public, for every act of the Executive. This is a cornerstone of our system of parliamentary government ... Now and again the House demands to know the name of the officer responsible for the occurrence. The proper answer of the Minister is that if the House want anybody's head it must be his head as the responsible Minister, and that it must leave him to deal with the officer concerned in the Department (Morrison, 1954, p.323 quoted in Chapman, 1987, p.52).

The second example Chapman uses is from the Parliamentary debate on the Sachsenhausen case, held on 5 February 1968. The details of the case are not directly relevant to this discussion, but what is important is a passage from the speech of the then Foreign Secretary, George Brown, who said, in relation to the convention of ministerial responsibility:

> ... we will breach a very serious constitutional position if we start holding officials responsible for things that are done wrong. In this country ... our Ministers are responsible to Parliament. If things are wrongly done, then they are wrongly done by Ministers ... I accept my full share of the responsibility in this case. It happens that I am the last of a series of Ministers who have looked at this matter and I am the one who got caught with the ball when the lights went up ... It is Ministers who must be attacked, not officials (quoted in Chapman, 1987, p.52).

In this system of accountability, the minister becomes the personification of the department. Parliamentarians have:

a real person, a public person, to whom they can address the grievances of their constituents. They have someone they can embarrass politically and thus someone over whom they can exercise some form of political control. Moreover, by being able to exercise some form of control over the person who represents, and very publicly represents, the department they have some form of control over the department. The consequence is that it would be a very foolish minister who did not make sure that, while he cannot know everything, his civil servants know what they are meant to be doing. It also means that if anything does go wrong the minister will take firm action to make sure that whatever went wrong does not go wrong again (O'Toole & Chapman, 1995, p.119).

This system of accountability may not be as important for the careers of individual ministers, as it is for the day-to-day work of public officials. While many commentators have concentrated on the former (that is, the resignation or otherwise of ministers), few have dealt adequately with the latter (see Woodhouse, 1994). The convention of ministerial responsibility has enormous practical significance for the everyday conduct of civil servants. The convention conditions the way they make decisions, sensitises them to the political environment and encourages them to document any action taken just in case a decision becomes politically sensitive. Such 'bureaucratisation' may be seen as inefficient (in terms of the so-called new public management), but it must also be seen as being essential to parliamentary democracy: it means that civil servants are constantly encouraged to act in ways which accord with the wishes of the elected government. In the British system it is the actions and decisions made in the name of ministers which must be accounted for; not the advice of civil servants. If these precepts continue to be followed then, given that the UK does have a system of parliamentary democracy, this would be a relatively effective system of accountability. It would be a system in which public servants, officials and politicians, would be aware that there is a public interest to be followed, would be better able to perceive what that public interest is and would be better able to act out of a sense of public duty.

What has Happened to the Public Service Ethic?

Recent trends and events have conspired to undermine all three of the characteristics of the public service ethic outlined above. This section of the chapter will deal with two aspects of this: first, the political trends which seem to have eroded the concept of the 'public interest'; and secondly, and very closely linked, the administrative trends which have undermined the concept of public duty, especially amongst civil servants.

It is in Sir Richard Scott's Report on the Export of Defence Equipment and Dual-Use Goods to Iraq in which the relationship between the public interest and questions of accountability is made most explicit. The Report makes it quite clear that the public interest is derived from parliamentary democracy. For democracy to work, ministers must be held accountable. For them to be held accountable they are under an obligation to disclose as full information as possible about their activities and the activities of their departments. In Scott's words 'The public interest in a full discharge of this obligation should be a constant heavy weight in the balance' (Scott, 1996, D1.165). As far as Scott was concerned, in relation to the actions of ministers and officials concerning the sale of defence equipment to Iraq and Iran, 'in circumstances where disclosure might be politically and administratively inconvenient, the balance struck by government [came] down, time and time again, against full disclosure' (D1.165). The main criticism of ministers was that they had, on innumerable occasions, and over many years, connived to prevent the full story from emerging about the sale of defence equipment to Iran and Iraq, and, in particular, they had not kept Parliament, MPs and the public as fully informed as they should. Ministers had, indeed, failed 'to comply with the standards set by paragraph 27 of the *Questions of Procedure for Ministers* and, more important, failed to discharge the obligations imposed by the constitutional principle of ministerial accountability' (D4.63; see O'Toole, 1997a).

Of course, the revelations of the Scott Report are not the first indications of the undermining of the principles of accountability referred to earlier. The constant refrain of much of the literature is that while the conventions remain in theory, in practice they have been undermined. Particular cases in the post-war years have been referred to as being watersheds in the decline of ministerial accountability. The two most referred to were the Crichel Down case of 1954 (see for example Finer, 1956; Chester, 1954; Nicholson, 1986) and the Vehicle and General Affair of the early 1970s (see for example Chapman, 1973; O'Toole, 1989, pp.144-152). In both cases, decisions made by civil servants led to major political controversies, to the establishment of inquiries and to the naming and blaming of civil servants. More importantly, but perhaps not so obviously, these cases, and others, have contributed to the general decline in the relationship of trust between ministers and civil servants, and to the emergence of a view of a career in the civil service which no longer sees public duty as necessarily the most important driving motivation in being a public servant.

At a superficial level the Scott Report may be compared to the earlier problem cases mentioned above. Closer examination, however, reveals the Scott revelations to be on quite a different scale. While individual civil servants are, indeed, referred to in the Report, and sometimes accused of culpability, it is the role of ministers and their personal day-to-day involvement in the attempts to prevent the disclosure of information which are at the heart of the Report's findings.

The implication of much of the Scott Report is that ministers, by failing to follow the requirements of the *Questions of Procedure for Ministers,* were acting contrary to the public interest. The question remains, however, about what the public interest is. While Scott is reasonably clear that the public interest derives from parliamentary democracy, and is manifested primarily in the relationship between ministers and Parliament and ministers and the public, it may not be unreasonable to suggest that ministers and officials genuinely believed that by acting in the ways that they did, including misleading Parliament, MPs and the public, they were still acting in the public interest. Indeed, it is clear from the Report and from evidence given by ministers that in many cases they believed that they were protecting Britain's commercial and diplomatic interests. Ministers and officials consistently argued that their actions were dictated by what they saw as being the public interest. To some extent this view of their actions relies on the conception of the public interest, referred to earlier, as being multifaceted. In other words, the ministers and officials involved had particular ideas about the public interest, peculiar to their narrow perspectives on public policy. They may genuinely have believed that it was best served in the ways outlined, including by the stifling of information. If so, they seem to have forgotten something which the non-politician Scott remembered, and put quite clearly at the forefront of his Report: Britain is a parliamentary democracy. His report is replete with examples of ministers misleading Parliament and the public and of them consistently failing to meet the requirements of ministerial accountability. As he states quite boldly: 'A failure by ministers to meet the obligations of ministerial accountability by providing information about the activities of departments, undermines ... the democratic process' (K.8.3). By implication, it also undermines the public interest (see O'Toole, 1997a, p.132).

The Scott Report is an intensely political document. It could be argued that it is unfair to alight on the Report as evidence of a general decline in the public service ethic. That would be a fair comment if there were no other indications for such a decline. However, there are other indications, and other examples to be cited, to indicate a general decline. Some relate to political matters; others to the changes to the administrative machine and to the administrative culture. All have had a significant influence on the public service ethic, and all, again, bring together the notions of the public interest, accountability and public duty.

There is no need here to catalogue yet again the enormous structural changes that have taken place in British central administration in recent years. It is sufficient merely to state that pluralism has replaced unity in organisational terms and that business values have replaced public values in cultural terms. In relation to the latter, of course, politicians and senior

94

officials are defensive. They assert that nothing could be further from the truth. Business-like methods, they have argued, sit hand in hand with public service values. Sir Robin Butler, who is the inheritor to the proud tradition of Fisher and Bridges, has presided over the dismantling of their creation. Yet he repeats, almost as a mantra, that the civil service is 'unified but not uniform' (Treasury and Civil Service Committee, 1989, Q.320) and that it is the values of 'integrity, impartiality, objectivity, selection and promotion on merit and accountability through Ministers to Parliament' which give it its unity (Cabinet Office, 1994, paragraph 2.7). The question we must ask ourselves is this: how do these values differ from the values to be expected in any decent private organisation? The answer is that, apart from the last, accountability through ministers to Parliament, they could apply to almost any organisation. Even this requirement has been severely tested by the organisational changes of the last ten years. No better examples can be given of this than those relating to the Home Office and the Prisons Agency or the Department of Social Security and the Child Benefits Agency. In both cases ministers have neatly side-stepped the issue of accountability by declaring their role to be that of policy makers and disowning any faults in operational matters (and they have themselves been the judges of what is a policy question and what is an operational question). Such evasions of responsibility, based again on one of the dubious distinctions of Robin Butler, that between accountability and responsibility, has not been lost on academic observers, and surely cannot have been lost on the civil servants whose careers are haphazardly, and in some cases unjustly, placed on the line.

The apparent breakdown, at least in high profile cases, of the relationship between ministers and civil servants, is, in itself, a cause for concern in relation to the concept of public duty. Civil servants may well be forgiven, in circumstances where ministers have disowned their officials and have consciously attacked what by some were seen to be their privileges, if they regard their personal well-being as being more important than their public duty. Civil servants have become increasingly demoralised since the Second World War, both in terms of their pay and in terms of the prestige of their profession. They have come under increasing pressure from their political masters. Their pay has declined relative to other professions. Their loyalty has increasingly come into question, most vividly as witnessed by the GCHQ Affair. Their profession has continued to be held in low esteem, both by politicians and more widely. All this has combined to create the conditions in which it cannot be surprising if their morale has declined. Nor can it be surprising if personal interests are allowed to come before public duty (see O'Toole, 1989). However, this demoralisation is not unique in being a factor which has encouraged civil servants to think of their personal interests. More recently there has been the positive inculcation of such attitudes by the

95

importation of business-like methods and values. This is related to the cases cited here, but, of course, is much more widespread and may be much more insidious.

It is in relation to questions of personnel management that these values are becoming increasingly evident. The work of Richard Chapman in relation to the Civil Service Commission (which now no longer exists) and the Recruitment and Assessment Service Agency (which is now no longer part of the public service) is especially valuable in considering these questions (see Chapman 1991; 1993; 1996; 1997). His work points to the inherent dangers associated with the abolition of the Commission and the privatisation, or at least 'Balkanisation', of the recruitment process, and the replacement of the old unified system with more pluralistic approaches. Most departments and agencies now have almost complete control over staffing matters and do not need to use any particular agency or private firm for recruitment. The civil service unions have pointed to the potential consequences of these changes, such as the 'trapping' of civil servants in 'employment ghettos' and the inability of the civil service to know about, let alone use, the great talent that is, in theory, at its disposal. This is unquestionably inefficient. In addition, it has implications for the perception which civil servants might have about their status as civil servants. In other words, questions might be raised about whether they perceive themselves as servants of the public or merely as employees of the organisation in which they happen to be employed. Such questions are even more pertinent in those areas of work which can no longer be carried out by civil servants. These, and other questions about public duty are raised in the admirable Report by the House of Lords Select Committee on the Public Service which considered the privatisation of the RAS (House of Lords, 1996).

Such ideas may also be explored in relation to other aspects of personnel management. The hoary old question of performance-related pay is one of these. Quite apart from the utility of PRP, the real problem is associated, yet again, with the potential for personal interests to obscure the needs of the public interest. Expressed in practical terms, personal ambition may stand in the way of collegial achievement. As Rousseau put it 'nothing is more dangerous to public affairs than the influence of private interests' (1913, Book III, Chapter 4). While dog-eat-dog may be appropriate in the business world, it must surely stand in the way of the efficient dispatch of public affairs. Collegiality has always been the basis of much of the work of the civil service, at all levels; individual enterprise and competition between agencies are the province of the business world. The production and selling of soap powder is not quite the same as the development and implementation of a policy in relation to the support of children living in single-parent families. The design and making of washing machines is not quite the same as dealing with the problems of financing local government. It is not just the tasks that are different, it is their importance. The people who are affected are not just customers; they are citizens. The arena is not the market place; it is society (see O'Toole, 1994, p.31).

These issues are merely examples of what might happen in the future if consideration is not given soon to the implications of the demise of public service in Britain. The reforms are storing up problems for the future. Yet the new Labour government seems equally as intent on pushing through more and more of these reforms as the old Conservative government. As far back as 1991, Mr John Smith, then Shadow Chancellor of the Exchequer, made it quite clear in a lecture at the Royal Institute of Public Administration that the Labour Party was sympathetic to the then Government's reforms. He said: 'Any Government will want a Civil Service which is as effective and efficient as possible... Next Steps provides the flexibility to enable the Civil Service to respond both to changes in what a Government wants and to changes in Government' (quoted in Treasury and Civil Service Committee, 1991, p.ix). This line was somewhat modified in the light of the fiascos of the Child Support and Prison Service agencies, which led Labour spokesmen to suggest that they would have clearer lines of responsibility. However, their support for the basic principles of 'new public management' remains. Indeed, the pace of change seems now as fast as ever. For example, Dr David Clark, the new Minister for Public Service, has inaugurated a 'Better Government' programme and, at the time of writing, a White Paper on reforming government bureaucracy is due to be published (*The Independent*, 8 July 1997, 'Network +' p.7). On the face of it the reforms may seem like 'common sense': examples of change currently considered to be good (see Chapman and Greenaway, 1980, pp.183-84). In fact they are undermining some of the cherished values of the British system of government. These values may seem old fashioned; in fact they lie at the very heart of administrative efficiency and sound democracy.

One final example, again from personnel management practice in the civil service, will illustrate the point. In 1993 the Efficiency Unit published what might be regarded in the future as being an even more important document than the Next Steps report itself. Known as the Oughton Report, it has the rather prosaic title *Career Management and Succession Planning Study* (Efficiency Unit, 1993) and suggested that, in the future, recruitment to the most senior positions in the civil service may be by open competition. This is already happening. Indeed, the 1997 Report from the Civil Service Commissioners deserves very close scrutiny (Civil Service Commissioners, 1997; Chapman, 1997). In addition the Oughton Report suggested that, in the future, even the most senior officials could be appointed on fixed term contracts and subject to performance measurement.

On the face of it, such possibilities may seem eminently reasonable. After all, the rationale behind such thinking is that these leading positions should be filled by the best possible people and that recruitment by open competition will secure this desirable state of affairs. Moreover, as the argument runs, new blood would surely lead to an injection of 'innovation' and 'imagination', the buzz-words which seem to earn management consultants such fat fees. The best practices of the private sector would revitalise the public sector. However, such thinking is blinkered and superficial. Surely, questions must be raised about the applicability of private sector practices in organisations dominated by the requirements of parliamentary accountability. Are business practices really appropriate when dealing with the rights of citizens and the delicate standards of democracy? Might not those brought in from the business world be frustrated by the 'inefficiency' of the requirements of democratic accountability? Might not ministers feel frustrated at the potential loss of the unique expertise of the 'mandarins' who know the machine so well? (O'Toole, 1994, p.31).

More important than these questions, however, are questions about the continuation of an impartial career civil service:

> Will competition for jobs be genuinely open? Or is there the possibility that they will be filled by placemen? Might there be scope for corruption of a more overt kind? Will those who have been recruited into the fast stream administrative grades, by rigorous open competition, feel cheated, even if the people appointed are not partisan appointees? Will those who are thinking of a career in the civil service be deterred by the idea that it might no longer be a 'career' civil service? (O'Toole and Jordan, 1995, p.170).

Such questions raise three sorts of doubts. First, what might be the implications for managerial efficiency of such possible changes? Secondly, what might be the constitutional implications of such changes? Thirdly, what becomes of the public service ethic?

The phrase, the Public Service Ethic, is an old fashioned phrase. However, it is a phrase which summarises the essential nature of political and administrative life in the United Kingdom. This is so because its essential characteristics are directly related to parliamentary democracy: the public interest; the concept of public duty; and accountability. In Britain, in the past, we have had faith in our system of government. Traditionally, we believed in our politicians and our public officials and assumed that our system was superior. Those days, of course, are long gone, and a cynicism pervades our view of public life – not just of politicians, but of the whole political and administrative system. This is a great pity, because there is much that is good about that system. Nevertheless, it seems that one of the reasons why cynicism prevails is that the public service ethic has been eroded. This chapter has argued that this is indeed the case. The public service ethic has been undermined partly because of the trends and events referred to here. We, both citizens and public servants, have lost 'faith' in our system.

Public servants have paid lip service to the notion of the public service ethic, but they have introduced so called reforms which have consistently undermined that notion. However, some public servants, politicians as well as officials, have themselves become concerned about the standards of public life and about the public service ethic. This has manifested itself in the setting up of the Nolan and Scott inquiries, the reports by select committees of the House of Commons and the House of Lords, and the promulgation of a civil service code, designed to inculcate a sense of public service ethics. Public officials too seem to have lost faith. And this brings the discussion back to the text for this chapter – 'we walk by faith – not by sight' – from the 2nd Epistle of St Paul to the Corinthians, chapter five, verse seven.

It is by believing in the public service ethic that it will be saved. Publishing a civil service code, or listing the 7 principles of public service as the Nolan Committee has done, will not make any difference if, at the same time, the public service is to have imposed on it values which are alien to it. Indeed, there may be additional problems if mechanistic formulas are relied upon. *Questions of Procedure for Ministers* (now *The Ministerial Code*), the civil service code, and Nolan's seven principles may be dangerous if dependence is placed on them at the expense of proper recognition and the practical application of the public service ethic. Statements of safeguards on their own are no substitute for the healthy life of ethical principles in a liberal democracy. This has been recognised in the past from time to time but nowhere more significantly than in the addendum by Ellen Wilkinson, MP for Jarrow in County Durham from 1935 to 1947, to the Report of the Committee on Minister's Powers: 'Nothing is so dangerous in a democracy as a safeguard which appears to be adequate but is really a façade' (Donoughmore, 1932, p.138). It is the spirit of democracy, the conscious attention to its inspiring qualities and values, that is the only effective safeguard for the rights and liberties of individuals: these have to be worked at and upheld by constant living attention; they cannot be achieved by formulas and codes, however worthy the intentions of such safeguards may be, and however skilfully their clauses may be drafted. Introducing them as a reaction to, or in an attempt to counterbalance, the invidious effects of market economies or New Public Management, is simply to recognise the problem. It is not a solution. The solution requires a belief in public service. Those who rely on formulas and codes to protect it are walking by sight and not by faith. Theirs is not a passionate distaste for public service; it is rather an undermining indifference born of a blinkered acceptance of virtues of personal ambition and personal gain. That indifference is the real enemy of public service.

'We walk by faith and not by sight' is the epitaph engraved on Green's tombstone. It is the principle which guided his life. Some might regard it as a great pity that it is not a principle writ large in the contracts of public servants. Unfortunately, it is those very contracts which might undermine any faith which citizens have in public service.

References

Cabinet Office (1994), *The Civil Service and Change*, Cm. 2627 (HMSO).

Chapman, Richard A. (1962), *An Examination of T.H. Green's Philosophy of the State with particular reference to its applicability to some theoretical problems of the twentieth century Welfare State*, unpublished MA thesis, Carleton University, Ottawa, Canada.

Chapman, Richard A. (1965), 'The Basis of T.H. Green's Philosophy', *International Review of History and Political Science*, Vol. III., pp.72-88.

Chapman, Richard A. (1970), 'Official Liberality', *Public Administration*, Vol. 48, pp.123-136.

Chapman Richard A. (1973), 'The Vehicle and General Affair: some reflections for public administration in Britain', *Public Administration*, Vol. 51, pp.273-290.

Chapman, Richard A. (1984), *Leadership in the British Civil Service*, Croom Helm.

Chapman, Richard A. (1987), 'Minister-Civil Servant Relationships', in Chapman, Richard A. and Michael Hunt (Eds.), *Open Government*, Croom Helm, pp.49-66.

Chapman, Richard A. (1988a), *Ethics in the British Civil Service*, Routledge.

Chapman, Richard A. (1988b), *The Art of Darkness*, University of Durham.

Chapman, Richard A, (1991), 'New arrangements for recruitment to the British civil service: cause for concern', *Public Policy and Administration*, Vol. 6, No. 3, pp.1-6.

Chapman, Richard A. (1993), 'Civil Service recruitment: fairness or preferential advantage?', *Public Policy and Administration*, Vol. 7, No. 2, pp.68-73.

Chapman, Richard A. (1996), 'Tragedy and Farce: the decision to privatise the RAS Agency', *Public Policy and Administration*, Vol. 11, No. 1, pp.1-7.

Chapman, Richard A. (1997), 'Civil Service Recruitment: the Civil Service Commissioners' Annual Report 1996-1997', *Public Policy and Administration*, Vol. 12, No. 3, pp.1-5.

Chapman, Richard A. and J.R. Greenaway (1980), *The Dynamics of Administrative Reform*, Croom Helm.

Chapman, Richard A. and Michael Hunt (Eds.) (1987), *Open Government*, Croom Helm.

Chapman, Richard A. and Barry J. O'Toole (1994), 'The Heroic Approach in the Historiography of Public Administration in the United Kingdom', *Jahrbuch Für Europäische Verwaltungsgeschichte*, Vol. 6, pp.65-77.

Chester, Norman (1954), 'The Crichel Down Case', *Public Administration,* Vol. 32.

Civil Service Commissioners (1997), *Annual Report 1996-97,* Office of the Civil Service Commissioners.

Donoughmore (1932), *Committee on Ministers Powers, Report,* Cmd. 4060 (HMSO) (Annex VI, Note by Miss Ellen Wilkinson on Delegated Legislation, with further Note by Professor Laski).

Dalyell, Tam (1996), 'Lord Bancroft', *The Independent.*

Efficiency Unit (1993), *Career Management and Succession Planning Study,* HMSO.

Finer, S.E. (1956), 'The Individual Responsibility of Ministers', *Public Administration,* Vol. 34.

Fisher, Sir Warren *et al.* (1928), *Report of the Board of Enquiry appointed by the Prime Minister to investigate certain statements affecting civil servants,* Cmd. 3037, HMSO.

Green, Thomas Hill (1900), 'Faith', *The Works of Thomas Hill Green Vol. III Miscellanies and Memoirs,* Ed. R.L. Nettleship, Longman.

Green, Thomas Hill (1931), *Lectures on the Principles of Political Obligation* (1879), Longman.

Green, Thomas Hill (1969), *Prolegomena To Ethics* (1883), Thomas Y. Cromwell.

House of Lords (1996), *Select Committee on the Public Service, 1st Report Session 1995-96, The Government's Proposals for the Privatisation of Recruitment and Assessment Service (RAS) with evidence, HL 109,* HMSO.

Morrison, Herbert (1954), *Government and Parliament,* Oxford University Press.

Nicholson, I.F. (1986), *The Mystery of Crichel Down,* Clarendon Press.

O'Halpin, Eunan (1989), *Head of the Civil Service,* Routledge.

O'Toole, Barry J. (1989), *Private Gain and Public Service: the Association of First Division Civil Servants,* Routledge.

O'Toole, Barry J. (1990), 'T.H. Green and the ethics of senior officials in British central government', *Public Administration,* Vol. 68, No. 3, pp.337-352.

O'Toole, Barry J. (1993), 'The Loss of Purity: The Corruption of Public Service in Britain', *Public Policy and Administration,* Vol. 8, No. 2, pp.1-6.

O'Toole, Barry J. (1994), 'The British Civil Service in the 1990s: Are Business Practices Really Best?', *Teaching Public Administration,* Vol. XV, No. 1, pp.24-35.

O'Toole, Barry J. (1995), 'Accountability', in John Wilson (Ed) *Managing Public Services: Dealing with Dogma,* Tudor.

O'Toole, Barry J. (1997a), 'Ethics in Government', *Parliamentary Affairs,* Vol. 50, 1, pp.130-42.

O'Toole, Barry J. (1997b), 'The Concept of Public Duty', in P. Barberis (Ed.), *The Civil Service in an Era of Change,* Dartmouth.

O'Toole, Barry J. and Richard A. Chapman (1995), 'Parliamentary Accountability', in O'Toole, Barry J. and Grant Jordan (Eds.), *The Next Steps: Improving Management in Government?*, Dartmouth, pp.118-141.

O'Toole, Barry J., and Grant Jordan (1995) (Eds.), *The Next Steps: Improving Management in Government?*, Dartmouth.

Plato (1941), *The Republic,* edited and Translated by F.M. Cornford, Clarendon Press.

Richter, Melvin (1967), *The Politics of Conscience: T.H. Green and his Age,* Weidenfeld and Nicolson.

Rousseau, Jean-Jacques (1911), *Émile,* Translated by Barbera Foxley, J.M. Dent and Sons.

Rousseau, Jean-Jacques (1913), *The Social Contract and Discourses,* with an introduction by G.D.H. Cole, Dent and Sons.

Rousseau, Jean-Jacques (1953), *The Confessions of Jean-Jacques Rousseau,* Translated by J.M. Cohen, Penguin.

Scott, Sir Richard (1996), *Report of the Inquiry into the Export of Defence Equipment and Dual-Use Goods to Iraq and Related Prosecutions,* HC 115, HMSO.

Treasury and Civil Service Committee (1989), *Fifth Report, Session 1988-89, Developments in the Next Steps Programme, HC 348,* HMSO.

Woodhouse, Diana (1994), *Ministers and Parliament: Accountability in Theory and Practice,* Clarendon Press.

7 Comparative Constitutionalism as a School for Administrative Statesmen

John A. Rohr

The most striking aspect of Richard Chapman's remarkable contribution to the literature of public administration is the abiding presence of the British Constitution at the heart of his interpretation of the administrative enterprise. Without neglecting the legal character of the constitution, Chapman lifts his readers' vision above the law's abstract technicalities and introduces them to a rich and complex set of normative principles to guide administrative behaviour.

It is no surprise that when Professor Chapman turns to the study of ethics, Lord Bridges emerges as the central figure (Chapman, 1988). The life of a prominent statesman provides the concrete focus that faithfully reflects Chapman's scholarship and the fact that this statesman is Lord Bridges reinforces the connection between the British Constitution and the ethical standards for public administration in the United Kingdom. Bridges was a constitutional specialist but, significantly, he was trained in history rather than law. His mastery of British constitutional history gave him a profound sense of the origins of the institutions he encountered in his daily routine. Unlike most constitutional specialists, however, Lord Bridges not only knew the British Constitution, but he developed it as well (Chapman, 1993, p.162).

I find in Chapman's concentration on the Constitution important pedagogical implications that go beyond the United Kingdom. The link between constitutionalism and public administration provides a useful counterweight to some of the more troubling aspects of recent developments in our field which are often grouped together under the convenient, if somewhat elusive, heading of the New Public Management (NPM). Although criticism of NPM is at times excessive and even alarmist, there can be no doubt that it raises legitimate fears for such traditional administrative values as a coherent public service, accountability to political masters, and, indeed, the rule of law itself (Butler, 1993, p.404; Carroll, 1995; Chapman, 1994, p.608; Drewry, 1995, pp.50-51; Greenaway, 1995; Lewis and Longley, 1994;

Moe and Gilmour, 1995). Professors of public administration who share these misgivings about NPM would do well to consider examining the constitutions of their own countries to see if they can find therein certain standards and principles that will provide an appropriate normative context for NPM's bold innovations. Instead of renouncing NPM and all its works and pomps, we would do well to tame its excesses by subjecting it to the discipline of constitutional scrutiny. Richard Chapman's work sets the standard in this endeavour because the British Constitution yields principles quite capable of sitting in judgement on NPM while, at the same time, its justly celebrated adaptability has the proven capacity to absorb innovations without undermining stability.

In the paragraphs that follow I shall try to develop the pedagogical possibilities of the study of comparative constitutionalism as the foundation for an international dialogue among professors, students, and practitioners of public administration concerned about ethical issues in our field of inquiry. By ethics, I do not mean conflict of interest, financial disclosure, bribery and other forms of corruption. I have in mind the more positive, albeit (alas) more nebulous, notion of the responsible use of administrative discretion which is central to the administrative statesmanship of governing wisely and well.

International discussions of ethics in public administration often founder on the shoals of the specific characteristics of various regimes: separation of powers versus parliamentary sovereignty, weak state versus strong state traditions, common law versus civil law, etc. Since nearly all nations have some sort of constitution, a discussion based on the relationship between public administration and constitutionalism will provide a common theme focused on how administrators respond to their respective constitutions. The responses, of course, will be different because the constitutions will be different; but the issue of the relationship between administration and its fundamental legal order is the same.

In this chapter, I shall try to apply this idea to four countries: the United States, France, the United Kingdom, and Canada. I have selected these four countries because I believe they are sufficiently similar to make the comparisons meaningful and sufficiently different to make them interesting. At a more personal level, candour compels me to admit I have chosen them because they are the only countries I feel I know well enough to write about and even for these four countries I must apologise in advance for any misinterpretations I may present of their constitutional traditions.

First, I shall present a very brief overview of the constitutions of each of the countries mentioned above. Then I shall examine those aspects of the relationship between administration and constitutionalism in each country which I believe are the most apt for structuring a discussion likely to yield insights into the normative foundations of the administrative systems in the four countries. In this part of the paper I shall paint with broad strokes; my findings will be merely suggestive, not exhaustive. The third and final section of the paper offers an academic reflection on the points reviewed in the first two sections.

An Overview

As noted above, each of our four countries has a very different constitutional tradition. The Constitution of the United States names the country; it is the United States of America only because its constitution unites the several states. It also creates a people. What do Hawaii and Vermont have in common save their federal constitution? In the United States, all federal officials, from the President to the lowliest clerk-typist, take an oath to uphold the constitution. It is no exaggeration to say that in the United States the constitution has an almost sacral character.

French constitutionalism is marked by its instability. Since the Revolution of 1789, the French have lived under at least thirteen constitutions that have embraced a dizzying melange of republics, monarchies and empires. In France, the constitution is more likely to be thought of in terms of purely positive law than in the other three countries. The French look elsewhere for deeper notions of national identity. Now nearing its fortieth year, the Constitution of the Fifth Republic has proved quite stable by French standards and yet, when grave crises arrive, patriotic Frenchmen can be heard to say without the least embarrassment that it may be time to try a new constitution (Poulard, 1990, p.249; Robert-Diard, 1990, p.8). Because of the frequent constitutional upheavals in their country, the French have learned to look to their well-established administrative institutions for the stability other nations find in their constitutions.

Because the British Constitution is unwritten or, to be more precise, written but uncodified (Norton, 1982, p.5) it is at once pervasive and ill-defined. British authors seem to find constitutional issues in situations where citizens of other countries would see only important issues that fall far short of constitutional significance. Since British courts cannot declare Acts of Parliament unconstitutional, constitutional law in the United Kingdom is not driven by questions of individual rights as is the case in the United States, and in Canada since the adoption of the Charter of Rights in 1982. Although there is no *Conseil d'Etat* in the United Kingdom, the marked tendency of British courts to nullify administrative action on the grounds of natural justice (Schwartz, 1996, pp.178-181; Wade and Forsyth, 1961, 1994 edn., p.494), suggests the development of a vigorous administrative law that must surely displease the shade of Dicey.

In Canada, the constitution is the great sign of contradiction. Although the present constitution was patriated in 1982, the Province of Quebec has never ratified it. Subsequent efforts to heal this rift through the Meech Lake and Charlottetown Accords have failed (Russell, 1992, 1993 edn., pp.127-228). A Quebec referendum in 1995 on the question of establishing a sovereign country, the second of its kind, failed by the narrowest of margins and plunged the country into a deep constitutional crisis. So profound is the problem that one hears Canadians speak of the C-word rather than even mention the name of the text that has wreaked such havoc. Remarkably, Prime Minister Jean Chrètien is on record as saying that the country's constitutional ills can be healed by good, solid, administration (Toronto Star, 1995, p.3).

The Constitutional-Administrative Relationship

With our brief constitutional overview in mind, let us now examine in more detail the precise connection between administration and constitutionalism in the four countries.

The United States

The United States is surely far less administered than the other three countries. This is because administration implies some sort of centralisation, even if it is nothing more than a centralised decision to decentralise as we saw in France during the early Mitterrand years (Aubry, 1988; Schmidt, 1990). American politics is profoundly decentralised. Of our four countries, only the United States has a constitution characterised by both federalism and separation of powers. France has separation of powers, but it is a unitary state. Canada is a federal country without separation of powers. Britain has neither federalism nor separation of powers.

These constitutional formalities have a serious impact on American administration. Aberbach and Rockman surely had it right when they said that if an American version of *Yes, Minister* were ever to be created, it would be called *Yes, Congressman* (Aberbach and Rockman, 1988, p.91). The active role of Congress in the day-to-day management of agency business is a defining characteristic of American administration. Although American administrators may frequently complain about congressional meddling and micro-managing, they forget the constitution they have sworn to uphold when they do so. Article 2, Section 2 of the constitution states quite clearly that offices are to be created by law, i.e., by Congress. This, of course, imposes severe limitations on the President's authority to restructure the executive branch of government as he sees fit.

The same text authorises Congress to vest the appointing power in one of

106

several officers: the President alone, the courts of law, or the heads of executive departments. If Congress is silent on how an officer is to be appointed, he or she must be nominated by the President and confirmed by the Senate. The recent controversy over President Clinton's choice of Anthony Lake as Director of the Central Intelligence Agency (CIA) was grounded in this text. Lake had served for four years without major incident as head of the National Security Council. He assumed this position without confirmation by the Senate because Congress chose to vest the power to appoint this officer in the President alone. Congress was not so accommodating when it came to the CIA. Here it reserved the Senate's authority to advise and consent to the President's choice with embarrassing consequences for both Anthony Lake and President Clinton.

The plethora of 'special counsels' who have been investigating alleged wrongdoing by high-ranking executive officers in the administrations of Presidents Reagan, Bush and Clinton can be traced to the same constitutional text. They have been appointed by federal judges, pursuant to an Act of Congress. Their benign title of 'special counsel' cannot conceal their true identity as independent prosecutors i.e., prosecutors who are independent of the Department of Justice which, of course, is part of the executive branch of the government. They play a role of enormous importance at the highest levels of contemporary federal administration.

To capture the significance of Congress in American public administration in comparison with, for example, the role of Parliament in British administration, we would do well to recall that Ollie North was indicted for lying to Congress while Clive Ponting met the same fate for telling Parliament the truth!

Over the past few decades, one of the most dramatic developments in American law has been the merging of constitutional and administrative law. Until the mid-1960s, American administrative law dealt primarily with regulation of industry and, for the most part, turned on questions of statutory construction. That is, did the agency act in accordance with the statute authorising its activity? The statute in question might be either the Administrative Procedure Act of 1946 or a statute drawn up for a specific set of circumstances such as labour-management relations, immigration, and so forth. During the past thirty years, however, the courts have become keenly aware of the profound impact administrative agencies can have on the lives of individual persons. Consequently, constitutional questions on due process of law and equal protection of the laws appear with increasing frequency in the administrative law books along side such traditional administrative law topics as rule-making, adjudication, exhaustion of administrative remedies, and judicial review of agency action. Of considerable significance is the recent appearance of a book on public law written for public administration students with chapters bearing such titles as 'The Individual as Public

Employee', 'The Individual as Inmate in Administrative Institutions', 'The Individual as Antagonist of the Administrative State'. These chapters, dealing almost exclusively with constitutional law, signal a remarkable transformation in American law as administrative institutions become increasingly integrated into the American constitutional tradition (Rosenbloom and O'Leary, 1997).

France

Of our four countries, France has the most powerful administrative institutions. When the last Parliament of the moribund Fourth Republic called upon General de Gaulle to draft a new constitution in 1958, he turned to Councillors of State, career civil servants, to carry out this task. Under the General's watchful eye, they drew up a document that would give France the strong executive that had been so woefully lacking in the Third and Fourth Republics. Whereas the Constitution of the United States explicitly creates the office of President and no less explicitly authorises Congress to establish unnamed 'executive departments', the Constitution of the Fifth Republic simply presumes the continued existence of such venerable administrative institutions as the *Conseil d'Etat* and the *Cour des Comptes*. They are not created by the constitution. They are just there as though it would be unthinkable to have a constitution without them.

A further contrast with the United States is found in the location of the residual powers in the two countries' constitutions. The Tenth Amendment to the American Constitution states that all powers not delegated to the federal government and not denied to the States 'are reserved to the States respectively or to the people'. The French Constitution, like its American counterpart, enumerates legislative powers and then adds, in Article 37, that '[m]atters other than those that fall within the domain of law shall be of a regulatory character'. Since Article 21 had already positioned the Prime Minister at the head of the government and had vested him with the 'regulatory powers', this means that the residual powers of the French State rest, not with Parliament, but with the government. That is, all powers not conferred upon Parliament are included in the regulatory powers of the government. This may well be the high-water mark of a constitutionalised administrative state (Rohr, 1995, pp.53-54).

A striking innovation in the Constitution of the Fifth Republic was the creation of the *Conseil Constitutionnel,* a quasi-judicial body empowered to declare Acts of Parliament unconstitutional. It is not a court because no litigants appear before it. Its jurisdiction is triggered by certain officers named in the constitution who have reason to believe that a given legislative enactment violates the constitution. The original purpose of this institution was to reinforce the distinction between legislative and regulatory powers

108

mentioned above. It was intended to be, as a French jurist once put it, 'a cannon aimed at Parliament' (Luchaire, 1980, p.31). As the history of the Fifth Republic unfolded, it became increasingly clear that French governments, headed by Gaullist prime ministers, had no trouble holding their own with Parliament. By the early 1970s, the Constitutional Council had managed to expand its jurisdiction to include the examination for constitutional defects of statutes violating individual rights enshrined in the Declaration of the Rights of Man and of the Citizen of 1789 and other important texts in French constitutional history. Today it is one of the most powerful institutions in the French State.

The remarkable development of the Constitutional Council goes far beyond questions of public administration, but it is relevant to our purposes because in developing its position on such cardinal constitutional questions as freedom of speech and freedom of the press and equality before the law, it has relied heavily upon the jurisprudence of the prestigious *Conseil d'Etat,* an administrative tribunal. Thus, French constitutional law followed a trail of individual rights originally blazed by French administrative law which for decades had defended individual rights against administrative transgressions. The *Conseil d'Etat,* like English courts, has no authority to strike down an Act of Parliament on constitutional grounds. Its writ runs only to administrative agencies. Prior to the creation of the Constitutional Council in 1958, no French jurisdiction could void an Act of Parliament. Under the Fifth Republic, however, this power has taken root and flourished in France, but, interestingly, the institution that exercises this power has been in tutelage to an administrative court. This surely suggests some salutary reflections for those who continue to stereotype administrative jurisdictions as insensitive to the rights of individuals (Rohr, 1995, pp.162-172).

The United Kingdom

A fundamental principle of the British Constitution is the doctrine of ministerial responsibility and its corollary, civil service anonymity. These principles bring constitutional considerations to the very core of public administration. There are few questions in the public administration of any country more fundamental than the political accountability of the highest officers of the state and the management of the civil service. Innovations such as the Next Steps agencies raise more searching constitutional questions in the United Kingdom than similar innovations might raise elsewhere precisely because administration is more firmly embedded in the constitution than it is, for example, in the United States. Long before these innovations appeared, the doctrine of ministerial responsibility had been under considerable pressure from political scientists in the United Kingdom and abroad who delighted in pulling back the veil that covered the real power exercised by career officials. These revelations, if pressed to their logical conclusions, threatened to reduce ministerial authority to a mere formality and to leave civil service anonymity hostage to the increasing demands for openness in government (Chapman, 1987, pp.56-57). Diane Woodhouse's exhaustive research has laid bare the unsettling gap between constitutional doctrine and administrative practice (Woodhouse, 1994). Nevertheless, I believe it is still accurate to consider ministerial responsibility a vital constitutional principle in British public administration without denying that it is also a likely candidate for constitutional reform.

One of the most striking aspects of constitutionalism in British public administration is its amazing breadth. Consider the vast range between the following two narratives. First, Henry Parris tells the story of the constitutional relationship between the civil service and the Crown as it developed from 1780 to 1830: 'As the monarchy rose above party,' he says, 'so the civil service settled below party. Constitutional bureaucracy was the counterpart of constitutional monarchy' (Parris, 1969, p.49). Next, consider Peter Hennessy's account of what he considers 'quite a significant constitutional change'. It involved changes in the public spending system introduced by Sir Leo Pliatzky in 1975-76. No longer could the Chancellor be overruled on a spending matter in a Cabinet committee. Only the full Cabinet could do this. Hennessy notes that 'shifting the onus of appeal on to the spending minister would make a great deal of psychological difference, as in [Prime Minister] Wilson's words, it would give the Treasury 51 per cent of the votes' (Hennessy, 1989, p.252). Thus, constitutional issues in British public administration seem to run the gamut from matters of such stunning importance as the flowering of constitutional monarchy to an interesting but surely less-than-monumental change in financial management.

The pervasive character of the British Constitution helps to explain why it adapts so easily to changing times, at least when compared with the Constitution of the United States. Take, for example, the unhappy fate of the 'legislative veto' at the hands of the Supreme Court in the 1983 case *Immigration and Naturalisation Service v. Chadha* (462, U.S. 952). Chadha arrived in the United States with a student visa which expired after seven years, at which time he could be deported. The statute creating these provisions also conferred upon the Attorney General a discretionary authority to suspend deportation. The same statute further provided that the Attorney General's decision to suspend deportation could be overruled by a vote taken in either house of Congress. This institutional arrangement was known as the 'legislative veto' because Congress conferred upon itself the power to 'veto' a discretionary judgement it had authorised to an administrative officer, in this case the Attorney General. By 1983, the 'legislative veto' had become quite routine in American public administration. Legislation with such provisions had been enacted over two hundred times dating back to the Hoover administration in the early 1930s. Although Presidents frequently questioned its constitutionality, they usually did so in the very act of signing bills authorising yet another legislative veto. As a practical matter, it seemed to be a sensible compromise between the need to delegate broad discretionary authority to the executive and congressional concern about keeping some sort of check on that same executive.

Although the practice had flourished for over half-a-century, and despite widespread recognition of its practical value, the Supreme Court struck it down as unconstitutional in the Chadha case. When Chadha's visa expired, the Attorney General suspended his deportation, but the House of Representatives overturned this decision and thereby rendered Chadha deportable. Whereupon, he brought suit challenging the constitutionality of the legislative veto and eventually prevailed. The Supreme Court's reasoning relied heavily on the constitutional text (Article I, Section 7) providing that all legislation must be passed by both houses of Congress and 'presented' to the President for his signature. Since the suspension of Chadha's deportation was voted by only one house of Congress, and since it was never presented to the President, it was constitutionally flawed on two counts: it violated both the 'bicameral' and the 'presentment' clauses of the constitution.

The explicit textual provisions of the constitution were as well known to the friends of the legislative veto as to its enemies. The former argued, however, that these texts applied only to legislation whereas the legislative veto was exercised over administrative rulings, such as a decision to suspend deportation. Over a vigorous dissent from Justice White, Chief Justice Burger held that legislation was involved because Chadha's legal status was changed and therefore the bicameral and presentment clauses had to be observed. Interestingly, the Chief Justice conceded that the legislative veto might have certain practical advantages, but these could not prevail against the stern letter of the law. This decision dealt a serious setback to sound public administration in the United States. In the United Kingdom, I believe such a well-regarded long-standing practice would probably have been considered a constitutional 'convention' precisely because it was well-regarded and long-standing. If my surmise is correct, I believe the Chadha case provides a useful insight into the different meanings of constitutionalism in the two countries. (If my surmise is incorrect, knowledgeable persons might point out my error and then the international dialogue I have in mind would be underway.)

In *Thatcher, Reagan, Mulroney: In Search of a New Bureaucracy,* Peter J. Savoie provides a fascinating account of the efforts of three prominent conservative statesmen to put their stamp on the administrative structures in their respective countries. He finds that Prime Minister Thatcher had the most success and President Reagan the least. Although Savoie relies on many factors to support this judgement, the difference in constitutional structures in the United States and the United Kingdom figures prominently among

111

them. Within two years of her arrival in office Mrs Thatcher had abolished the Civil Service Department, transferring its pay and manpower planning functions to the Treasury and its efficiency, recruitment and selection functions to a newly-created Management and Personnel Office within the Cabinet Office. A few years later she abolished the Management and Personnel Office and transferred its functions to the Treasury (Savoie, 1994, pp.201-204). The free hand that Mrs Thatcher enjoyed in shaping the bureaucracy to her liking contrasts sharply with President Reagan's utter failure to abolish the Departments of Energy and Education, despite unequivocal pledges in his 1980 campaign that he would do so.

Constitutional structures go a long way in explaining Thatcher's success and Reagan's failure. The Prime Minister could effect these changes by executive means without a statute, but the President needed an Act of Congress, which was not forthcoming. The two departments targeted by Reagan had far too much support in Congress to let the President redeem his campaign pledge. Reagan was not the only President to undergo such frustration. President Carter failed to persuade Congress to give him a Department of Trade (Campbell, 1983, p.113) and President Clinton just barely succeeded in preventing a congressional effort to abolish the Department of Commerce. Thus, the American executive, unlike his British counterpart, cannot rearrange administrative structures to suit his managerial style. President Carter could not get the executive department he wanted, President Clinton almost lost one he wanted, while President Reagan had to continue to manage two departments he did not want! This, of course, expresses the logic of separation of powers and has nothing to do with classic doctrines of management which seem more closely attuned to the British constitutional doctrine that has traditionally treated civil service matters as falling under the prerogative powers of the Crown.

Canada

The fundamental structure of Canadian government is stated with extraordinary brevity in the preamble to the British North America Act of 1867, which was renamed 'The Constitution Act, 1867' by the Constitution Act of 1982. In the preamble to the 1867 Act, we read that the three provinces of Canada (which, at that time, included both Ontario [Upper Canada] and Quebec [Lower Canada]), Nova Scotia, and New Brunswick 'desire to be federally united into One Dominion under the Crown of the United Kingdom of Great Britain and Ireland, with a Constitution similar in Principle to that of the United Kingdom'. No mention is made of a prime minister or a cabinet. Although the 1867 Act covered some topics in excruciating detail, the most fundamental structure of the regime was left to the implications to be derived from 'a Constitution similar in Principle to that of

112

the United Kingdom'. Thus, from the outset, Canada was to develop its own form of Westminster government that would necessarily depart dramatically from the British model because of the federal structure of the new Dominion.

One of the most striking aspects of Canadian constitutional history centres on the distribution of powers between the federal government and the provinces. Canada has always been far more 'federal' than the United States in the sense that no American state (at least since the end of the Civil War) has ever been as powerful as a Canadian province in relation to their respective federal governments. The premiers of the Canadian provinces are far more significant figures than the governors of the American states. What makes this interesting is that the constitutional texts of the two countries would suggest just the opposite. We have already seen that the residual powers of the United States remain with the States or with the people. The American federal government possesses only those powers delegated to it by the constitution. The Canadian Constitution Act of 1867 reverses this order. Article 91 confers upon the federal government the power 'to make Laws for the Peace, Order and good Government of Canada, in relation to all Matters not coming with the Classes of Subjects by this Act assigned exclusively to the Legislatures of the Provinces'. Thus the Canadian Constitution explicitly states that all powers not assigned to the provinces belong to the federal government.

Despite this explicit language, the 1867 Act goes on to enumerate a long list of specific powers that fall to the federal government e.g. the public debt, the regulation of trade and commerce, the borrowing of money on the public credit, legal tender, etc. All these provisions would seem to be superfluous in view of the statement we have just seen to the effect that all powers not given to the provinces belong to the federal government. Anticipating this objection, the Constitution Act of 1867 states that these federal powers are explicitly conferred only 'for greater Certainty, but not so as to restrict the Generality of the foregoing Terms of this Section' – that is, the previous language empowering the federal government to make laws 'for the Peace, Order, and good Government of Canada' in all matters not assigned exclusively to the Provinces.

This language was hotly disputed by the participants in the Confederation Debates of 1865 where the text was drafted. Since these debates took place in February and March of that year, while the American Civil War was still raging, the Fathers of Confederation were determined to learn from the unhappy American experience of excessive decentralisation and, consequently, wrote a constitution intended to insure federal hegemony. Subsequent events soon revealed that the political will to support a vigorous federal government was sadly lacking and, by the turn of the century, provincial leaders, ably assisted by key constitutional opinions rendered by

113

the Judicial Committee of the Privy Council in London, had turned the tide in favour of the provinces (Vipond, 1991, pp.151-190).

Thus Canadian administration has been, and still is, carried on under a constitutional text which distributes powers between Ottawa and the provinces in a manner virtually antithetical to political realities, while at the same time giving Canada a governmental structure 'similar in Principle to that of the United Kingdom' for the purpose of ruling over a federal regime unknown to the laws and traditions of the mother country.

We noted above Prime Minister Chrètien's comment on the heels of the nearly disastrous (or glorious, depending on one's point of view) Quebec referendum of 1995, that the nation's constitutional ills could be healed by 'good solid administration'. One can hardly imagine a more high-toned view of administration. It still remains to be seen just what this might mean in practice and, more importantly, what results it will achieve. Be that as it may, the Canadian press regularly reports federal initiatives aimed at strengthening national unity through a variety of administrative programmes in such traditional areas as the environment, disaster relief, education, manpower and training, crime-fighting, etc. (Rohr, 1997, p.22). In addition, attention is being increasingly given to detailed examination of the economic consequences of the separation of Quebec from the rest of Canada. These consequences include such mundane administrative matters as the distribution of the national debt and the pensions of civil servants. Thus, Canada today provides a fascinating example of the constitutional-administrative interface. These down-to-earth administrative initiatives are underway while there is pending litigation before the Supreme Court of Canada on the absolutely momentous question of whether the Constitution of Canada, which Quebec does not recognise, would allow Quebec to secede from the Canadian Confederation if a majority of its citizens supported separation in a province-wide referendum.

While Chrètien's critics might not take seriously his idea of solving constitutional crises by administrative means, his idea is not altogether without precedent. The Confederation Debates of 1865 reveal that a projected 'Intercolonial Railway' played an extremely important role in the decision to approve the confederation project that would link the several provinces. Here was an administrative matter of the greatest importance, involving nothing less than the new government's management of the 'high tech' of the day. Indeed, there are numerous examples of participants in the debates stating quite explicitly that without the Intercolonial Railway there would be no confederation (Parliamentary Debates, 1865, pp.52, 87, 251, 356). Chrètien's reliance on administration to bind up the nation's wounds may be unrealistic, but one must acknowledge that he touched upon an idea with a solid precedent in Canadian constitutional governance. If 'good solid administration' helped to create the Canadian Confederation, it may help to preserve it as well.

An academic reflection

Since this paper has been prepared for a *festschrift* in honour of a distinguished scholar, it seems only fitting to conclude with a reflection on how the constitutional – administrative relationship might contribute to research and teaching in the field of public administration. My remarks fall under three headings: constitutional scholarship, professional enhancement, and a dialogue on ethics.

Constitutional Scholarship

Academicians from a wide variety of disciplines examine constitutional issues for diverse purposes. Philosophers probe constitutional decisions to advance the fields of jurisprudence and legal theory. Historians look for the development of broad themes over several decades or even centuries and then generalise about 'the John Marshall Era' or the great movement from 'status to contract'. Political scientists lower their sights and tell us about judicial behaviour and the 'role of the courts' in the political process. The law journals deal with all of the above and include as well articles exposing inconsistencies in judicial reasoning and shrewd advice on courtroom strategy. Perhaps students of public administration could make their own distinctive contribution to constitutional scholarship by concentrating on constitutional practice, i.e., on how the constitutional word becomes flesh through administrative action. Over a century ago, Woodrow Wilson said that in his day government was becoming so complicated that it was harder to run a constitution than to write one (Wilson, 1887, p.210). His insight is even more valid today. Administrators operate constitutions; they make them work; they reduce their majestic generalities to practice. Those who study administrators systematically should tell the world how they do it.

Professional Enhancement

The New Public Management movement has little respect for the traditions of the public administration profession. When Mrs. Thatcher called the Civil Service Department she was about to abolish 'a pack of poachers turned gamekeepers', she captured all too nicely the spirit of what was to become the NPM (Savoie, 1994, p.201). Because NPM ideas play an increasingly important role in the public administration curriculum, it is important for professors of public administration to provide a balanced picture of the profession by reminding their students of the richness of its culture and the nobility of a calling that can lead to administrative statesmanship. I believe an awareness of the constitutional foundations of the profession in various countries provides a singularly apt means toward this most desirable end.

115

This is a far more positive way of taming the excesses of NPM than a frontal assault on its most fundamental principles which, if successful, would deprive the profession of NPM's many useful suggestions.

Thoughtful jurists trained in the common law have always been interested to learn how their civil law counterparts carry on their professional duties. Professional soldiers study with considerable interest the command structures of friendly and hostile armies. Similar observations would apply to professionally alert teachers, physicians, entrepreneurs, athletes, and even spies. As far as I know, there is no utilitarian justification for indulging such curiosity. An admiral does not necessarily improve his skills as a warrior by routinely visiting naval museums in other countries. A bishop is not a holier man because he reads extensively in the theology of Islam. The admiral and the bishop are simply enhancing themselves professionally and no doubt finding considerable satisfaction in so doing.

I have found that the same is true for students and practitioners of public administration. When American administrators discover that in France there is no appeal to a higher court from decisions of the *Conseil d'Etat*, they often want to know more about the entire French administrative system. Their curiosity is similarly aroused when they learn that the increasing importance of select committees in the United Kingdom has affected the traditional role of British civil servants. Constitutional questions related to administration are particularly suitable candidates for broadening the horizons of our students because it is the nature of constitutions to address fundamental principles. Such inquiries need no practical justification to be added to the public administration curriculum. They are their own reward.

A Dialogue on Ethics

At the beginning of this chapter I noted that international discussions of ethics in public administration are often hampered by the considerable constitutional differences between one country and another. I went on to argue, however, that since administration in virtually every country must necessarily have some sort of relationship to its fundamental legal order, that relationship could be the basis of an international discussion regardless of how different the fundamental legal orders might be from one country to another. I would like to revisit this question and examine it more closely with the four countries in mind that we have studied in this paper. There follows a brief description of questions of ethics based on the administrative structures of each of our four countries which I believe may be of interest to public administration professionals from all four countries.

Since American administrators take an oath to uphold the Constitution of the United States, public administration professionals in all four countries might want to know just what practical significance this oath might have for high-ranking administrators who find themselves caught in a seemingly intractable struggle between the political leadership of their agency and a congressional committee charged with overseeing and evaluating the agency's performance. As a variation on this separation-of-powers theme, what practical steps should conscientious American administrators take in response to an unwelcome court order imposing a firm deadline on an agency to perform certain tasks when the immediate performance of these tasks will seriously jeopardise carefully developed long-term plans?

Public administration literature from the United Kingdom frequently quotes the following statement by Sir Robert Armstrong, Head of the Home Civil Service, on civil servants' relationship to Parliament: 'Civil servants are servants of the Crown. [I]n general, the executive powers of the Crown are exercised by and on the advice of Her Majesty's Ministers, who are in turn answerable to Parliament. The civil service as such has no constitutional personality or responsibility separate from the duly elected Government of the day' (Armstrong, 1985). Sir Robert's comments were delivered in the aftermath of Clive Ponting's trial and echoed Judge McGowan's ineffective instructions to the jury in that *cause celebre*. Nearly all the authors who write on this topic condemn Armstrong's position, but I cannot find a consistent and clear statement of what the constitutionally correct version of the civil servant's relationship to Parliament might be. I would also be interested in learning what moral or legal restraints there are on civil servants, or even ministers, who violate some constitutional principle or convention. I pose the question with the adaptability of the British Constitution in mind. How does one know when it is time to change an outmoded principle or convention and, once one has decided that the time is right, how does one change it without violating the constitution? Is it only with the wisdom of hindsight that one knows which apparent constitutional violations were really violations and which ones were actually positive contributions to constitutional growth and development?

French administrators do not take an oath to uphold the Constitution of the Fifth Republic. Indeed, one knowledgeable commentator maintains that 'the very thought of such an oath makes Frenchmen shiver' (Toinet, 1987, p.196). Many reasons are given for this repugnance to state-sponsored oaths, but the most important are (1) that oath- taking is inevitably associated with the Vichy regime of Marshall Petain and (2) that the instability of French constitutions make them inappropriate objects of an oath. Given the vagaries of French constitutional history, the rejection of state-sponsored oaths seems quite plausible. Nevertheless, the question remains as to what moral obligation a public official in France should have toward the legal order established by the present constitution. If the answer is none at all because all constitutions are purely matters of positive law then the next question is, where does one look for the moral foundation of French public life. The State? The people? The republican tradition?

The present constitutional turmoil in Canada raises important questions about how administration fares amidst chronic constitutional instability. The most interesting ethical dimension of this broader problem focuses on francophone *Quebecois* who work for the federal government. At present, questions of how they sort out the various loyalties they justly feel within themselves are probably too sensitive for systematic inquiry. When the crisis is finally resolved, it will be time enough to study this painful question of divided loyalties.

References

Aberbach, J. and B. Rockman (1988), 'Political and Bureaucratic Roles in Public Service Reorganisation', in Campbell, C. and B.G. Peters (Eds), *Organising Governance: Governing Organisations*, Pittsburgh: University of Pittsburgh Press.

Armstrong, Sir Robert (1985), 'Note by the Head of the Home Civil Service', *The Duties and Responsibilities of Civil Servants in Relation to Ministers*, Cabinet Office.

Aubry, F.X. (1988), *Essai sur la decentralisation*, Paris: Groupe des Publications Periodiques Paul Dupont.

Butler, R. (1993), 'The Evolution of the Civil Service', *Public Administration*, Vol. 71, Autumn, pp.395-406.

Campbell, C. (1983), *Governments Under Stress: Political Executives and Key Bureaucrats in Washington, London, and Ottawa*, Toronto: University of Toronto Press.

Carroll, J. (1995), 'The Rhetoric of Reform and Political Reality in the National Performance Review', *Public Administration Review*, Vol. 55, May-June, pp.302-312.

Chapman, Richard A. (1987), 'Minister-Civil Servant Relationships', in Richard A. Chapman and Michael Hunt (Eds), *Open Government*, Croom Helm, pp.49-66.

Chapman, Richard A. (1988), *Ethics in the British Civil Service*, Routledge.

Chapman, Richard A. (Ed), (1993), *Ethics in Public Service*, Edinburgh University Press.

Chapman, Richard A. (1994), 'Change in the Civil Service', *Public Administration*, Vol. 72, Winter, pp.599-609.

Drewry, G. (1995), 'Public Law', *Public Administration*, Vol. 73, Spring, pp.41-57.

Greenaway, J. (1995), 'Having the Bun and the Halfpenny: Can Old Public Service Ethics Survive in the New Whitehall?' *Public Administration*, Vol. 73, Autumn, pp.357-374.

Hennessy, P. (1989), *Whitehall*, New York: The Free Press.

Lewis, N. and D. Longley (1994), 'Ethics and the Public Service', *Public Law*, Vol. 57, pp.596-608.

Luchaire, F. (1980), *Le Conseil Constitutionnel*, Paris: Economica.

Moe, R. and R. Gilmour (1995), 'Rediscovering Principles of Public Administration: The Neglected Foundation of Public Law', *Public Administration Review*, Vol. 55, March-April, pp.135-146.

Norton, P. (1982), *The Constitution in Flux*, Basil Blackwell.

Parliamentary Debates on the Subject of the Confederation of the British North American Provinces, (1865), 3rd Session, 8th Provincial Parliament of Canada, Quebec: Hunter and Rose.

Parris, H. (1969), *Constitutional Bureaucracy*, New York: Augustus M. Kelley.

Poulard, J. (1990), 'The French Double Executive and the Experience of Cohabitation', *Political Science Quarterly*, Vol. 105, pp.243-267.

Robert-Diard, P. (1990), 'En attendant la Vie Republique', *Le Monde*, 8 December, p.8

Rohr, J. (1995), *Founding Republics in France and America: A Study in Constitutional Governance*, Lawrence, KS: University Press of Kansas.

Rohr, J. (1997), 'Canadian Constitutionalism and the Confederation Debates', unpublished paper prepared for the Canadian Studies Research Grant Program, Washington, D.C.: Canadian Embassy.

Russell, P. (1992, 1993 edn), *Constitutional Odyssey: Can Canadians Become a Sovereign People?* Toronto: University of Toronto Press.

Savoie, D. (1994), *Thatcher, Reagan, Mulroney: In Search of a New Bureaucracy*, Pittsburgh: University of Pittsburgh Press.

Schmidt, V. (1990), *Democratizing France: The Political and Administrative History of Decentralisation*, New York: Cambridge University Press.

Schwartz, B. (1996), 'Wade's Seventh Edition and Recent English Administrative Law', *Administrative Law Review*, Vol. 48, Winter, pp.175-190.

Toinet, M. (1988), 'La morale bureaucratique: Perspectives transatlantiques et Franco-Americaines', *Revue Internationale de Science Politique*, Vol. 9, pp.193-204.

Vipond, R. (1991), *Liberty and Community: Canadian Federalism and the Failure of the Constitution*, Albany, N.Y.: SUNY Press.

Wade, W. and C. Forsyth (1961, 1994 edn), *Administrative Law*, Clarendon Press.

Wilson, W. (1887), 'The Study of Administration', *Political Science Quarterly*, Vol. 2, pp.197-222.

Woodhouse, D. (1994), *Ministers and Parliament: Accountability in Theory and Practice*, Clarendon Press.

Part Three

LEADERSHIP IN PUBLIC SERVICE

8 The Changing Role of Senior Civil Servants Since 1979

Peter Barberis

Introduction

The summer of 1997 seems an appropriate time to examine the changing role of senior civil servants. The Conservatives have just been roundly rejected by the electorate after more or less a generation in office. Under their stewardship the civil service has been subjected to a succession of initiatives collectively greater in magnitude than those unleashed during any comparable time-span this century. Clearly some change is to be expected over any eighteen year period – things never stand still. Yet it is tempting to say that developments in the civil service between 1979 and 1997 have brought fundamental transformation with potentially far reaching consequences. Whitehall may never be the same again. It is therefore the purpose of this chapter to examine the substance of these assertions, focusing upon the extent and character of changes in the role of the higher civil service.

Implicit in much of the discussion will be the idea that there are broadly two types of change. On the one hand there are the formal, observable and (usually) measurable shifts. On the other hand there is a different kind of change – something less determinate and certainly less measurable but which may nevertheless bring perhaps more profound transformation in the 'gut' or character of an institution like the senior civil service. These two types may loosely be described as changes of 'body' and 'soul' respectively. It is possible to have one kind of change without the other and indeed to mistake one for the other. In particular, we may mistake changes in the outer face, or body, for those in the interior character or soul of the civil service. Sometimes the outer manifestations of change may be indicative of interior convulsions; or they may bear upon the interior, so effecting a deeper transformation of character. But the two are not the same and we cannot adduce evidence of one as proof of the other. Moreover, change does not emerge from a vacuum. It comes from a particular historical trajectory, proceeding within a specific context. This is not to adopt an unduly deterministic perspective, simply to help deepen our understanding of the changes in process that have occurred within Whitehall's senior echelons.

With these points in mind this chapter is organised into four parts. First, there is a brief sketch of the historical trajectory from which the changes of 1979-97 unfolded – the legacy, or heritage. Second, the context of change is examined. This charts the changing landscape of Whitehall and of its key personnel. Presented in measurable and largely quantitative terms it shows the crude, exterior face of change. Such evidence can be illuminating and interesting in itself but cannot capture the full significance of role change. The third section therefore discusses the alleged 'managerialisation' of Whitehall and the shift of emphasis from policy to management work. Such a shift may have wider implications, especially when allied to other developments which permeate the essential values and constitutional position of the civil service, the focus of the fourth and final section.

A couple of preliminary points should be made. First, the term 'senior civil service' is open to precise interpretation. The now officially designated Senior Civil Service includes *all* officials at grade 5 and above. In hierarchical terms this provides a useful point of demarcation – but not quite. For, second, the focus here is narrower in that it concentrates upon Whitehall and those operating close to the centre of government, ignoring, for example, those who work in the regions and other outposts. Core officials have on the whole been shielded from the icier blasts of change – more so at any rate than some of the agency chief executives. They continue to enjoy a position of relative, if declining, privilege which brings a corresponding burden of responsibility. The point was nicely put by the former prime minister Lord Callaghan, when he told the Treasury and Civil Service Committee (1993, Q. 622) that the civil service is one of the bulwarks of the constitution. Senior officials in the core departments are the custodians in chief of the bureaucracy's constitutional role. They, above all others, are Whitehall's body and spirit. If the changes of 1979-1997 have been more apparent than real, then it is among this group and its activities that this reality will remain most visible. If, on the other hand, there has been fundamental change in the roles played by these officials, and in their collective personality, then we can be sure that the changes of the last eighteen years have reached to the very soul of Britain's central bureaucracy.

The Heritage

It is widely believed that Margaret Thatcher's assumption of office marked a watershed in the development of the civil service, as indeed it did in other and wider affairs: 1979 has come to be seen as a pivotal date, almost equal in significance to 1945 or 1914. Allied to this, there is a good deal of caricature about the nature of the senior civil service down to and including the 1970s. For many years such caricature was sustained by the echoes of the Fulton Report (1968) and in the media images of *Yes, Minister* and *Yes, Prime Minister.* Caricature has its place but is no substitute for careful appraisal. It may be many years, if ever, before we begin to get a true picture of the higher civil service over the last thirty, forty or fifty years. It is nevertheless worth considering the traditional role of the higher civil service; its essential characteristics and values; and the extent to which it has changed in the years down to 1979. This will the provide a baseline for assessing the changing role of senior officials during the years of the Thatcher and Major governments. In what can be no more than a brief, scene-setting, sketch the Whitehall tradition may be outlined by considering each in turn of four classic assertions:

> that the higher civil service was overwhelmingly and symbiotically minister-orientated, giving little if any credence to 'management';

> that the vast majority of its members were career officials, recruited by open competition directly into an elite corps, the Administrative Class;

> that they were an homogeneous, socially exclusive group of generalists or 'all-rounders'; and

> that they were sustained in a closely woven network by commonly held values, mores and patterns of professional behaviour – part of a distinct phenomenon sometimes known as the 'public service ethic'.

The higher civil service was overwhelmingly and symbiotically minister-orientated, giving little credence to 'management'.

The Fulton Committee (1968, para.18) opined that senior officials spent too much time serving ministers, too little attention being given to running their departments. This was one of the Committee's basic critiques, perhaps nearer to the mark than many of its other broadsides. It was a highly credible observation given the constitutional role of the mandarinate and the peculiarly British philosophy of administration. Constitutionally, senior officials are supposed to advise their political chiefs. This is sometimes equated with policy work, though by no means all minister-orientated activities can be strictly, or even loosely, defined as policy work. At the same time, the British philosophy of administration features a fusion of the political and the administrative (Thomas, 1978, pp.33-37). There is no such thing as pure or abstract administration: its spirit lies in political and practical realities to which all must be ready to respond. There can be no finite rules or principles of administration, no sweet maxims or universal structures of bureaucracy. Neither the organisational classicists of continental Europe nor the American technique-mongers held much sway in the British tradition. Administration, if not quite an art, was nevertheless something of a craft, brought to perfection or at any rate to tolerable satisfaction through practice informed by accumulated experience and contextual sensitivity (Sisson, 1966; Vickers, 1965). There was something to be learned from textbooks, 'vocational' training, and even from modern management methods – but not very much.

This portrait fits with much that is known about the civil service of the past. Few senior officials were, in any modern sense, conscious managers of their departments. Certainly they would never let it intrude into, or disturb, their relationships with ministers. Sir Peter Carey (1984, p.82) has said that the first managerial role he had was upon becoming a permanent secretary and nothing in his previous career in Whitehall had prepared him for this. Carey was Second Permanent Secretary and then Permanent Secretary at the DTI/Department of Industry, 1973-83. His testimony broadly accords with those of his contemporaries and near contemporaries (Barberis, 1996, p.87). Two further points should be made. First, much depends upon what exactly is meant by 'management'. Some top officials in previous generations did try to manage their departments (Barberis, 1996, pp.47-50). They were the minority and proceeded with little sophistication – certainly nothing systematic. But they did run their departments – more so than the Fulton Report led many to believe – usually maintaining quite a tight grip. To the extent that the British philosophy assumed the fusion of political and administrative work, this necessarily left its mark on the routine functioning of many departments. However, this should not be exaggerated since, (secondly), things were already beginning to change in the 1970s, and indeed before that. Sir Patrick Nairne (1983, pp.251-52) has noted the increasing weight of management work at the DHSS of which he was permanent secretary between 1975 and 1981. Other things confirm that a shift of emphasis was taking place – for example the use of special ministerial advisers from the 1960s, gaining in momentum with the creation in 1974 of the Policy Unit (Donoughue, 1987). This brought some initial unease but no permanent or substantial disfigurement to the symbiotic relationship between mandarins and ministers.

The vast majority of senior civil servants were career officials, recruited by open competition into an elite corps, the Administrative Class.

This second classic assertion is more easily verified. From the end of the Great War, the vast majority of top officials had spent all, or nearly all, of their careers in Whitehall – peaking at 87 per cent among those who became permanent secretaries between 1946 and 1964 (Barberis, 1996, p.153). A few more outsiders had begun to enter the portals of Whitehall in the 1960s and 1970s but not many, and constituting nothing like the presence of their counterparts during the mid and late nineteenth century. Broadly, this preponderance of careerists corresponded with entry by open competition, long the norm for all civil servants. But it did not always mean entry into the elite corps, the Administrative Class. Throughout the present century and down to the 1970s a significant minority of senior people began their careers in one of the clerical, executive or specialist grades. If nothing else, the steady expansion of the *corps d'elite* brought the necessity to draw from other quarters. Whitehall may have been relatively closed to the outside world but was internally rather more egalitarian than its critics were usually prepared to allow.

The Higher Civil Service was an homogeneous, socially exclusive group of generalists or 'all rounders'.

Senior mandarins of the 1960s and 1970s were a relatively homogeneous group, though never the exclusive social caste portrayed by critics. Over 69 per cent of those who became permanent secretaries between 1965 and 1979 were Oxbridge products, 20 per cent having been to one of the top twenty public schools. This compares with figures of 66 per cent and 35 per cent respectively during 1919-64, showing some mixed evidence of decomposition before the age of Thatcherism. Again, the notion of the generalist or non subject specialist is more true than false, yet with more exceptions than often acknowledged. Even at permanent secretary level a significant minority possessed a specialist qualification or had some specific professional expertise (Barberis, 1996, pp.158-60). Moreover, many of these were deployed in positions appropriate to their specialism.

Senior mandarins were sustained in a closely woven network by commonly held values, mores and patterns of professional behaviour – part of a distinct phenomenon sometimes known as the 'public service ethic'.

The fourth and final classic assertion is the most difficult. The evidence is patchy and there are no longitudinal survey data. It is easy to assume that the likes of Sir Warren Fisher and Sir Edward Bridges spoke for all when they pronounced from on high. Fisher was Head of the Civil Service 1919-39, Bridges his successor between 1945 and 1956. We will never know, and must indeed be healthily sceptical about, the extent to which their lofty sentiments of public service were shared within the civil service at large. But we must avoid the opposite and almost perverse assumption that because their positions within Whitehall were unique, so too were the values they held and espoused; or that others a little way down the line took delight in confounding them. That Fisher, Bridges and others of the period upheld a purity of ethic and a distinct public service ethos there can be no doubt (Chapman, 1988; Chapman and O'Toole, 1995). That they did so with sincerity and confidence is scarcely less to be denied. We can be less certain, though still fairly confident, that the relative homogeneity and hierarchical character of Whitehall ensured that such values were widely shared. Fisher and Bridges did not invent or inaugurate any new set of values. Rather they consolidated and embellished a tradition that was already deeply rooted. If Sir William Armstrong (Head of the Home Civil Service, 1968-74), Sir Douglas Allen (1974-77) and Sir Ian Bancroft (1978-81) failed to leave their mark in ways comparable to Fisher and Bridges it was largely because they were forced by the climate of their times to lay the emphasis elsewhere. But there is little to suggest that they wished, or consciously attempted, to disengage from the public service values of their predecessors.

What, then, did Mrs Thatcher inherit in 1979? She inherited a senior civil service with some, though only rudimentary, management acumen, otherwise largely orientated towards ministers. It was still a career meritocracy, though less socially homogeneous or exclusive than once it had been. The seeds of change were in soil but had yet to flower. In particular the public service ethic was probably as deeply etched as ever in the Whitehall psyche. The quasi-business ethos of such as the Property Services Agency and the Defence Procurement Executive stood in stark contrast to the traditional public sector norm. The Whitehall of the 1970s would have been recognisable to those who had graced its corridors in the 1950s and 1960s – probably also to those of the 1940s if not the 1920s or 1930s.

The Context of Change 1979-97

The context of change may be set out at two levels – the quantitative and the qualitative. Quantitatively, it is worth considering change as reflected both in the characteristics of senior officials and in the shape of Whitehall itself. Bold figures can tell us something, though by no means all we need to know. For many informed observers, there has also been a qualitative change in the character of Whitehall, having implications for the roles played by all senior officials.

Table 1 shows the main background and career profiles of all Whitehall mandarins at grade 3 and above. The table offers a snap-shot comparison of those in post in 1997 as against the class of 1979. It covers all departments in and around Whitehall, including (for 1997) agency chief executives but otherwise excluding those located outside central London. Broadly the

Table 1
Civil Servants Grade 3 and above in Whitehall and related Locations: 1979 and 1997

	1979	1997
Personal		
Age (years)	52.3	51.6
	%	%
Men	95.0	88.0
Women	5.0	12.0
Education		
School:		
Top 20 Elite	14.0	11.7
HMC (exclusive top 20)	32.9	33.1
Other non-state	15.1	12.9
State	38.0	42.3
TOTAL	100.0	100.0
University:		
'Oxbridge'	55.0	53.8
Other	28.4	37.6
None	16.6	8.6
TOTAL	100.0	100.0
Class on Entry to the Civil Service		
Admin/Admin Trainee	49.5	52.3
Executive/clerical	12.6	6.4
Specialist	32.0	31.2
Other/Senior entry	5.9	10.1
TOTAL	100.0	100.0
Service in Whitehall		
20 years and over	85.6	87.4
10-19 years	9.7	5.5
under 10 years	4.7	7.1
TOTAL	100.0	100.0
Experience Prior to Civil Service		
Some outside experience	20.5	29.8
At least 5 years experience	15.1	10.3

Source: Civil Service Yearbooks; Who's Who; Whitehall Companion

figures show how relatively little change there has been in the collective characteristics of the *corps d'elite*. Those in post today are slightly younger than their 1979 counterparts. In terms of education the state schools have made a modest advance at the expense of the minor public (other non-state) schools and the top twenty elite schools – but nothing dramatic. Over half (54.8 per cent) of today's senior officials went to Headmasters' Conference schools, only slightly less than the 56.9 per cent among the 1979 group. Oxbridge retains its position, while the civic (or redbrick and new) universities now lay claim to a greater share, largely because there are fewer who did not go to a university. The latter is partly a function of the expansion of higher education, partly also a reflection of the smaller proportion in 1997 who began their career in a clerical or executive grade. This decline in upward internal mobility is one of the more noticeable contrasts and is itself the product of sustained contraction (see below). Thus the administrative elite – those who entered directly into the Administrative Class or Administrative Trainee Scheme – has retained and even strengthened its hold on the senior echelons. Yet the figures show that this is nothing like the near exclusive monopoly sometimes implied by the critics and that specialists have always assumed quite a strong minority presence.

It is necessary to offer some comment about those who began their Whitehall careers in the category described as 'other'. These include the various departmental classes (e.g. tax inspectorate) as well as those who entered Whitehall directly at more senior levels. Such outsiders have been the subject of some controversy, especially where they have been associated with crude attempts to import private business methods or where their appointments have been seen as violating the principles of open competitive recruitment. Their presence in strategic positions may well exceed their numerical weight in Whitehall (Corby, 1997, p.72). They are an increasing minority but remain a fairly small minority nonetheless. The Whitehall elite continues to be predominantly comprised of career civil servants, the vast majority of whom have had over twenty years service. At the same time, nearly one third of today's mandarins had some other employment prior to becoming civil servants – half as many again, proportionately, as the 1979 group. Moreover, one in five have spent at least five years outside the civil service. This, together with the modest but steadily increasing number of women, marks a growing heterogeneity in the ranks of the mandarinate. This said, the overall impression is of a group which remains a recognisable entity, in so far as such can be inferred from a quantitative profile.

As an institution the civil service has changed more dramatically than its senior personnel. Most obviously it has contracted from 733,176 staff in 1979 to 494,292 in 1996, a reduction of 33 per cent (Source: *Civil Service Statistics*). The effects have been felt the length and breadth of the service. Numbers in the three most senior grades fell from 814 in 1979 to 593 in 1995, a reduction of 27 per cent; those at grade 5 and above fell by 29 per cent during the same period. The latter category broadly corresponds to what, since April 1995, has been called the Senior Civil Service (SCS). The creation of the SCS was an attempt to knit together the senior grades to form a recognisable entity conscious of its own existence. In particular, it was hoped to embrace those located outside Whitehall and was thus an acknowledgement of the need to counteract potentially centrifugal tendencies.

One measurable manifestation of these centrifugal tendencies is the growing geographical dispersal of officials. In 1979, two-fifths of all civil servants were located in the south east: now the proportion is approximately one third (*Civil Service Yearbook, 1997*). More importantly, there are now 129 executive agencies in which 74 per cent of all civil servants are engaged (Office of Public Service, 1997, p.v). These executive agencies are now a fixed feature of the administrative landscape, having established some, if by no means all, the freedoms claimed to have been necessary for their effective operation. They remain part of the civil service but have semi-independence in personnel and other related matters of day-to-day management, as indeed do most core departments within Whitehall. In matters of nomenclature as well as of remuneration the *Civil Service Yearbook 1997* reflects a variety and an eschewal of uniformity greater than anything that could have been predicted in 1979. Alongside this there has been the process of delegation, the watchword not only of the Next Steps programme but also of the Financial Management Initiative and much else at the heart of Whitehall itself. There has been the open government initiative and the more general temper of transparency of which it is the product.

One way or another all these things have impinged upon the roles of senior officials. Not surprisingly, the continued integrity of the system in which they operate has been called into question. Richard Chapman himself (1991, p.5) has wondered whether the civil service any longer exists – at least as a 'distinct institution of the public service, identifiable primarily through certain characteristics or qualities rather than through an authoritative and/or legal definition'. Even the definition, he now says, is less clear (Chapman, 1997). Others see evidence of dissolution in different ways. It has been said that the old style Weberian, hierarchical pattern of bureaucracy in Whitehall has begun to dissolve, calling into question the 'constitutional-representative' government perspective with which it was associated (Dowding, 1995). As suggested above, it is doubtful if Whitehall ever bore the hallmarks of pure Weberian classicism and one may question the links with 'constitutional-representative' government – but some sort of change in this direction may well have taken place. Civil servants may have felt some sense of ownership and attachment to initiatives such as the Next Steps programme (Dowding, 1995, p.106). A much bolder claim is made by Campbell and Wilson (1995). They talk of the death of the Whitehall paradigm – that is of a 'professional civil service (which) provided politicians with both fearless advice ... and a smoothly running machine for implementing decisions once they had been made' (*Ibid.*, p.5).

It is not the task here to establish the truth or otherwise of these claims; it is enough for our purpose to note that they have been made. For they are not the wild assertions of the ill-informed or of those who would wish the system ill. They are claims rooted in genuine concerns about the very character of the British mandarinate and about the efficacy of the system in which it operates. These are not trifling matters: they go well beyond the managerial concerns of Fulton and Ibbs. They imply that some sort of basic, qualitative, change has been taking place. Even if exaggerated, talk about the end of the civil service and about the death of the Whitehall paradigm implies something profound about the context in which senior officials operate and about the tasks they perform. In the next two sections their changing roles are therefore examined – first in terms of the greater emphasis upon management that now pervades Whitehall, then in terms of their position in the wider constitution.

They're all Managers now?

The one theme which unites the reformers of the 1980s and 1990s with those of the Fulton era is the desire to make civil servants more management-conscious. At times this has taken more direct form, as in the Financial Management Initiative and, more recently, in the introduction of resource accounting (Likierman, 1995). On other occasions it has been less direct but no less compelling in intent, as in the Ibbs Report. Some – usually those who see the move as a change for the worse or who have misgivings – are apt to emphasise the extent to which managerialism has taken root in Whitehall and elsewhere in the public sector (Elcock, 1995). Others who see greater merit in the principle are more sensitive to the apparent durability of the old ways (Metcalfe and Richards, 1990).

To which of these positions does the evidence lend the greater weight? Are all senior civil servants now managers? Is the managerialisation of the civil service (if such it is) compatible with traditional policy roles, and has the policy role itself changed? The reality, in as much as anyone can yet be sure, is almost certainly more complex than is commonly supposed. The role of senior officials is now more managerial than was the case in 1979. At the same time, a good part of their work remains policy-orientated, or at least minister-orientated, albeit with a subtle shift in the nature of such work. Similarly, many elements of the traditional ethos remain extant, though subsisting in a climate less conducive to its full nourishment.

In a sense all senior officials are now managers. This is most clearly true of agency chief executives (ACEs). It is also true of nearly all core department officials, not least those who have extensive contacts with the executive agencies. This is part of the transformation from management *by* contract to the management *of* contract (Greer, 1994, p.77). As noted above, there have been changes of nomenclature, almost certainly indicating a shift in substance as well as in appearance. It is unlikely that anyone now would be appointed to a permanent secretaryship without some serious consideration of his or her managerial capacity. In contrast to the career of Sir Peter Carey, progress through the middle and senior hierarchy would involve an explicit management 'charge' – at least for most people most of the time. In recent years this has meant the fulfilment of various specified performance targets and outputs, a utilitarian manifestation which is the essence of modern management. It is also a product of the conscious desire of successive governments of the 1980s and 1990s to make Whitehall more businesslike – not merely tighter and more efficient but also bearing many of the mannerisms of a private business organisation. Senior officials right up to permanent secretary level talk the language of management: no longer do they scoff, even if (privately) a few may remain sceptical.

If this seems to be an overstatement it is partly because it is accompanied by another manifest reality – that many senior officials continue to be involved in 'policy' work. This is most obviously true of the more senior officials, the policy advisers and those close to ministers. It is perhaps more the norm among those in the central departments (Cabinet Office, Treasury) than of those in the service departments though the latter, where they are involved, will often have a deeper involvement on particular policies. Even ACEs are not straightforward managers; they too make policy inputs. This is nearer the mark than the alternative interpretation which sees ACEs as having absorbed much of the managerial work, so leaving core officials to concentrate even more heavily upon 'pure' policy. Such a view merely confirms that policy and management work are closely interlinked – again nothing new but a brute reality which explains why it is possible to see civil servants as either policy or management orientated, according to inclination.

To leave it there would be incomplete and misleading. The nature of policy work in Whitehall has almost certainly changed – not dramatically, but subtly, and in a number of ways. First, among the most senior mandarins, the permanent secretaries, it is now much more difficult for any one individual to imprint him or herself upon the policy process. Departments are much less the personal fiefdoms of the man or woman in charge – less so, for example, than in the days of Sir Charles Cunningham or Dame Evelyn Sharp during the 1950s and 1960s. Most modern permanent secretaries orchestrate, or act as brokers of, policy, usually as leaders of a team. Nowhere in Whitehall do they or anyone else monopolise the channels of advice to ministers as was still fairly common (though not universal) thirty or forty years ago.

133

Secondly, senior officials collectively share the policy role with others, inside and outside Whitehall. Special advisers and political aides now play a more active and visible role. They are no longer seen by the mandarinate as an alien force. On the whole relations between the 'irregulars' and the permanent Whitehall residents have long since bedded down. But the accommodation has had a lasting effect upon the policy roles of the latter. So, too, has the external presence of think tanks, the influence of which during the 1980s and 1990s has been the subject of much interest (Cockett, 1994; Denham, 1996; Stone, 1996). Think tanks are by no means a recent phenomenon but they have been more prominent during the Thatcher and Major years than hitherto. At the very least they have given ministers another 'string', a counterweight to the cocoon once described by Richard Crossman as a 'padded cell'.

A third factor has been at work. During the past eighteen years there has been a loss of faith in planning. At its height during the 1960s and 1970s planning could be linked, however implicitly, with the growth of so called corporatism (Schmitter, 1985; Cawson, 1986). As Cawson put it 'the defining characteristic of corporatism is the *fusion* of representation and (bureaucratic) intervention, so that the same actors within the same institutions negotiate both the formation of policy and its implementation' (p.135). In even more controversial fashion it bore traces of the infamous adage 'the man in Whitehall usually knows best'. Except among the more ardent Fabian socialists of a now departed generation no one took this literally, any more than the deeply committed libertarian believes that the customer is always right. But the assumptions of planning from the centre, and the process of integrated governance placed a premium on the 'steering' role of the bureaucracy. Senior officials were granted a central, highly active role. This was reflected in a network of departmental and interdepartmental committees operating at the official level – Whitehall's 'digestive system'. Much business at the intersection of policy and administration could be, and indeed was, ironed out among officials, leaving only the loose ends and issues of higher politics to be resolved by ministers. This was of course open to the objection that it could become difficult for ministers to set or change the scene; that the centre of gravity lay too much with officials. Be this as it may, the process seems in recent years to have become more streamlined, making Whitehall more acutely sensitive to the whims and wishes of ministers. The entire Whitehall machine has become much more directly minister-driven. There have been recurrent bouts of administrative indigestion.

Again, it should not be thought that there has been a complete reversal from one extreme to the other. Rather there has been a shift of emphasis – and even then not a simple one. The new managerialism is not the old, hierarchical pattern of bureaucracy to which Whitehall never conformed in all respects anyway. All senior officials are now managers – managers of a sort.

But management has not displaced the minister-orientation of most senior Whitehall officials. In some ways they have worked more than ever under the shadow of ministers during the last eighteen years. They have become perhaps more deeply immersed in the fine tuning, 'lubrication' or 'finessing' of policy, less so in its initiation and fundamental appraisal. This raises a further question about the role of senior officials in ensuring good government, or in averting the dangers of bad government. It is partly what Lord Callaghan had in mind when he spoke about the civil service as a bulwark of the constitution.

The Mandarinate and the Constitution

'Good piano won't play bad music'. So wrote Sir Kenneth Stowe (1992), sometime PPS to successive premiers and Permanent Secretary at the DHSS, 1981-87. The unstated assumption was that the Whitehall machine invariably acted to ensure that policies were at least tolerable and workable; that major disasters would be averted. Presumably, senior officials are, or were, adept at weaning governments away from the sillier and potentially more damaging courses of action – or, as the late Lord Bancroft once put it: 'handling matters so that, somehow or other, the garbage is made into something edible' (Hennessy, 1989, p.510). In this sense, senior civil servants are a bulwark of the constitution. They will, moreover, help to uphold the proper conduct of public business – a bulwark against corruption, fraud, deception and anything else that may undermine the integrity of the system. These, then, are the two main dimensions of the bulwark role: good government (or deliverance from bad government); and proper conduct. The former is essentially to do with performance, the latter with style and values, though the two are connected. In both senses the roles of senior mandarins have been subject in recent years to critical scrutiny where once they were taken almost for granted.

There has been a suspicion that senior officials of the 1980s and 1990s have been less adept at 'snag hunting' – that is, offering fair, objective yet searching analysis in the hope that policy proposals may thereby be better informed, sounder and capable of effective exercise. The result has been allegedly poorer policies. A minor literature on policy disasters has ensued, replete with claim and counter-claim (Dunleavy, 1995; Thompson, 1995; Gray, 1996). The case for the prosecution implies that officials have failed to 'head off' or 'sanitise' ministerial policy initiatives which, from their very conception, seemed destined for trouble. The poll tax and penal policy are among the examples cited (Butler *et al*, 1994; Faulkner, 1993). In the former case, the Permanent Secretary, Sir Terence Heiser, is said to have 'squared' senior colleagues at the Department of the Environment and elsewhere, so allowing an apparently flawed proposal to be firmed up without full critical appraisal. In the case of penal reform, ministerial initiatives were allegedly launched and pushed through the Whitehall machine in relatively undigested form, especially during the Home Secretaryship of Michael Howard, 1993-97. Officials right up the line are said to have been uneasy at the minimal levels of consultation and deliberation. They were unable or unwilling to curb interventions which went against the grain of earlier policies, carefully honed and nurtured within the Home Office over a sustained period under ministers of the same government.

To what extent has the provision of objective policy analysis been compromised and does this have any deeper implications for the constitutional role of senior officials? In truth, we cannot be certain. First, it is by no means obvious that the policies of the 1980s and 1990s have been intrinsically more defective than those of earlier periods, though some among Whitehall's own elite seem to detect a secular trend to this effect (Cubbon, 1994, p.109). Second, assuming that policies are worse, or that a greater number of flawed policies have emerged from the Whitehall machine, we do not know (and may never know) to what extent civil servants tried but failed to inject the legendary dose of realism, as distinct from rolling over in spineless acquiescence. Perhaps Whitehall never did possess the capacity to save a government from itself on more than a certain number of occasions during any one Parliament. It is just conceivable that the mandarins of the last eighteen years headed off as many potential disasters and embarrassments as usual but were simply overwhelmed by the constant waves of ministerial ineptitude! This may be unfair to ministers and unduly charitable to civil servants. Third, then, one must wonder whether officials have indeed been more obsequious than their predecessors and, if so, why. They may well have been anxious to accede to minister's wishes, though this itself is nothing new (Shapiro, 1981; Pliatzky, 1989, p.164).

This raises a fundamental point about the constitutional role of senior civil servants. They are supposed to criticise, to help sharpen up policy proposals and even to weigh in with proposals of their own – so long as they do so with constructive impartiality, acknowledging that, in the end, the minister's decision is final. They must avoid being wantonly negative or obstructive; never should they backtrack or subvert the course of an initiative once it has the ministerial imprimatur. At what point, though, does constructive criticism shade off into obstruction, impartiality into half-heartedness? To this there can be no clear answer: it all depends upon the precise circumstances. Similarly, to paraphrase the famous words of Lord Bancroft, conviction is the forte of the politician, not of the civil servant. Officials must be ready at short notice to put their shoulder to the wheel of new and different policies – sometimes policies which are at a tangent or even diametrically opposed to those on which they have just been working. If they are effectively to transfer their loyalty from one minister to another then there must be the capacity to disengage, to retain an element of reserve. This demands a careful balancing act, one which some believe to be near impossible and which may indeed have become more difficult to perform as the spotlight of publicity exposes more than was ever known before about the work of individuals. It demands a professional loyalty and what Wass (1984, p.53) described as energy without enthusiasm, eschewing the heartfelt personal attachment of nineteenth century Whitehall crusaders such as Sir Edwin Chadwick or Sir Rowland Hill. There may nevertheless have been a partial resurgence of the enthusiast civil servant in recent years. This was seen most clearly in the behaviour of Ros Hepplewhite at the Child Support Agency – not an encouraging example. It may have found fainter echoes closer to the heart of Whitehall but not, as with Chadwick or Hill, in the form of officials pursuing their own policy initiatives rather than attaching themselves to those of their ministers.

If civil servants in recent years have sometimes appeared to yield too readily to ministerial initiatives then this may have had more to do with ministers and with the political context in which they have operated than with the disposition of officials. With one party in office for eighteen years there has been a broad consistency of political direction – the very circum-stances in which officials are most likely to follow ministerial leads. Under Mrs Thatcher and, to a lesser extent, under John Major, this meant a government with a clear Parliamentary majority and sustained sense of direction; conditions quite different from the 1970s. Should there ever arise political uncertainties akin to those of the 1970s then the Whitehall machine may again assume a more powerful presence.

The implication of all this is that, at one level, the constitutional role of senior officials has not changed dramatically during the 1980s and 1990s: the role looks to have been played out in different fashion because it has been played in different circumstances. Change has been more apparent than real. What, then, about the other level or dimension of the bulwark role – that is as guardians of propriety? If civil servants have not manipulated, and perhaps should not be able to manipulate, policies that ministers are determined to pursue, it may be held that they should at least insist that such policies and other activities be conducted properly and with due integrity.

There is a widespread belief that standards of conduct in public life have fallen in recent years. As Lord Nolan (1995, para.7, p.16) says, the fact that this belief exists is itself a matter of concern, whatever the validity of the supporting evidence. The Scott Report (1996) highlighted instances of deception, disingenuity, and even dishonesty in the way in which ministers conducted themselves, especially towards Parliament and the public. Certain officials seem to have been almost as bad – at least in aiding and abetting their miscreant political chiefs, perhaps even putting them up to some of their tricks. Yet no one was claiming that civil servants (or ministers) had broken the law. On a charitable reading, officials were simply acting out to a fault their constitutional loyalty to ministers. Until the Code of Practice, adopted in 1996, there had never been any *formal* acknowledgement that civil servants should owe a duty to Parliament, least of all if this meant compromising ministers. But there was certainly an informal presumption that senior officials would give a sharp reminder to ministers who seemed set to break the bounds of propriety; and that ministers would heed the warning. Sir Warren Fisher hoped that his colleagues would, where necessary, say to their ministers: 'That's a damned swindle, sir, and you can't do it' (Chapman, 1984, p.170). Is there any reason to suppose that civil servants of today are less worthy custodians of propriety? What, if anything, can the mandarins do when ministers look set to kick over the traces?

As with objective policy advice, and for the same reasons, it is difficult to know for certain whether contemporary senior officials are any more or less sensitive to the canons of propriety than were their predecessors. In general, the traditional values which underpin proper conduct probably remain extant. The Major government stated and restated its commitment to the values of fairness, impartiality, justice, recruitment and promotion by merit and so forth (Cabinet Office, 1994, 1995). Rumour had it that such endorsement was pressed upon lukewarm ministers by top officials keen to retain the Whitehall 'Gold Standard'. If so, this suggests two things: that the mandarins continue to recognise the validity of public service values and standards of conduct; and that they are prepared to defend those values and standards.

If this is all that there was to be said then it could quickly be concluded that there has been no change in the role of senior civil servants as custodians of propriety. In fact the reality is more complex and slightly less reassuring. Some of the factors noted earlier have taken their toll – in particular the stronger business culture and the 'debureaucratisation' of Whitehall. These phenomena are not synonymous with impropriety but the corner-cutting, 'can do' approach with which they are sometimes associated can find itself in tension with the procedural, protocol-orientated mores of proper conduct in the public sector. The public service ethos has become less clearly defined, less confidently asserted, having for many years been downplayed in deference to that of the private business organisation. All this has given rise to greater uncertainties. The boundaries are less clearly drawn between proper and improper conduct and between what is constitutionally proper or otherwise in the roles performed by civil servants. Officials are supposed to serve their ministers; and they are supposed to see that things are done properly. So where should their loyalties lie if ministers want to violate the bounds of propriety and seek to enlist the help of civil servants in this as well as in any subsequent dissembling? And on what strength may officials draw in seeking to keep ministers (and other mandarins) on the 'strait and narrow'?

The question of loyalty is a large one beyond the scope of this chapter and requiring no further comment save for the observation that, during the 1980s and 1990s, senior officials have almost certainly experienced more acute role conflicts than did their immediate predecessors. The principal strengths upon which their predecessors drew when necessary were a slight detachment, an 'other worldly' high mindedness and a system of values often unstated but largely shared with the political establishment. It is difficult to prove, but these common understandings are perhaps now less common, hence the need for formal codes. Traditional values count for less; perhaps the political and the mandarinate establishments no longer share quite the same assumptions.

Conclusions

To suggest that politicians and mandarins no longer share quite the same values may seem to contradict the earlier assertion that policies have been more explicitly minister-driven and that civil servants have breezed happily along in the slipstream, occasionally exuding an enthusiasm that some would think unwise if not unbecoming. Such enthusiasm should not be exaggerated or misunderstood. There have been relatively few Ros Hepplewhites or, for that matter, Bernard Inghams and Charles Powells close to the heart of Whitehall. Not only few in number, the enthusiasts have enacted their roles in the specific and unusual circumstances of one party in office for eighteen years. Perhaps the official machine was never geared up to a dominant party state. The notion of a permanent, politically impartial, bureaucracy always assumed periodic changes of political rule. To this extent, the constitutional role of senior civil servants has been severely tested, if never quite to its limits. Add to this changes in the Whitehall landscape, and in the nature of management and policy work, and the appearance or outer manifestation of substantial change becomes difficult to deny. The mandarins have been on the defensive; they are a less confident elite. Yet for all this, and for their greater heterogeneity, they remain a more or less cohesive elite with some sort of 'collective personality'. The 'Whitehall village' has not been destroyed, though centrifugal tendencies are undoubtedly at work. Some, though by no means all, of these tendencies have been endorsed or encouraged by ministers who, after all, are the scene-setters. Much will therefore depend upon the behaviour of ministers in the newly elected Blair government. But for the time being, Whitehall's *corps d'elite* has absorbed substantial and perhaps unprecedented change on a number of fronts while maintaining a semblance of integrity, sometimes against the odds. It has, so to speak, taken a succession of cold baths which have chilled the body but not frozen the soul.

References

Barberis, P. (1996), *The Elite of the Elite: Permanent Secretaries in the British Higher Civil Service*, Dartmouth.

Butler, D., A. Adonis and T. Travers (1994), *Failure in British Government: The Politics of the Poll Tax*, Oxford University Press.

Cabinet Office (1994), *The Civil Service: Continuity and Change*, (Cm. 2627), HMSO.

Cabinet Office (1995), *The Civil Service: Taking Forward Continuity and Change*, (Cm. 2748), HMSO.

Campbell, C. and G.K. Wilson (1995), *The End of Whitehall: Death of a Paradigm?* Blackwell.

Carey, P. (1984), 'Management in the Civil Service', *Management in Government*, 39, pp.81-5.

Cawson, A. (1986), *Corporatism and Political Theory*, Blackwell.

Chapman, Richard A. (1984), *Leadership in the British Civil Service: A Study of Sir Percival Waterfield and the Creation of the Civil Service Selection Board*, Croom Helm.

Chapman, Richard A. (1988), *Ethics in the British Civil Service*, Routledge.

Chapman, Richard A. (1991), 'The end of the Civil Service?', *Teaching Public Administration*, Vol. XII, No. 2, pp.1-5.

Chapman, Richard A. (1997), 'The end of the British Civil Service', in Barberis, P. (Ed), *The Civil Service in an Era of Change*, Dartmouth, pp.23-37.

Chapman, Richard A. and Barry J. O'Toole (1995), 'The role of the civil service: a traditional view in a period of change', *Public Policy and Administration*, Vol. 10, No. 2, pp.3-20.

Cockett, R. (1994), *Thinking the Unthinkable: Think Tanks and the Economic Counter-Revolution, 1931-1983*, Harper Collins.

Corby, S. (1997), 'Industrial relations in the civil service', in Barberis, P. (Ed), *The Civil Service in an Era of Change*, Dartmouth, pp.69-81.

Cubbon, B. (1994), 'Memorandum of evidence to the Treasury and Civil Service Committee', Fifth Report, Session 1993-94, *The Role of the Civil Service*, Appendices to the Minutes of Evidence, HC27 – III, HMSO, pp.108-110.

Denham, A. (1996), *Think Tanks of the New Right*, Dartmouth.

Donoughue, B. (1987), *Prime Minister: The Conduct of Policy Under Harold Wilson and James Callaghan*, Jonathan Cape.

Dowding, K. (1995), *The Civil Service*, Routledge.

Dunleavy, P. (1995), 'Policy disasters: explaining the UK's record', *Public Policy and Administration*, Vol. 10, No. 2, pp.52-70.

Elcock, H. (1995), 'The fallacies of management', *Public Policy and Administration*, Vol. 10, No. 1, pp.34-48.

Faulkner, D. (1993), 'All flaws and disorder', *The Guardian*, 11 November.

Fulton, Lord (1968), *The Civil Service*, Vol. I: Report of the Committee, (Cmnd. 3638), HMSO (Fulton Report).

Gray, P. (1996), 'Disastrous explanations – or explanations of disaster? A reply to Patrick Dunleavy', *Public Policy and Administration*, Vol.11, No.1, pp.74-82.

Greer, P. (1994), *Transforming Central Government: The Next Steps Initiative*, Open University Press.

Hennessy, P. (1989), *Whitehall*, Secker and Warburg.

Likierman, A. (1995), 'Resource accounting and budgeting: rationale and background', *Public Administration*, Vol. 73, No 4, pp.562-570.

Metcalfe, L. and S. Richards (1990), *Improving Public Management*, 2nd ed., Sage.

Nairne, P. (1983), 'Managing the DHSS elephant: reflections on a giant department', *Political Quarterly*, Vol. 54, pp.243-56.

Nolan, Lord (1995), *Standards in Public Life, First Report of the Committee on Standards in Public Life*, (Cm. 2850-I), HMSO (Nolan Report).

Office of Public Service (1997), *Next Steps Agencies in Government: Review 1996* (Cm. 3579), The Stationery Office.

Pliatzky, L. (1989), *The Treasury Under Mrs Thatcher*, Blackwell.

Schmitter, P.C. (1985), 'Neo-corporatism and the state', in Grant, W. (Ed.), *The Political Economy of Corporatism*, Macmillan, pp.32-62.

Scott, Sir Richard (1996), *Report of the Inquiry into the Export of Defence Equipment and Dual-Use Goods to Iraq and Related Prosecutions* Vols. 1-5, HC 115, HMSO.

Shapiro, D. (1981), 'When in doubt blame the bureaucracy', *Times Higher Education Supplement*, 12 June.

Sisson, C.H. (1996), *The Spirit of British Administration and Some European Comparisons*, 2nd Ed, Faber and Faber.

Stone, D. (1996), *Capturing the Political Imagination: Think Tanks and the Policy Process*, Frank Cass.

Stowe, K. (1992), 'Good piano won't play bad music: administrative reform and good governance', *Public Administration*, Vol. 70, No.3, pp.387-94.

Thomas, R. (1978), *The British Philosophy of Administration: A Comparison of British and American Ideas 1900-39*, Longman.

Thompson, H. (1995), 'Joining the ERM: analysing a core executive policy disaster', in R.A.W. Rhodes and P. Dunleavy (Eds), *Prime Minister, Cabinet and Core Executive*, Macmillan, pp.248-75.

Treasury and Civil Service Committee (1993), Sixth Report, Session 1992-93, *The Role of the Civil Service*, Interim Report, Vol. II – Minutes of Evidence and Appendices, HC 390-II, HMSO.

Vickers, G. (1965), *The Art of Judgement*, Chapman and Hall.

Wass, D. (1984), *Government and the Governed*, Routledge and Kegan Paul.

9 Leadership in the American Civil Service

David L. Dillman

My intellectual debt to Richard Chapman runs deep. The most relevant source of this debt for purposes of this chapter is his researches on individual leaders in the British civil service. In particular, *Leadership in the British Civil Service* (1984) and *Ethics in the British Civil Service* (1988a) are significant contributions to the study of leadership. Both are public biographies – the first, of Sir Percival Waterfield and his role in the creation of the Civil Service Selection Board, the second, of Lord (Edward) Bridges during his tenure as Head of the Civil Service – and much more. Each study attempts to determine why these civil servants were successful – what motivated them, what standards guided them, and how they went about their work – and to expand our understanding of the day-to-day workings of the higher civil service, especially its administrative culture. It is a tribute to Professor Chapman that although his work on leadership focuses on the British civil service, it has been a constant source of stimulation for my thinking about my own civil service and its leaders. This chapter will briefly compare the administrative culture in the US to that of Britain. Secondly, it will examine how a particular leader in the United States civil service, John W. Macy Jr., went about his administrative tasks and discuss his widely acknowledged contributions to the operations and character of the civil service. Thirdly, guided by themes found in Chapman's work on leadership, I will explore the implications for leadership of the current effort in the United States to 'reinvent' government.

Leadership and Administrative Culture

Leadership in the British and American civil services takes place in distinctive administrative cultures. The administrative culture of each country 'can be observed in the attitudes and standards, values, beliefs and assumptions of individual civil servants. It has a variety of sources: some aspects have social and educational origins; some are developed from the structures and processes of the civil service; some come from precedents and have evolved into traditions and into working philosophies of administration' (Chapman, 1984, p.167). In Britain, the foundation laid by the Northcote-Trevelyan Report in 1853 resulted in an administrative culture characterized by a relatively closed, elite corps of liberally educated generalists who are committed to the principle of anonymity, nonpartisanship, and public service. Within the constraints of constitutional conventions, such as the doctrine of ministerial responsibility, British civil servants exercise broad authority. As Professor Chapman has noted, those called to be leaders in the British civil service historically have been widely known for being 'outstandingly able' and 'free from corruption' (Chapman, 1988b, p.3). British citizens in general 'have high expectations of their politicians and officials, and their expectations have usually been met' (Chapman, 1996a, p.1).

In contrast, the higher civil service that emerged in the United States in 1883 with the passage of the Pendleton Act evolved into a culture characterised by relative openness, professional-technical specialisation, and commitment to particular policies and programmes. American citizens are generally suspicious of public authority and expect, if not tolerate, a certain amount of corruption. Thus, a pervasive ethos of limited government long ago resulted in constitutionally determined fragmentation of power and responsibility designed to circumscribe administrative discretion and authority. Ironically, the demands of the late-twentieth century have resulted in a nation with a large, complex, and professional civil service 'but [also] a mixture of disdain for and suspicion of its civil servants. Rarely is the American higher civil service respected as an elite corps, as it is in Britain ...' (Marmor, 1990, p.210).

The relationship between civil servants and ministers further distinguishes the two administrative cultures. In Britain the line between politicians and officials 'is marked most clearly and rigidly, and associated with a definite and well understood differentiation of roles. Moreover, each of the groups principally concerned is highly cohesive' (Self, 1972, p.163). Chapman makes it clear in his valediction (1996a) that the well understood roles and standards that guide the relationship between British politicians and officials are being undermined. Nonetheless, British career officials are much better integrated into the governance role than their American counterparts. The American administrative structure 'produces neither a clear differentiation of politics and administration, nor a cohesive pair of political and administrative elites' (Self, 1972, p.173). It has produced an administrative culture in which tension between career and political officials is the norm and is no closer to resolution than it was in 1883.

The source of this 'government of strangers' (Heclo, 1977) is found in the

143

prehistory of the American civil service system. As Pat Ingraham notes, 'the American civil service emerged as a kind of hybrid' of merit and patronage (Ingraham, 1995, p.xix). Merit selection of public employees was instituted in the form of a civil service system designed to secure efficient delivery of services and to check political power. At the same time, political control of career officials was intended to promote bureaucratic responsiveness to the popular will. Historically, one of the most direct means to exert political influence over the bureaucracy has been through patronage appointments. Thus, though patronage has greatly diminished since the late nineteenth century, 'the United States [still] has the largest number of political appointees of any major Western nation, and those numbers have increased substantially in the past twenty years' (Ingraham, 1995, p.xix) to approximately three thousand appointments available to the President. By comparison, the prime minister has only about one hundred and twenty such appointments. Given the fragmented, decentralized, highly political, and often partisan administrative culture in the United States and the fact that 'our leading civil servants ... are without the benefits of great formal authority and wide public respect it is no wonder ... that we can regard determined, effective public leadership as worthy of exceptional note' (Marmor, 1990, p.210).

Efforts to secure effective public leadership to overcome the effects of fragmentation and to achieve the great purposes of state can be traced to the Progressive Era, if not earlier. The Brownlow Committee Report (1937) established – and later management studies, such as the first Hoover Commission Report (1949), the second Hoover Commission Report (1955), and the Ash Council Report (1971), reiterated – the orthodox doctrine of American public administration: 'Presidential control of administration is the way to vigorous, effective government in the service of democratic purposes' (Mainzer, 1973, p.84). The orthodox doctrine or what Ronald Moe calls the 'administrative management paradigm', 'accepted as its fundamental premise that the government of the United States is a government of laws passed by the representatives of the people assembled in Congress .... For laws to be implemented, authority and accountability had to be centralized in the President' (Moe, 1994, p.112). Though hierarchical accountability centralized in the President, his political appointees, and central management agencies was stressed, administrative delegation and some degree of discretion were assumed. The ideal was for central management to set standards, 'but not so detailed as to discourage initiatives by agency administrators' (Moe, 1994, p.113). The doctrine also recognizes that in the American democratic polity the Congress shares an interest in the administrative process. Consequently, because both President and Congress claim a legitimate role in bureaucratic oversight, administrative reforms have typically reflected broader political debates within the governing system. In short, administrative leadership cannot be separated from the political forces swirling in the larger political system.

Furthermore, the orthodox doctrine 'had a second premise that there were two distinctive sectors of society, government and private, governed by different sets of laws and generally kept distinctive in organizational management terms'(Moe, 1994, p.112). Though government might borrow management tools from business, government's distinctive character was rooted in a vision of the broad public interest achieved through democratic accountability. As Newland recently noted, 'support of a political system of constitutional democracy that works has been an enduring purpose of American public administration'(1997, p.ii).

Whatever else one may say about the American administrative doctrine and culture, it is clear that public leadership in the American context does not come easy. Nonetheless, working within this particular administrative culture, John Macy rose to positions of authority, made significant contributions, and exemplified the highest of professional standards. After a brief sketch of his background, Macy's contributions to public service and leadership style will be examined.

Background and Career – A Sketch

John Williams Macy Jr. was born into comfortable affluence in the suburbs of Chicago on the day the United States entered the First World War, 6 April, 1917 (Macy, 1969, Tape 1). His father, an advertising executive with *Field and Stream* magazine, had migrated to the Midwest from New York two years earlier. His mother was a school teacher. Living a rather privileged suburban life Macy attended North Shore County Day School, a progressive and comprehensive private school, graduating in 1934.

By this time the depression was taking an economic toll on the Macy household. However, the young Macy was able to secure a university scholarship that reflected economic needs as well as academic merit and attended Wesleyan University, a small liberal arts college in Middletown, Connecticut. There, given his rising interests in public affairs, which was stimulated by the economic consequences of the depression that he had observed on the Chicago streets and by the inspired teaching of political scientist E.E. Schattschneider, Macy majored in government. He excelled as a student, was elected to Phi Beta Kappa, and was nominated for, though failed to receive, a Rhodes scholarship. By the 1936 presidential election he had completed a political conversion from suburban Republican to New Deal Democrat.

Toward the end of his education at Wesleyan, Macy became interested in a newly created government intern programme at the National Institute of

145

Public Affairs. Financed by the Rockefeller Foundation, the programme was designed to attract young college graduates to Washington by assigning them to a government agency as unpaid interns, offering seminars with well-known public officials, and providing graduate work at The American University. Macy applied and was accepted, and at the age of 21 selected the Social Security Board as his intern assignment. According to Macy, the Social Security Board was the place to be for someone eager to learn about the social programmes of the New Deal. There he met and worked with Wilbur Cohen, Robert Ball and many others who were also beginning their careers at that time. Given his intellect, youthful enthusiasm, and the opportunities afforded by the New Deal and wartime administration of Franklin Roosevelt, Macy, like others of his generation, became a high flier. Entering public service at age 21, he attained by age 36 what was then considered the highest career position in the federal merit system – executive director of the United States Civil Service Commission, the nation's central personnel office.

In November 1940 Macy became an administrative assistant in the Civilian Personnel Division of the War Department – his first professional entry into the personnel field – and, in November 1942 at the age of 24, he was promoted to assistant director of the Division. He remained in the personnel field – broadly conceived – for most of the rest of his career.

Though he was a registered Democrat, Macy was never active in political party work. Yet his party affiliation and his activism on behalf of the career service were antagonistic to key conservative Republicans in the Eisenhower Administration and in Congress in the 1950s. Nonetheless, by virtue of his professional reputation, he was appointed to be executive director of the Civil Service Commission in 1953. Through the years of partisan Republican revenge directed at the civil service, Macy stayed on as executive director, saying, 'it is much better to stay with it and see if you couldn't moderate it [extremism] than to get outside and throw rocks at it because that wasn't likely to have any particular effect' (Macy, 1969, Tape 2, p.7). Like the quintessential British civil servant, he would not divulge his innermost feelings. However, there is no doubt that his belief that the Republican leadership on the Commission was thwarting positive change on behalf of the career service prompted his departure from the government in 1958 for a brief stint as vice president at Wesleyan University, his alma mater.

Macy's energy and commitment to public service symbolized the new frontiersman of President Kennedy and the activists in the Great Society of President Johnson. Likewise, his proven ability and policy views were welcomed in the Kennedy and Johnson White Houses. Thus in 1961 Macy was appointed to serve as chairman of the Civil Service Commission by President Kennedy, who made it clear he wanted a career person in that particular position. Macy became chairman of a Commission he 'not only knew but to an appreciable extent had built up during ... five years as

146

Executive Director' (Macy, 1964, p.7). As chairman, he began to thaw many of his projects that had been placed in a deep freeze by the Republican leadership. Though Macy's primary focus during the Kennedy years was on the career service, Kennedy also looked to him as a 'quality conscience' for many high-level political appointments (Macy, 1964, p.8).

After President Kennedy's assassination President Johnson asked Macy to continue to serve as chairman of the Civil Service Commission and in 1965 reappointed him for another six-year term. Shortly after the 1964 presidential election, Macy was asked by President Johnson to serve also in the Executive Office as a presidential aide who would identify, evaluate, and refer individuals for possible presidential appointment. It is in this role of talent scout for Johnson that Macy is most widely remembered.

After Macy announced that he would resign as chairman of the Commission at the end of President Johnson's term, he was approached by the board of the newly created Corporation for Public Broadcasting. Responding affirmatively, Macy 'assumed office as CPB president in February 1969, fifteen months after the passage of the act that established the corporation and in the first month of the new Nixon Administration' (Macy, 1974, p.32). He was only fifty-two years of age and beginning a job in which he had no substantive experience but, on the other hand, for which he had spent his entire career preparing. At the CPB he was instrumental in funneling federal funds to public television and radio broadcasting stations and programmes. In this Macy was a pioneer, and his skills of persuasion served him well. Indeed, a former chairman of the Federal Communications Commission remarked that 'under John's leadership, public broadcasting remained nonpolitical and independent. He did irrigate a wasteland, and the seeds left by that irrigation left roots which will grow, flourish, and prevail' (Macy, 1974, p.x). Three years later Macy resigned under pressure from the Nixon White House due to a dispute with the administration over the direction and financing of public television public affairs programmes. It was a source of some notoriety that his name appeared on the Nixon 'enemies list' for his work in behalf of public television.

Leaving the government in 1972, Macy joined David Lilienthal and other former public servants in consulting on international management and development projects. He returned to government service for the last time during the Carter Administration, where he served as the first director of the Federal Emergency Management Agency from 1979 to 1981. After leaving government service for the final time in 1981, he dedicated himself to developing and training leaders, serving as vice president of the National Executive Service Corps and chairman of the Alliance for Leadership Development. He organized and taught in the John W. Macy, Jr. Leadership Seminar designed to encourage and prepare high school students for leadership responsibilities. He also served as chairman of an effort to bring

147

attention to hunger and homelessness. John Macy could never do nothing. He died in 1986 at the age of sixty-nine.

Leadership in the American Civil Service

Macy was a leader in the American civil service, serving five Presidents at senior levels. Donald Harvey has written that Macy's tenure at the United States Civil Service Commission resulted 'in change of nearly revolutionary proportions in the Commission's attitudes and activities as well as the structure of the career service itself' (Harvey, 1970, p.69). Bernard Gladieux believes that Macy was responsible for bringing the United States civil service into the modern age despite resistance and inertia (Gladieux, 1991). Frank Sherwood concludes that Macy is 'the most important single figure in the approximately 100 years while [American] public personnel administration has been a matter of conscious public concern' (1987, pp.221, 225). Macy received the Presidential Medal of Freedom from President Johnson on January 20, 1969. The citation, in part, reads:

> John Macy recruited more talent of proven ability into government service than any other man of our time. In demanding only the best and in seeking it out, he set a standard of excellence that will serve as a benchmark for many years to come. Our government is stronger today from top to bottom because of his efforts. The government is fairer too because John Macy insisted that equal employment opportunity meant what it says. He insisted only on ability and character without regard to religion or race or color or section (Macy, 1969, Tape 3, p.1).

It is an assessment with which no one disagrees.

Through more than forty years of public service, John Macy came to epitomize the intelligent, able, and dedicated career federal government official he so often spoke about in public speeches. Macy was a man of handsome physique who enjoyed a game of tennis but who put most of his energies into his work. He never wasted time, typically arriving at airplane departures with only minutes to spare. Exceptionally well organized, he was never far away from a spiral notebook or a dictating machine to produce 'a continuous stream of memos asking questions and making suggestions' (Harvey, 1970, pp.68-69). Macy drove himself, but was never overbearing with others. With clerks he was kind and considerate; with associates he was collegial. He surrounded himself with capable employees who, though they might not always agree with his decisions, appreciated his decisiveness and knew that he had deliberated on their requests or ideas rather than simply reacted. They felt a part of decisions because he explained *why* he needed something or *why* he did something. Macy was a good listener, but by the force of his intellect, facility with language, and reputation for straight-talking, he was also persuasive and could bring people on Capitol Hill and on K Street around to his viewpoint.

O. Glenn Stahl's assessment (Stahl, 1991) that Macy had a genuine regard for what was good and what was in the public interest echoes the views of many of Macy's contemporaries. No doubt the source of Macy's standards, his deep commitment to public service, and his generalist orientation was rooted in his rather strict upbringing and in his university education. At the same time, his public service attitude was enhanced by post-entry socialization. His early intern experience clearly brought him into contact with others of like mind, gave him opportunities to work early on at high levels, and provided a generalist perspective. Though the American administrative structure and process tend to reward specialized skill and deter lateral movement, Macy succeeded by negotiating 'an interesting balance between specialist and generalist roles.' Sherwood goes on to note that 'it can be argued that his most enduring reputation comes from his work in a specialized area, personnel administration. Interestingly, he may have played a dominant role in personnel largely because he would not allow himself to be specialized' (Sherwood, 1987, p.221). He sought lateral moves and consciously broadened his perspective.

In his adult years Macy was a religious man who had what appeared to be rigid ethical standards – he did not drive faster than the speed limit, did not complain about paying taxes, and felt that things should be done properly – but he was fair and generous of spirit. Likewise, in his public life he was guided by an ethical ideal:

> In accepting his public responsibility, [the public servant] must recognize that he accepts a special code of conduct and a special set of ethical standards. Not only must he obey statutes and regulations that relate to his performance as a public servant; he must also avoid any behavior that creates the appearance of violation of the code or the standards or will undermine the confidence of the public in his impartiality, objectivity, and integrity. He must bring to his public performance a set of personal values that transcend his own success, satisfaction, or advancement. He must be prepared to apply a moral measure in the public interest to every act or decision (Macy, 1971, p.249).

In short, formal safeguards – statutes and regulations – were respected but insufficient guideposts. What Chapman calls informal safeguards – 'the values and beliefs that contribute to the set of patterns and guidelines for behaviour' (Chapman, 1988a, p.306) – were also important sources of guidance to Macy.

Given his high profile in the Johnson White House, Macy had many offers to join prestigious executive search firms. But he had no interest in the task of recruitment for its own sake; his interest was in securing leadership for the public service. Furthermore, his high regard for the public interest precluded taking advantage of his relationship with the President. In January 1969 as Johnson and Macy were about to leave office, the President called Macy to ask him if there was anything he wanted; you are the only one that has not asked a favour, Johnson reportedly said. Macy's strong sense of propriety would only allow him to ask Johnson to meet his mother, who had never met the President. Johnson willingly obliged (Macy, Joyce, 1991). Because his own public (and private) life was consistent with the highest of standards, Macy, without appearing self-righteous or sanctimonious, was a source of moral authority inspiring and influencing associates to achieve high quality performance with integrity.

Leadership in the civil service takes place in a political environment. As Chapman notes, 'this is a uniquely important aspect of the situation in which officials find themselves working; it is essential that officials find it compatible with their individual qualities and attitudes; it is also essential that they develop sensitivities relevant to it' (Chapman, 1984, p.189). If an appreciation of the political environment is important for the British civil servant, in the explicitly politicised American higher civil service such an appreciation is crucial for survival and for developing constructive relationships with political superiors. Though understanding the inherent difficulty of reconciling neutral competence and political responsiveness, Macy believed that 'a merger of these two quests in the public interest' was possible. Indeed, attempts to separate them are fruitless because 'these two basic functions are closely intertwined as a means of combined action on the part of the careerist and the political manager' (Macy, 1959, p.16). At a minimum Macy's career illustrates his ability to cross political barriers by being appointed to senior positions by two Republican and three Democratic administrations. More importantly, Macy's success in balancing the values of professional competence with the political needs of his superiors resulted in competent governance.

Though there were critics who believed that Macy's dual appointments as personnel advisor to the President and Civil Service Commission Chairman compromised the merit system, Macy disagreed. The appointment as personnel advisor was, he said, 'a logical extension of the responsibility of the Chairman of the Civil Service Commission and ... there was no reason why rational individuals should criticize this' (Macy, 1969, Tape 3, p.5). The arrangement was, in fact, very close to that recommended by the 1937 Brownlow Committee and the first Hoover Commission. Working one shift at the Civil Service Commission and one shift in the West Wing at the White House, Macy took on the two jobs for the duration of the Johnson presidency. In the White House, Macy's purpose was to recruit and recommend professionally competent people for senior jobs requiring presidential appointment, that is, to bring merit standards into a highly politicised environment. Macy 'established a personnel presence in the White House that has not been duplicated before or since' (Sherwood, 1987, p.223). According to Bill Moyers, President Johnson 'felt that Macy was a man who was devoted to finding good civil servants, but who was aware of the fact that if you have a choice between a good civil servant who is apolitical and a good civil servant who is political, you choose the latter because our government is built on politics ... He liked Macy for that; ... he had an umbilical cord to the political process without compromising the integrity and the intelligence of the government' (Schott and Hamilton, 1983, p.15). Associates of Macy believe few others could have succeeded in maintaining the appropriate balance.

Certainly Chapman is correct that 'not all persons who reach senior positions in the civil service are leaders in the sense that they have made a contribution to the public service that is both known and significant. For the accolade to be bestowed on particular individuals it is necessary to know ... what their achievements were and whether in retrospect some years later they are seen as having made an important contribution to the public service' (Chapman, 1984, p.193). Macy was a leader in this special sense. Like many, if not most, civil servants, he was not creative in the sense of identifying imaginative solutions or inventive programmes, but he was able to overcome obstacles to implement programmes effectively. To take only one example, while chairman of the Civil Service Commission, Macy took the initiative to develop the Federal Executive Institute, a federal executive training programme and facility. Sherwood notes that 'it is important to understand that this highly important leadership institution has never had a legislative basis and, throughout almost its entire history, no appropriations' (Sherwood, 1987, p.225). Given his broad charge as chairman, Macy single-handedly leased the facility without any specific authority, assumed he could pay the lease and faculty salaries by charging tuition to federal agencies for training opportunities, and hired its first director (Sherwood, 1991). Without his willingness to take risks and his sustained leadership, the Federal Executive Institute would not exist.

Macy's guiding concern seemed to be with the question, 'how does a government get the best possible people to perform its socially critical tasks?' (Sherwood, 1987, p.223). The creation of the Federal Executive Institute was one answer to the question. Throughout his years at the Commission, his efforts to answer the question led to 'more attractive salaries; more flexibility in the examination process; more recognition of superior performances; and dramatic increases in the hiring and promotion of blacks and women' (*Washington Post*, 1986). He was at the forefront of changing the organiza-

151

tional structure of the Commission and its relationship with the executive agencies. In particular, he succeeded in achieving greater decentralization between the Commission and agencies with government-wide standards established by the Commission. During the Johnson presidency, Macy's leadership contributed to the selection of more than six hundred 'exceptionally talented individuals who by and large shared the president's belief in government as an instrument of social reform and a mechanism for the amelioration of social ills. These were, finally, also persons of substantial character and high ethical standards who led an administration remarkably free of scandal, personal pettiness, and adventurism' (Schott and Hamilton, 1983, p.209). Although Macy's impact may have been greater at lower levels in the political executive ranks, the selection of John Gardner as Secretary of the Department of Health, Education and Welfare is an example of how 'the White House had become so socialized in respect to merit that Gardner's [professional] superiority was, in fact, the essential reason for his appointment' (Sherwood, 1987, p.224). According to Macy the President was unaware of Gardner's party affiliation until a few minutes before his appointment was announced; he was a Republican. These and other accomplishments suggest Macy's lasting legacy is his quest for quality. Sherwood's conclusion aptly summarizes Macy's impact: 'a comparable record cannot be found in public personnel annals' (Sherwood, 1987, p.225).

Reinventing Government: At What Cost to Leadership?

Macy's career was a lifetime away in political and organizational time from the contemporary public service. Nevertheless, his career has much to say to current efforts in the United States to change civil service structures and processes and, ultimately, its administrative culture. The United States, of course, is not alone in this type of effort. In Britain, for example, the aim of The Next Steps initiative, according to Sir Robin Ibbs, 'should be to establish a quite different way of conducting the business of government' (Efficiency Unit, 1988, para. 44). Similarly, in the United States, the report of the National Performance Review (NPR), which is headed by Vice President Al Gore, calls for a structural and cultural shift away from 'bureaucratic government' toward a reinvented 'entrepreneurial government' (Gore, 1993).

Rooted in public choice and market theories, the report of the National Performance Review seems to assume that the public and private sectors are essentially alike in their fundamental processes and purposes and further implies that leaders in the public service are – or should be – subject to the same set of economic incentives and disincentives as leaders in the private sector. Consequently, a reinvented government would be based on four principles: cut red tape and make employees accountable for achieving results not just following rules; put customers first and meet their needs through using surveys and focus groups; empower employees to get results by decentralizing authority; and make government work better and cost less by cutting back to basics (Gore, 1993, pp.6-7). More specifically, civil servants – now entrepreneurs – in the reinvented culture would be held accountable for achieving measurable results and satisfying customers and would be empowered with greater authority to use their own judgment; spend money more freely; hire, reward, motivate, and fire workers; and create agency mission statements and performance standards.

Richard Chapman reminds us that we should always inquire how organizational change in the public sector will affect the administrative culture and socialization process which so much influence the ethos and standards of public life. The process of socialization is 'learning attitudes of mind, accepted codes of behaviour, knowing what is done and what is not done, forming a mental picture of the ideal civil servant'(Chapman, 1970, p.132). Have advocates of wholesale reinvention of the American civil service given adequate attention to the consequences of change with regard to the democratic values and safeguards that are promoted by or embedded in its orthodox administrative doctrine? No one argues that many of the attitudes of mind held by some civil servants do not need changing. But if Chapman is correct that 'one of the values of such socialization is probably to instil acceptable codes which may temper the possible excesses of bureaucratic power' (Chapman, 1970, p.132), then one must ask if a reinvented government will change the socialization process in unanticipated ways and thereby undermine standards and safeguards thought to be essential to America's democratic administration. By way of example, I will touch on four broad areas that give cause for concern.

The standards and values which have guided and defined American public administration emphasise 'the Constitution, statutory controls, hierarchical lines of responsibility to the President, distinctive legal character of the governmental and private sectors, and the need for a cadre of nonpartisan professional managers ultimately responsible not only to the President but to Congress as well ...' In short, one principal source of guidance for public management is public law 'supplemented by comprehensive, yet flexible, general management laws' (Moe, 1994, p.114). The NPR, on the other hand, 'seeks to replace the legal paradigm, which has provided the basis for public administration values, with the market paradigm,' which assumes that efficiency is the predominant value (Moe, 1993, p. 47). John Macy was motivated by a passion for excellence in implementation, but he had a clear understanding of the role of public law in administration. Where the report of the NPR suggests to managers that laws and regulations which interfere with effective and responsible administration 'should be either ignored or not enforced with vigor'(Moe, 1994, p.115), Macy's example counsels openly trying to change the law but, if unsuccessful, implementing the law to the best of one's ability, or resigning.

Secondly, a reinvented government may not only undermine the rule of law in administration, it may weaken democratic accountability. 'While political accountability may have once been properly the highest value for government executives, this is no longer true. The highest value in the entrepreneurial paradigm, by all accounts, is customer satisfaction'(Moe, 1994, p.114). Putatively, as in America's best run businesses, accountability to the customer is achieved by devolving management responsibility to the lowest possible level and empowering those employees to make decisions. 'This will let front-line and front-office workers use their creative judgment as they offer service to customers and solve problems'(Gore, 1993, p.72). Historically, both presidents and congresses have regarded such administrative discretion as a problem to be confined and checked with a variety of formal safeguards. In order to achieve their political and policy ends, presidents and members of congress attempt to impose their policy views on the bureaucracy by micromanaging discretion. In short, the presidential and congressional view of public administration does not draw a sharp dichotomy between politics and administration.

In a sharp break with this view, the reinvented culture would empower 'federal managers to make decisions in a competitive mode, without feeling so bound by regulations and hierarchical accountability' (Moe, 1993, p.48). Hence, the NPR report attempts to create a culture in which political leadership from both President and Congress is enervated and in which administrative discretion is enhanced. While the report voices allegiance to the value of accountability, the structural changes it recommends would actually undermine the orthodox normative doctrine of political accountability.

Thirdly, a reinvented government may undermine administrative competence. The orthodox administrative doctrine attempts to differentiate carefully 'the expectations surrounding political officials and career executives [in] an attempt to provide a way for each to exert the appropriate influence over the other' (Heclo, 1987, p.199). Heretofore, senior levels of the American public service – career and political – have been 'heavily dependent on people knowing what is expected of them, on people sensing the institutional subtext that should shape personal calculations and appropriate behavior' (Heclo, 1987, p.199). As noted earlier, the report of the NPR places paramount importance upon achieving customer satisfaction through empowering employees and liberating agencies from overcontrol. 'We can be sure,' Hugh Heclo concludes, 'that a governing community in which "anything goes" among the participants will be one in which nothing goes particularly well.' The reinvention effort is thus not only at odds with the fundamental normative standards of American public administration but, thirdly, conflicts with its essential competence.

Fourthly, if Chapman is correct that leaders uphold standards in public life, one should ask what standards the new entrepreneurs will be motivated to uphold. The qualities emphasized in the reinventing government literature are those of the market. The reinvented culture would reward entrepreneurial energy and creativity, reaching clearly defined contractual objectives, achieving quantifiable results. These may or may not be the qualities that are desired by politicians and citizens. In any case, one should ask, as does Caiden, 'whatever happened to the virtues of public interest, guardianship, integrity, merit, accountability, responsibility, and truth?' (Caiden, 1994, p.128). Is it possible to provide 'better customer service' without weakening the values that have characterized many leaders in the American civil service in the past? Where the report is clearly interested in results not process, Macy and other outstanding leaders are remembered as much for how they went about their day-to-day activities as for what they accomplished. A successful leader in the public service, in Macy's view, is one 'who can blend and mesh into a coherent and unified program of action the products from a variety of professional disciplines, who can relate human effort to specified public program goals, who can marshal resources to serve public programs, and who can mediate basic differences among group interests in search of viable relationships' (Macy, 1959, p.15) while applying 'a moral measure in the public interest to every act or decision' (Macy, 1971, p.249). What Macy is pointing out is that leaders must not only have technical or managerial skills but must also have negotiation skills, an appreciation of democratic political processes, and an understanding of what Chester Barnard calls the 'moral element' of leadership (1938, p.262). Macy's career exemplified these qualities not because they were contractual obligations but because they were inculcated through a complex socialization process involving parents, teachers, public service leaders with whom he worked, particular organizational structures, rules and procedures, and an adminis-trative culture that fostered democratic accountability.

The public service ethos that Macy exemplified includes loyalty, integrity, civility, energy, impartiality – particularly his ability to work with people of all political persuasions – personal propriety, respect for democratic processes, and the pursuit of quality for *public* purposes. 'To change such an ethos without careful attention to all the relevant evidence and without properly considering the potential consequences,' Chapman reminds us, 'seems as dangerous as settling a difficulty by ordering [like the Queen of Hearts in Alice in Wonderland] "Off with its head", without even looking around' (Chapman,1996b, p.14).

Leadership and Change

There are, of course, numerous approaches to thinking about leadership and even leadership in the particular setting of the American civil service. Here I have been guided by themes and concerns raised by Professor Chapman, who concludes that 'top civil servants may be regarded as leaders because by the examples they set and by the quality of the decisions they make, they influence those under them to make judgments according to similar criteria' (Chapman, 1988a, p.300). John Macy could not have agreed more:

> Those who carry public responsibility as top managers and professionals set the tone. They determine the patterns of administration to carry out the legislative mandate. It is through their offices that proposals for new or revised programs must pass to initiate public progress. It is their planning and their acts that enter the record upon which Presidents, governors, and mayors must go to the people. Within government, they set the style of vigor and imagination and efficiency or they deflate those qualities among their subordinates (Macy, 1971, p.215).

Described by the *Washington Post* as 'an outstanding role model for career civil servants,' Macy indeed 'contributed to the standards expected of civil servants and was an exemplar of them' (Chapman, 1988a, p.295).

In addition, Macy was a leader because he reached a position of authority in the civil service and, further, was vested with authority by the President, supplemented his positional authority by his personal qualities and moral standing, made a mark in the public service not only through his tireless advocacy of the public service but also through his success in instituting structural and programmatic change, and negotiated the interstices of politics and administration with finesse.

Macy would, no doubt, place in a positive light many of the NPR proposals to make the civil service more responsive to the 'customer.' On the other hand, he would be troubled by attempts to change administrative structures, processes, and culture without appropriate thought and study as to the likely consequences of such changes for what generally has been regarded as a public service which has achieved 'an impressive record combining competence, dignity, and responsibility' (Mainzer, 1973, p.151). He would be anxious about recommendations which strike at the normative foundations of American public administration: rule of law, political accountability, and the standards and values which promote informal but essential democratic safeguards.

For his part, Professor Chapman reminds us that leaders with the qualities of John Macy are essential for democratic governance. He also reminds us that organizational change has consequences for the socialization process and administrative culture which influence the qualities that our leaders possess, the standards that guide them, and the safeguards that discipline them. Finally, Professor Chapman reminds us that it would be tragic if change for change's sake were allowed to undermine the values and standards that have sustained democratic administration. But change for change's sake will do so unless the importance of developing leaders who model such values and standards in public life is asserted by adept defenders. Professor Chapman is one of those adept defenders.

References

Barnard, C. (1938), *The Functions of the Executive*, Cambridge, Massachusetts: Harvard University Press.

Caiden, G.E. (1994), 'Administrative Reform – American Style', *Public Administration Review*, Vol. 54, No. 2, pp.123-28.

Chapman, Richard A. (1970), 'Official Liberality', *Public Administration*, Vol. 48, Summer, pp.123-36.

Chapman, Richard A. (1984), *Leadership in the British Civil Service*, Croom Helm.

Chapman, Richard A. (1988a), *Ethics in the British Civil Service*, Routledge.

Chapman, Richard A. (1988b), *The Art of Darkness*, University of Durham.

Chapman, Richard A. (1996a), 'Standards in Public Life: A Valediction', *Teaching Public Administration*, Vol. XVI, No. 2, pp.1-19.

Chapman, Richard A. (1996b), 'From Croquet Mallets to Flamingos: Perspectives on Change', *Public Policy and Administration*, Vol. 11, No. 4, pp.1-17.

Gladieux, B. (1991), Interview with the author, 25 July.

Gore, A., National Performance Review (1993), *From Red Tape to Results: Creating a Government That Works Better and Costs Less*, New York: Random House.

Harvey, D.R. (1970), *The Civil Service Commission*, New York: Praeger.

Heclo, H. (1977), *A Government of Strangers*, Washington: Brookings.

Heclo, H. (1987), 'The In and Outer System: A Critical Assessment', in G.C. Maskensie (Ed.), *The In and Outers*, Baltimore: Johns Hopkins University Press.

Ingraham, P.W. (1995), *The Foundation of Merit*, Baltimore: Johns Hopkins University Press.

Macy, J.W. (1959), 'Leadership in the Public Interest', *Leadership and the Vigorous Mind, Advice to Young Public Administrators*, Syracuse, New York: Maxwell Graduate School, Syracuse University.

Macy, J.W. (1964), Transcript of personal interview by F. Holborn, John F. Kennedy Library Oral History Program, Boston: John F. Kennedy Library.

Macy, J.W. (1969), Transcript of personal interview by D.G. McComb, LBJ Library Oral History Project, Tapes 1-4 Austin, Texas: Lyndon B. Johnson Library.

Macy, J.W. (1971), *Public Service: The Human Side of Government,* New York: Harper and Row.

Macy, J.W. (1974), *To Irrigate a Wasteland,* Berkeley, California: University of California Press.

Macy, Joyce (1991), Interview with the author, 31 July.

Mainzer, L.C. (1973), *Political Bureaucracy,* Glenview, Illinois: Scott, Foresman.

Marmor, T.R. (1990), 'Entrepreneurship in Public Management: Wilbur Cohen and Robert Ball', in Doig, J.W. and E.C. Hargrove (Eds.), *Leadership and Innovation,* pp.210-45, Baltimore: Johns Hopkins University Press.

Moe, R.C. (1993), 'Let's Rediscover Government, Not Reinvent It', *Government Executive,* June, pp.46-48, 60.

Moe, R.C. (1994), 'The "Reinventing Government" Exercise: Misinterpreting the Problem, Misjudging the Consequences', *Public Administration Review,* Vol. 54, No 2, pp.111-22.

Newland, C.A. (1997), 'Realism and Public Administration', *Public Administration Review,* Vol. 57, No. 2, pp ii-iii.

Rosenbloom, D.H. (1993), 'Editorial: Have an Administrative Rx? Don't Forget the Politics!', *Public Administration Review,* Vol. 53, No. 6, pp 503-07.

Self, P. (1972), *Administrative Theories and Politics,* George Allen and Unwin.

Schott, R.L. and D.S. Hamilton (1983), *People, Positions, and Power,* Chicago: The University of Chicago Press.

Sherwood, F.P. (1987), 'The Legacy of John W. Macy, Jr.', *Public Administration Review,* Vol. 47, No.3, pp. 221-26.

Sherwood, F.P. (1991), Letter to the author, 28 May.

Stahl, O.G. (1991), Interview with the author, 22 July.

Washington Post (1986), 'John Williams Macy, Jr.,' 27 December.

10 'As others see us': Administrative Leadership and Biographical Research for the Public Service of a Microstate: The Maltese Experience

Edward Warrington

A Pen Portrait

Picture the Hon. Edgar Cuschieri, CBE, Official Secretary to the Government of Malta, presiding at a meeting of the Economic Committee of the Advisory Council in May 1958, a week after the onset of Malta's last constitutional convulsion prior to Independence – the Emergency, 1958-1962.[1] His spare figure, his angular face, his modest stature, his anonymous garb, belie the influence that he wields within the government.

He is the Governor's adviser on the Island's economy and finances at a time of crisis when thousands are being discharged from the Naval Dockyard and Air Force establishments, and the Exchequer is kept afloat by transfusions of aid from the United Kingdom. It is these issues that have precipitated the constitutional crisis; Maltese politicians refuse to treat with the United Kingdom and pass a unanimous resolution in the Legislative Assembly to 'Break with Britain' (Blouet, 1987, pp.216-217). Worse still, after a week of rioting and a general strike, the Malta Labour Party has begun a campaign of civil disobedience intended to discomfit the colonial administration, and has branded as 'collaborators' those civil servants who continue to carry out their duties (Advisory Council, Minute 4/59, 26 January 1959). It is the Official Secretary's job, as Head of the Civil Service, to steady the administration, to discipline officers convicted of rioting, to reassure anxious heads of departments newly propelled into the limelight, to cajole the apathetic majority into the brave enterprise of the First Development Plan (Advisory Council, Minutes 8/58, 28 August 1958; Minutes 14/58, 8 August 1958; Minutes 5/58, 18 June 1959).

Edgar Cuschieri served with distinction. The figure that speaks to us from official minutes and files is both cautious and astute; adept at wearing down the opposition in negotiations; a master of the pithy minute and the cryptic reply; a moderniser and an innovator within the constraints of Malta's circumstances and the strictures of his profession. The Emergency was not the first nor the last episode to call upon, and draw attention to, his distinguished abilities. He presided over the Malta Civil Service, as Treasurer, Official Secretary and Administrative Secretary, for the better part of four decades. During that time, he chaired the post-war reconstruction committees (see Warrington, 1994, for a detailed review of his role). As Chairman of the Malta Government Joint Council throughout its troubled existence (1950-1968), he successfully held Malta's fractious unions to a policy of wage restraint. As Chairman of the Public Service Commission until 1959, he filled public offices with men of his choice: those whose merits he first recognised hold senior posts in the present-day civil service. He led the Service through the achievements and upheavals of the first decade of Maltese statehood. The loyalty with which he served the Crown in the difficult days of the Emergency was transferred to the State of Malta when it came into being in 1962.

The institution over which Edgar Cuschieri presided was itself unique (see Pirotta, 1996). As a fortress since the sixteenth century, Malta had been closely-administered for upwards of four centuries by an extensive, paternalistic administration staffed largely by Maltese officials. By the middle of the nineteenth century, the Malta Civil Service was localised as a result of deliberate British policy, the first such institution in the colonial empire. The members of this established elite rated a status and influence at least as great as that of the clergy, another established elite and, informally, a pillar of British rule (see Koster, 1984, for a history of church/state relations in Malta). However, status and influence attracted the envy and ire of Malta's disenfranchised political elites. The post-war history of Malta is as much the story of the displacement of its traditional elites from a position of constitutional and social pre-eminence, as it is the story of national emancipation from colonial rule.

Given this backcloth, it is perhaps not surprising that Cuschieri was cast in the same mould as the post-war generation of Malta's political and ecclesiastical leaders. He presided over the Malta Civil Service from 1943 until his retirement in 1970. By comparison, the redoubtable Archbishop Gonzi led the Catholic Church in Malta from 1943 until 1977; Dom Mintoff led the Labour Party from 1949 to 1984; and Giorgio Borg Olivier, the father of Maltese independence, took the helm of the Nationalist Party while its leader was interned during the War, then again from 1950 to 1977 (see Mizzi, 1995, pp.3-7). Power gravitated towards Edgar Cuschieri no less than it did to the politicians and prelates who dominated post-war Maltese history. Like them, he cultivated a personal following within the public service; and, also like them, he did not groom successors who might aspire to an early succession. Above all, like the politicians and the archbishop, he was responsible for the welfare of a great estate of the Maltese commonwealth through times of unsettling change. By the time he retired, the civil service – like the Catholic Church – had been displaced from a position of constitutional pre-eminence, a prey to the ambitions or mistrust of politicians. The profession faced, as it still does, acute difficulties in recruiting and retaining men of talent. The ethic of neutrality that the civil service professed, the financial austerity that it practised, its preoccupation with due process and control – these characteristics were poorly attuned to the strident partisanship of Maltese politics, to the rising expectations of a newly-affluent society, and to the impatience of the wealth-producing commercial classes.

A Duty Statement

Long after Edgar Cuschieri retired, with the public service 'caught in the throes of a prolonged crisis of morale', the Government of Malta launched an ambitious programme of administrative renewal intended to create 'a new public service for Malta' (Public Service Reform Commission, 1989, p.2). The Public Service Reform Commission, which reviewed the condition of the service a quarter-century after Independence, found an institution lacking in leadership, burdened with a legacy of mistrust between politicians and civil servants, and poorly-served by decades of austerity (*ibid*, pp.1-2). While lauding the contribution of the public service to national development, the Commission criticised the 'highly centralised' management systems:

> There seems to be little understanding of management concepts, and such management talent as has been retained is dissipated in 'crisis management' arising from the predominance of short-term considera-tions (pp.2-3).

The Commission prefaced its recommendations about 'building organisational capacity' by drawing attention to its deliberate use of the terms 'manager' and 'management', in preference to 'administrator' and 'administration':

> This symbolises and emphasises the changes that we have in mind. The image of the administrator is congruent with a system that is unchanging and operates by the centralisation of authority and control. The alternative image, that of the manager, is congruent with a decentralised system, held together by mechanisms for planning and accountability and emphasising efficient use of resources and flexible response (p.27).

161

In drawing this distinction, the Commission was inspired by a body of ideas and initiatives that were then rapidly gaining currency in the English-speaking world and among leading multi-lateral institutions (see, for example, Metcalfe and Richards, 1987). The new paradigm in public administration emphasises the role of public managers in providing high quality services that citizens value (Borins, 1994, p.6). In support of that role, the paradigm advocates managerial autonomy, particularly by reducing central agency controls, as well as recognising the importance of providing the human and technological resources that managers need to meet their performance targets. In return, it demands, measures and rewards both organisational and individual performance, as well as maintaining receptiveness to competition and open-mindedness about which public purposes should be performed by public servants as opposed to the private sector (Borins, 1994, pp.7-12).

The recommendations submitted by Malta's Reform Commission fall squarely within the terms of the paradigm (Pirotta, 1997). It posited eleven goals of renewal that have been adopted by many other states, large and small, developed or developing: win public confidence in the Service; create a culture of excellence and integrity; define the role of the public service; develop administrative structures and management systems; define and develop employee confidence; select and retain the brightest and ablest; improve the quality of management; invest in technology and plant; increase planning and audit capabilities; define and contain executive discretion; institutionalise change (Public Service Reform Commission, 1989, pp.5-7). It must be said that the Commission did not merely substitute a plausible set of ideas conceived in a different setting for a judicious prescription addressing distinctive local issues. In advocating a managerial orientation to the ethos of the public service it responded to informed views about the *malaise* afflicting administrative performance (Public Service Reform Commission, 1990). The higher civil service, too, was dissatisfied with current operating systems. The Reform Commission itself examined features of Malta's political system, notably the large patronage in the gift of ministers that adversely affected the performance of public services or corroded the ethic of politically-neutral, impartial administration (Public Service Reform Commission, 1989, pp.9-18). The Commission believed that

> The public service is part of the institutional framework of government; it has a distinct identity and value system which have been obscured. The Commission wishes to see the distinction made once more, with the public service recognised and respected as an institution in its own right (*ibid*, p.3).

It was undoubtedly for this reason that the Commission gave great importance to administrative leadership, and not only insofar as the implementation of its recommendations were concerned. In its view

> The leadership role of heads of department is, or should be, oriented towards the attainment of goals established by official policy. It must be complemented by the development of a professional identity, collegiality and *esprit de corps* that bring unity and cohesion to the public service. Such a role would fall naturally to the Administrative Secretary, who is already acknowledged as the Head of the Civil Service, a courtesy title that can be given much greater substance (*ibid*, pp.31-32).

The fate of the Commission's recommendations is, perhaps, of greater interest than the recommendations themselves. As they were implemented, the managerial bias of the Commission's proposals overshadowed almost every other consideration. In particular, they may have obscured two facets of public administration about which the Reform Commission evinced particular concern, namely, 'the distinct identity and value system' of the public service as well as its 'professional identity, collegiality and *esprit de corps*'.

This was not an unexpected outcome. The business community, a natural constituency of the government in office at the time, was vociferous in its dissatisfaction with the performance of various public services. Secondly, in order to increase administrative capacity and thereby accelerate *ir-riforma*, as the programme of renewal came to be known, numerous British and Canadian management consultants were recruited into the Management Systems Unit, which was established to drive and support the reforms. Finally, the ruling Nationalist Party had itself been revitalised during sixteen difficult years in opposition by the application of the managerialism that it now advocated for the public service (Pirotta, 1994). In the course of six years the departments of state were reorganised as 'business units'; business planning was instituted; unprecedented investments were made in information technology and training; and top posts in the public service were filled by career officers appointed above their substantive grade on three-year, renewable 'performance contracts' (Commonwealth Secretariat, 1995). As a result of this effort, several government departments that had acquired a reputation for chronic under-performance were transformed into model organisations. The Commonwealth Secretariat singled out Malta as a model reformer among small states.

The reorganisation of top posts in the public service was accompanied by definitions of the roles and responsibilities of the office holders. In itself, this was a positive development: it re-stated the importance of sound management. More significantly, perhaps, it addressed an issue that had bedevilled relations between civil servants and ministers. The duty statements deserve attention.[2]

Within the framework of their constitutional responsibility for the 'direction and control' of government business, ministers were to 'oversee the development of strategic and business plans' and to chair management committees within their ministry. As vice-chairmen of management committees, permanent secretaries were to be accountable to ministers for implementing major projects, for policy formulation and direction, and for sectoral strategic and business plan development. They were to co-ordinate the utilisation of all resources available to the ministry. Heads of departments were *inter alia* to answer to permanent secretaries for 'programme development, management and results, customer services, Operational Plan development'. The duty statements and organisation structures were subsequently refined. At present, the managerial responsibilities of civil servants are placed firmly within the context of the legal framework of administration and the policies of the government, as well as centrally-mandated policies and operating procedures (Office of the Prime Minister, 1992, pp.23-27). The managerial role of permanent secretaries and heads of departments is, furthermore, supported by Departments of Corporate Services that furnish personnel, accounting and information technology services (Office of the Prime Minister, 1992, pp.23-27).

A concern for results permeates the performance management system adopted for the top four grades.[3] Performance agreements specify 'objectives, functions and responsibilities attaching to [a] position and for which the officer shall be held accountable...' (Office of the Prime Minister, 1992, pp.23-27). Providing leadership (defined as 'teamwork, motivation of subordinates, sense of direction to staff'), managing financial resources and human resources effectively, and improving 'client services' feature as standard objectives. 'The opinion of stakeholders (superiors, subordinates, customers, clients and other parties who have an interest or are affected by executive performance...)' is sought in evaluating an officer's performance (Office of the Prime Minister, 1994).

An official survey of the performance management system at the close of the first cycle of reviews revealed considerable support for it: 'the majority recognised that the system is effective for top executives and contributes to a greater focus on results' *(ibid)*. Furthermore, 'the majority stated that the Business Plan, financial policies and guidelines, and position description were very important as a basis for drawing up the performance agreement' *(ibid)*. What could be said against a system that addresses long-standing problems in Maltese public administration and also appears to enjoy the support of the higher civil service?

In the best of worlds, of course, a duty statement is shorn of colour, emphasis and nuance: it cannot entirely encompass either the scope or the circumstances of a particular role. In essence, the duty statements devised for the top grades of the Malta public service casts their incumbents in the role of corporate executives pursuing well-defined goals in an organisation strangely divorced from the vagaries of politics, and wholly concerned with meeting the needs of customers. By comparison with the pen portrait of Edgar Cuschieri, sketched out above, this is an impoverished view of leadership in public administration. The comparison needs to be explored.

Leadership in Administration: Pen Portrait vs. Duty Statement

Drawing on the concerns evinced by the Reform Commission, one can postulate three reasons for comparing the perspectives on leadership conveyed, respectively, by the pen portrait and the duty statement. These are, first, to assess which of the two better satisfies the contemporary needs of society in so far as administration is concerned; second, to determine which does the greater honour to the 'distinct identity and value system' of the public service and, third, to discover which is better calculated to secure the 'professional identity, collegiality and *esprit de corps*' of the administrative profession.

The duty statement emphasises what is currently expected of the public service by a wide range of constituencies. With its emphasis on efficiency, resource utilisation, business processes, results, accountability, and client-orientation, it reflects the ascendancy – political and ideological – of the entrepreneur in independent Malta. It reflects a view of government in which the rights and obligations of 'citizenship' are displaced by discrete transactions between business units (government agencies) and users (clients). It is, in that respect, a reaction by an affluent, articulate and enterprising populace against the *ideals* embodied in the acquisition of independent statehood, as well as against the *excesses* of patronage operating through the machinery of government. Finally, the duty statement also reflects a current of thought that had been steadily gaining ground among members of the higher civil service. In short, it is not – as some critics have argued – merely a fashionable, alien implant: the managerial view of leadership in the Maltese public service responds to historical realities that are a compound of long-standing grievances, heightened expectations, vocal interests, and vigorous habits of thought and action. The *symbolic value* of the duty statement is that it promotes values such as accountability, a concern for results and concern for the needs of users of public services, upon which the legitimacy of Maltese administration increasingly rests. The *substantive value* of the duty statement lies in the standards set, and the material incentives assured for high-performing officers. However, certain deficiencies of the duty statement become apparent when it is measured against the pen portrait.

165

The pen portrait discloses the political context in which, and through which, the business of government is transacted; it reveals the official mind at work on affairs of state; it gives depth to conventional views about the duties and responsibilities of civil servants. The duty statement, grounded in a managerial view of leadership, discounts the political context, except to the extent that it encourages 'managers' to be 'pro-active', or to think strategically. Even in ordinary circumstances, however, high-ranking civil servants are closely involved in the political life of their country: by giving advice to ministers; translating electoral commitments into practical policy; drafting policy statements or replies to parliamentary questions; and by negotiating on behalf of their government.

In the circumstances of a micro-state, such as Malta, the minutiae of administration gravitates towards ministers and top officials: in a sharply-partisan political culture, they are potentially embarrassing. They are therefore removed from the sphere of bureaucratic competence: rather than being decided by the application of rules, they become the subject of political interaction, where official paternalism, ministerial patronage, the intervention of brokers, and the supplication of citizens determine outcomes (Boissevain, 1974; Zammit, 1984, pp.31-42). Civil servants negotiate these hazards with a mixture of guile and discretion, as well as expertise and integrity. The entrepreneurial attitude which the duty statement encourages them to adopt could become hazardous: on the one hand, it might encourage an unscrupulous official to set up as a broker and dispenser of patronage while, on the other hand, a narrow zeal for managerial excellence could lead to conflict with ministers and users of the service concerned.

In times of crisis, the political character of government business overshadows every other quality. In a society negotiating a difficult constitutional transition, such as the acquisition of statehood, a change of regime, or a military coup, civil servants may be required to fill a political vacuum. We have seen this to be the case in Malta during the Emergency when political parties refused to work within the constitution. The civil services of numerous former colonies have experienced similar disturbances. The common view that such experiences belong to the past is, however, mistaken. In the early 1990s, the collapse of long-established regimes in Eastern Europe and sub-Saharan Africa propelled their public services into the centre of national affairs, both as arenas for political struggle as well as entrenched interests confronting the ambitions of newly-enfranchised political elites (see, for example, Hesse, 1993 and Dia, 1993). Micro-states other than Malta also experienced challenges to the democratic order, with similar consequences for their public services: Fiji, Trinidad and Tobago, Grenada, the Gambia and the Seychelles provide examples of this. In circumstances such as these, the qualities of leadership demanded of the public service bear little comparison with those necessary to satisfy the material expectations of

166

citizens of a stable, democratic polity. The portrait of Edgar Cuschieri becomes, then, a surer guide than the managerialist duty statement: political acumen takes the place of resource management; conflict-resolution displaces business process re-engineering; innate qualities of judgement and integrity may become more important constraints on official behaviour than watchful external scrutineers; tenacious crisis-management and holding operations necessarily substitute visionary strategy or planning. During periods of instability, the stabilising nature of civil service systems becomes a critical counter-weight to destabilising forces at work.

In fact the pen portrait suggests that leadership in public service is as much about preserving continuity as promoting change. Thus, during the first weeks of the Malta Emergency, Edgar Cuschieri's principal task was to ensure the continued operation of the civil service in the face of political intimidation and financial insolvency. After the crisis passed, and Malta settled down to an indefinite period of direct rule, the civil service was absorbed by the task of containing the destabilising effects of large-scale unemployment and emigration. Without social stability and political quiescence, the ambitious plans for economic development would not attract the interest of investors. Later, as the prospect of ministerial government drew closer, Edgar Cuschieri and his colleagues sought – successfully – to secure a smooth transfer of power.

That said, the idea current in the 'New Public Management' that leadership is essentially concerned with bringing about desired, planned change has a superficial attraction to a developing country such as Malta, ambitious for rapid affluence and undergoing wide-ranging social change. In a competitive political system, where appearances garner votes, tokenism – the illusion of innovation – may take the place of substantive developments in policy. Maltese civil servants on performance agreements considered the number of objectives and tasks listed in their contracts to be unrealistic (Office of the Prime Minister, 1994). The effect of this may be to encourage tokenism, by altering the balance of incentives decisively in favour of innovation.

In devising models of administrative leadership, the task is not to choose between change or continuity, but to reconcile the two powerful tendencies in governance. Terry proposes the model of *administrative conservatorship* for career civil servants. The administrative conservator 'is summoned to perform different leadership roles ranging from initiating to protecting as a means of preserving institutional integrity. These roles specify, in a general way, the behaviours and orientations needed to address conditions and problems associated with a given institution's stage of historical development' (Terry, 1995, pp.64-65). This is an important insight: there is no single, all-purpose, unchanging set of behaviours and values appropriate to administrative leaders. They must be able to consider the significance of unfolding events in historical perspective, and exercise judgement in responding to contingencies.

In Terry's view, administrative conservators perform three 'critical functions'. First, they conserve 'the mission of public bureaucracies' by preserving the executive authority vested in them by their constitutional masters, as well as the non-executive authority conferred by reason of their expertise and official position (*ibid*, pp.65-66). Secondly, they preserve the external support of a wide variety of 'stakeholders' who are interested in and affected by the activities of their organisations, as well as the internal support of staff for the larger purposes of the organisation (*ibid*, p.67).

Thirdly, administrators conserve the values 'that help to maintain an agency's distinctive competence and role (*ibid*, p.66). The principal task in this respect is that of maintaining 'a viable executive cadre' who, as 'custodians of policy', are sufficiently strong 'to protect the values of public bureaucracies from serious corruption'(*ibid*, p.117). This signifies rather more than the efficient human resource management enjoined by the duty statement. It recalls the Reform Commission's concern with restoring 'the distinct identity and value system' of the public service, 'recognised and respected as an institution in its own right', as well as developing 'a professional identity, collegiality and *esprit de corps* that bring unity and cohesion to the public service' (Public Service Reform Commission, 1989, pp.5, 32). The managerialist duty statement submerges the distinctive ethos of the public servant in the bland, professional anonymity of the corporate world. By emphasising individual effort, and promoting competition for reward, it may undermine collegiality and intra-professional solidarity.

What can be said, then, about the respective merits of the duty statement and the pen portrait? The former is designed to satisfy the *expectations* of contemporary Maltese society in regard to government and administration. That is not to say that *needs* are thereby met. In themselves, the expectations of greater economy, efficiency and accountability are ambitious in a public service still suffering from the effects of chronic under-investment in corporate infrastructure (Pirotta, 1997, p.206). However, by promoting entrepreneurial public administration, they run counter to the paternalism that has long characterised Malta's system of government. The question naturally arises whether they can be sustained for long. Some doubts must remain as to whether the rhetoric of strategic planning and business process re-engineering is relevant to the uncertainties associated with Malta's economic vulnerability, or the ambiguities produced by its intensely-partisan political culture.

We set out to determine whether the duty statement or the pen portrait does the greater honour to the 'distinct identity and value system' of the public service, and which is better calculated to secure the 'professional identity, collegiality and *esprit de corps*' of the administrative profession. The answer seems to be that the pen portrait illuminates and, indeed, celebrates what the duty statement merely prescribes. In short, the perspective on administrative leadership grounded in the 'New Public Management' and enshrined in the duty statements of the Maltese civil service and its peers is useful but incomplete. Its understanding of the setting in which administration is transacted lacks depth and, in some circumstances, relevance. This limits its usefulness as a tool for training newly-promoted civil servants, socialising recruits, or guiding the exercise of judgement by an office holder. Against that, what the pen portrait lacks in prescriptive authority, it makes up for in description and analysis. Clearly, a strong case exists for biographical research on eminent civil servants. The remainder of this essay attempts an answer to two questions. What can biographical research contribute in terms of administrative renewal in a small, newly-independent state? How can such research be conducted and its findings disseminated?

The Contribution of Biographical Research to Administrative Renewal

The comparatively anonymous figures of civil servants, however distinguished, are not, generally speaking, a common subject of scholarly research. Terry attributes the comparative neglect of bureaucratic leadership to various factors, including scholars' emphasis on the influence of interest groups in decision-making; the attention devoted to studying the consequences of bureaucratic routines; the failure of scholars to discover patterns that make leaders comprehensible; the belief that bureaucracies are guided by powerful forces beyond the control of individual leaders; and deeply-rooted hostility toward career civil servants (Terry, 1995, p.3). Raadschelders points out that, in the Anglo-Saxon world, administrative scientists feel the need to justify research into administrative history more on the grounds of utility than on scholarly inquiry (Raadschelders, 1994, p.122).

The question whether administrative history, and (still more) biographical research, are useful pursuits may be more awkward in a small, newly-independent state.[4] Newly-independent states are, perhaps, not thought to have an administrative history, nor administrative traditions. Where, as in Malta, a history and tradition are acknowledged, their importance tends to be discounted by administrators and scholars: not unexpectedly, the drama of the struggle for independence and the heroic figures of the State's founding fathers attract greater attention.[5] Besides, new states have a bold agenda of development to pursue, past shackles to cast aside. The enlarged scope of government action, the large-scale recruitment of new professions into the public service and the adoption of new structures, technologies and operating procedures alters the colonial civil service out of recognition. If that is indeed so, there is little to be gained from studying administrative history; still less from biographical research into the lives of a handful of administrators. The public services of newly-independent states, struggling to enlarge their limited administrative capacity, may consider investments in management expertise and training as giving better value for money than a scholarly assessment of eminent figures and past events.

This is not to say that no valuable research is carried out on the administrative cadre. In the past, in the Maltese public service, this has taken the form of demographic surveys, tracer studies and surveys of the values of top officials (Public Service Reform Commission, 1990). These were commissioned as 'background papers' to administrative reviews. However valuable they are in contributing to our knowledge of the profession, they construct a static, one-dimensional view. Cuschieri, his contemporaries, and hundreds of other officials who administered societies negotiating the transfer of power from colonial rule to independent statehood, are overlooked, or have been merely mythologised in the folk memories of the civil service, harking back to the chimera of a past 'golden age'.

One of the noteworthy facts disclosed by a demographic survey of the Maltese civil service is that, until the 1970s when the Service began to age and terms of office shortened, heads of departments tended to hold office for a decade or more. Terms of office as long as Cuschieri's were unusual but not by any means exceptional. The pattern seems to be replicated in other small, newly-independent states, including Barbados, Fiji and Mauritius (see, for example, Carroll and Joypaul, 1993). The evidence suggests, therefore, that even newly-independent states have an administrative history stretching back several decades and, in some instances, centuries. If, during colonial rule, conventional politics – involving parties, elections and legislatures – was proscribed or embryonic, then *administrative history* constitutes the core political experience of that territory, as Pirotta demonstrates in his study of Malta's nineteenth century public service (Pirotta, 1996). Within that history, the careers of long-serving officials constitute distinct time-scales that offer researchers natural points of entry to their subject. This answers the argument that, in the absence of an administrative history, there is little scope for biographical research, but does not explain what may be gleaned from such studies.

If one accepts the view that knowledge of the past is not valuable for its own sake, it is still possible, following Raadschelders, to argue for the contemporary relevance of biographical research. Studies of the lives of eminent civil servants such as Edgar Cuschieri can contribute to administrative renewal in small, newly-independent states in a number of different ways. First, 'by acquiring knowledge for itself to serve (better) understanding of the present' (Raadschelders, 1994, p.192). The lives of eminent officials disclose much about their societies, as well as about the individuals themselves. In a small, intimate society such as Malta's, where personalities tend to overshadow institutions, biographical research offers, as it were, the key to the inner workings of government and administration. By documenting patterns of leadership and decision-making and by probing the official mind, a fresh perspective may be brought to widely-held views about politics and the public service. This will provide insights into political interaction and political culture, the origin and development of policies, interest groups and political organisations, and patterns of leadership and decision-making. The elementary pen portrait of Edgar Cuschieri with which this chapter began discloses, for example, important parallels between the institutions that dominated Maltese affairs during the past half-century. The comparison with the Catholic Church is especially instructive: it puts into perspective the loss of professional status of the administrative elite. It explains a phenomenon that successive reviewers have attributed merely to the uncompetitive salaries offered by the civil service.

This brings us to the second reason for undertaking biographical research; 'Listing practical lessons from this knowledge about developments' *(ibid)*. The findings of scholars can yield important practical lessons for leaders in administration, as well as for reformers. If, to pursue the example cited above, reviewers recognised that loss of status for the administrative elite was a concomitant of national emancipation, they might have better understood the reasons for the government's persistent failure to raise salaries to competitive levels: ministers undoubtedly saw, in salary restraint, an instrument for trimming the influence and pretensions of the administrative elite whom they had displaced. For senior civil servants, an understanding of the Catholic hierarchy's transition 'from lordship to stewardship' (Vassallo, 1979) may have yielded clues as to the fate of their own profession, as well as pointers for coping with their altered circumstances.

Biographical research, therefore '[contributes] to the solution of current problems and the shaping of society in the future' *(ibid)*. Together with more conventional organizational and sociological studies, biographical research can contribute to administrative revitalization by examining the origins and assessing the strengths of established leadership patterns, by drawing on the 'institutional memory' of Malta's oldest governing institution and by reinforcing a professional identity rooted in collective, historical experiences. Certainly, the depth of understanding of *local values, behaviours and circumstances* afforded by biographical research would considerably enhance the relevance of prescriptions for administrative renewal. The 'new public administration' as, indeed, the 'development administration' and other paradigms that preceded them, suffered from a tendency to advocate stock remedies. Knowledge of the lives of former officials unearths the rich deposit of tradition and experience on which Maltese public administration rests, adding an intangible but invaluable resource to *material* instruments applied in reform initiatives – enhanced salaries and career prospects, information technology applications, reorganisation, and delegation of operational authority.

Furthermore, by presenting 'heroic' leadership figures as models for contemporary administrators, well-written biographies can be applied, in education, training and apprenticeship, to the socialisation of junior officers earmarked for advancement. The warmth and immediacy of a biography could inspire them to excellence or, indeed, alert them to the occupational hazards and the follies attending their profession. It may, in that sense, offer more effective incentives to appropriate behaviour than the material rewards of a performance agreement.

An apologist for biographical research to revitalise administrative leadership in a small, developing state is acutely aware of the practical difficulties attending any such enterprise. For, as long as the value of such research is not widely acknowledged in the civil service and in universities, financial constraints will certainly limit the volume and, perhaps, the quality of studies. Within the universities, the rewards for scholarship may favour projects that have greater 'practical' value. Malta is unusual among small states in having its own long-established university: dozens of other small states in the Caribbean, the Pacific and the Indian Ocean share regional institutions, or make use of universities in neighbouring countries. The smallest, remotest states simply do without. One way around their difficulty may be to encourage multi-lateral institutions such as the Commonwealth Secretariat, which is already sponsoring 'profiles' of the public services of Commonwealth states, to sponsor selected studies of official lives that hold extraordinary interest for their native land, and for others. Institutions that receive the papers of former colonial service officers and therefore attract the interest of numerous biographers (such as the Rhodes House Library in Oxford) could selectively extend the scope of their holdings to include the papers of local officers such as Edgar Cuschieri. They would share the custody of the administrative heritage of small states that may be ill-equipped to discharge the responsibility alone.

Judged from the standpoint of world affairs, the lives of officials in small, isolated territories merit, perhaps, little more than a footnote in the history books. Edgar Cuschieri and his peers were, almost to a man, engaged in managing contingencies and applying initiatives conceived far from their jurisdictions. The professions to which they belonged did not rank alongside those of the great powers that imposed their stamp on local events and developments. They played little part in the innovations that transformed public administration into the handmaid of the welfare state. But, within their own communities, they were men of substance. The image of Edgar Cuschieri presiding over the Economic Committee of the Advisory Council at a time of national distress is as important for contemporary Malta as the image of the national flag heralding Malta's statehood. His portrait deserves a place in the gallery of Maltese history.

Notes

1. Malta, a naval fortress of the British Empire since 1800, acquired a dyarchical constitution in 1947, with an elected 'Maltese Ministry' responsible for local affairs, and a 'Maltese Imperial Government' responsible for 'reserved matters' associated with the fortress. The constitutional settlement, never satisfactory, broke down in April 1958, and the Island reverted to direct rule under a state of emergency. The Governor administered the Island's civil government, first through a secret Advisory Council and later through a nominated Executive Council. Direct rule continued until March 1962. Malta became an independent state within the Commonwealth in September 1964.
2. Unless otherwise stated, the references that follow are from Prime Ministers Office, 1991.
3. Permanent Secretary (Scale 1), Permanent Secretary (Scale 2), Director-General, Director.
4. The author will not easily forget the disappointment expressed by a Maltese permanent secretary, himself a man of some distinction, when he learned that a full biography of Edgar Cuschieri was contemplated.
5. In contrast to the rich literature on nineteenth-century Maltese politics, for example, only one study of its public service has been carried out (Pirotta, 1996).

References

Blouet, B. (1987), *The Story of Malta*, Malta: Progress Press.

Boissevain, J. (1974), *Friends of Friends: Networks, Manipulators and Coalitions*, Basil Blackwell.

Borins, S. (1994), 'Summary: Government in Transition – A New Paradigm in Public Administration' in S. Borins (Ed), *Government in Transition*, Toronto: Commonwealth Association for Public Administration and Management.

Carroll, B.W. and S.K. Joypaul (1993), 'The Mauritian senior public service since independence: some lessons for developed and developing nations', *International Review of Administrative Sciences*, 59(3), pp.423-440.

Commonwealth Secretariat (1995), *A Profile of the Public Service of Malta*, Commonwealth Secretariat.

Dia, M. (1993), *A Governance Approach to Civil Service Reform in sub-Saharan Africa*, Washington DC: World Bank.

Hesse, J.J. (1993), 'Administrative Transformation in Central and Eastern Europe: A Symposium', *Public Administration*, 71(1/2), pp.219-257.

Koster, A., (1984), *Prelates and Politicians in Malta: Changing Power Balances between Church and State in a Mediterranean Island Fortress 1800-1976*, Assen: Van Gorcum.

Metcalfe, L. and S. Richards (1987), *Improving Public Management*, Sage.

Mizzi, E. (1995), *Malta in the Making: An Eyewitness Account*, Malta: Mizzi.

Office of the Prime Minister (1991), *Instruction on Roles and Responsibilities*, Malta.

Office of the Prime Minister (1992), *Top Structures: Papers on Structures, Responsibilities and Performance Agreements*, Malta.

Office of the Prime Minister (1994), *Malta Public Service: Category 'A' Officers Performance Agreement – Assessment Guidelines for 1994*, Malta.

Pirotta, G. (1994), 'Maltese political parties and political modernisation' in Sultana, R. and G. Baldacchino, *Maltese Society: A Sociological Review*, Malta: Mireva.

Pirotta, G. (1996), *The Maltese Public Service 1800-1940*, Malta: Mireva.

Pirotta, G. (1997), 'Politics and public service reform in small states: Malta', *Public Administration and Development*, 17(1), pp.197-207.

Public Records Office, London (CO 926/584-587), *Administration of Government after Declaration of Emergency – Malta* (contains minutes and memoranda of the Advisory Council).

Public Service Reform Commission (1989), *A New Public Service for Malta: A Report on the Organisation of the Public Service*, Malta: Government Press.

Public Service Reform Commission (1990), *Supplementary Papers*, Malta: Government Press.

Raadschelders, J.C.N. (1994), 'Administrative history: contents, meaning and usefulness', *International Review of Administrative Sciences*, 60(1), pp.117-129.

Terry, L.D. (1995), *Leadership in Public Bureaucracies: The Administrator as Conservator*, Sage.

Vassallo, M. (1979), *From Lordship to Stewardship: Religion and Social Change in Malta*, The Hague: Mouton.

Warrington, E. (1994), *The Making and Un-making of a Great Estate: An Essay on the Malta Civil Service from War to Self-Government 1943-1947*, Malta: Staff Development Organisation.

Zammit, E.L. (1984), *A Colonial Inheritance: Maltese Perceptions of Work, Power and Class Structure*, Malta: University Press.

11 Reform, Ethics and Leadership in Public Service

Michael Hunt and Barry J. O'Toole

Reform, ethics and leadership in public service are central to our understanding of public administration. They have inspired Richard Chapman's teaching and research. Although they may be treated separately (particularly in some management textbooks) they are not, in reality, discrete elements of public service. For example, as Professor Chapman has demonstrated in his study of Lord Bridges, a vital attribute of leadership is the capacity to inspire and encourage commitment to particular organisational goals of service, even if these goals are to be inferred rather than clearly articulated (Chapman, 1988a). Further, as some of his other writings have demonstrated, reform undertaken without reference to the values of an organisation, or without recognising the need to relate any changes to an agreed, different, set of values, may easily lead to organisationally corrupt behaviour (Chapman and O'Toole, 1995; Chapman, 1996). The capacity to recognise such inter-relationships from both a theoretical and a practical perspective is, it may be argued, one of the functions of an academic, particularly an academic whose interests lie in the study of the governmental process. Such an academic should be in a position to stand back from particular policy issues or policy problems and provide informed comment on the way in which the policy is developing. This may include identifying some of the unforeseen consequences to which the policy might lead. Such an external observer also possesses the advantage of being able to monitor changes, whether planned or not planned, over a period of time, including changes in process, in order to be able to draw attention to those changes that seem to threaten wider public interests.

If there is to be any value in the role described above, the perspective provided by the academic needs to be considered, if not adopted, by those who determine public policy. This is the case in some countries; L.J. Sharpe, for example, has drawn attention to the contribution made by academic social scientists to the policy making process in the United States (Sharpe,

175

1975). This contrasts with the situation in some other countries, including Britain, where contact between policy makers and academics is rarely as close or as purposive as that described above. Academics may be involved in the policy process, in ways discussed below, but it is rare for unsolicited comments, however eminent the source from which they originate, to be accepted simply as a contribution to knowledge. More usually, they may lead to defensive behaviour on the part of practitioners who doubt the value of the academic's contribution. The purpose of this chapter is to examine the contribution to policy making made by social science academics in Britain, and by one distinguished academic in particular, to consider some of the reasons for the limited role played by UK academic social scientists and to comment on the implications of this for 'good government'.

Social Scientists and Policy Making

At first sight there would appear to be ample justification for including those who study and research in the disciplines of politics (including public administration), economics or sociology in the process of policy making. Such specialists might be assumed to have a knowledge that would be of benefit to those decision makers whose own undergraduate education has not included a study of these subjects. However, the link between academic social scientists and the world of policy makers, particularly in the UK, has proved to be much more tenuous than many might have expected. Erik Albaek has noted that 'it is a common view that we have not been very successful in applying social science in policy making' and goes on to suggest that this may be because of 'unrealistic and normatively problematic expectations' about how social science could and should be utilised in policy making (Albaek, 1995, p.79). He points out that expectations of the linkage between the two have traditionally been informed by positivist and rational concepts of science and decision making – concepts that, as a number of commentators have indicated, do not necessarily have a direct applicability to the policy making process. S.S. Blume has argued that the claim that social scientists 'should' have a contribution to make to policy making misunderstands the nature of policy making, which is not driven by facts but rather by the accommodation of different perspectives (Blume, 1979, p.320). Although there is obvious truth in this, it does not invalidate the role of the social scientist – not only do policy makers need facts in order to justify their decisions but there are other contributions that academics might make to policy making.

It may be useful to draw a distinction between the social scientists employed by governments in order to provide information that will assist policy makers, and the academic social scientist who may perform this role but also has a role as a disinterested observer and critic of processes of government. In the case of the former, J.E. Frank and R.A. Smith have identified three kinds of possible involvement by social scientists in the policy process. These are *inclusive* involvement where social scientists make a contribution to all parts of the process, *limited* involvement where the social scientist is involved both in the examination of alternative policies before implementation, as well as in measuring outcomes and, finally, *post hoc* involvement, where their contribution is restricted to measuring the effects of policies (Frank and Smith, 1976, pp.106-109). Naturally, this is a generalisation about the policy process as well as about the involvement of the social scientist – different social scientists may be involved to a greater or lesser extent in all of these. However, it appears largely true that most academic social scientists find that their direct involvement in the policy process is limited to the third of these categories. Whilst there are plenty of examples of social scientists being used to conduct evaluation studies, particularly of pilot programmes in anticipation of a major policy development, only a handful of academics find that their expertise is called upon in the formative stage of policy making. This contrasts, of course, with the American experience where, even in 1975, Sharpe could argue that it was normal for politicians at both state and federal level to involve their local social science academics in the policy process (Sharpe, 1975). While part of the reason for this discrepancy is to be found in the different political systems of the two countries and in the fact that the American Congressman has a much greater opportunity to affect policy making than the British MP, as well as a larger budget for the purpose, it still seems unfortunate that policy makers in the UK find such a limited need to involve academic social scientists in the policy making process.

It is a pity that money for research is entirely directed to the immediate needs of contracts rather than to the more reflective, less practical research that academic social scientists might want to engage in. To assert that the latter is other worldly is to miss the point – such reflections need to be developed in discussion with those directly involved in the process of government. It is likely that some ideas from social scientists will be appropriately ameliorated in the light of practical advice from those directly involved in day to day operational matters. However, the description 'other worldly' works two ways. Civil servants appearing before Lord Justice Scott's Committee may have been surprised to discover that many of their practices for avoiding giving complete answers to Parliament were completely out of touch with public expectations about their behaviour. Listening to advice from those with a more dispassionate perspective might have proved valuable. Richard Chapman's own criticisms of the creation of the Recruitment and Assessment Services agency in 1991 (Chapman, 1992) might have appeared, to some 'insiders', to be out touch with the practical world of the New Public Management, but such a perspective hardly invalidates his comments. The result of being ignored by politicians and officials is that academics tend to end up publishing their work in journals that are only read by other academics (and the universities' Research Assessment Exercise does nothing to discourage this). It seems unlikely that many politicians or practitioners read the special edition of *Parliamentary Affairs* which considered the implications of the Scott Report. Whilst the Report itself was highly critical of the actions of the government, the comments by academics drew attention to the wider implications of the report for the way in which the country is governed. These should have prompted some response either from the government or from senior members of the civil service. However, as with so many other issues, the government's reaction to Scott's report was essentially political; to apply casuistry to his findings and pretend that these exonerated the government from any blame. Although this attitude has been convincingly rebutted by journalists as well as academics it offers clear evidence that, without a political will to address the issues that they raise, the work of academics as contributors to policy making is effectively wasted.

Alternative Roles for the Academic Social Scientist

There are, therefore, plenty of plenty of possible roles for academic social scientists besides that of fact gatherer to evaluate particular policies. One clear role is that of challenging the existing norms and assumptions of policy makers. For a variety of good reasons, well articulated by writers such as Herbert Simon, policy makers seeking to resolve a problem are unlikely to find solutions that are substantially different from those already existing. As Simon's study of decision making has pointed out, they are already committed by habit and memory, not to mention pressure of time, to adopt solutions that 'satisfice' (Simon, 1957). However, the lack of radicalism inherent in this may lead to a series of temporary solutions when fresh thinking, from a new perspective, might be valuable. Frank Heller (1987, p.13) has referred to the importance of sunk and opportunity costs in affecting resistance to change and thus negating the role of the academic in devising 'rational' policies. Sunk costs refer to the effort and commitment to particular policies made by policy makers. Opportunity costs refer to the costs of not introducing a change. If the latter is, or appears to be, too low, whilst the former is too high, there is every reason not to undertake change – whatever the arguments put forward by academics. The difficulty for social scientists is that challenging existing orthodoxies is unpopular and it is easy to portray criticism as 'unworldly' or unrealistic. There may, of course, be some truth in this. It is easy for academics to ignore, possibly because they do not know, the bargaining and negotiation processes that have been gone through in order to arrive at a particular decision. In such circumstances, as

Lindblom's model of successive limited comparisons indicates, decisions arrived at may be the best ones because they are the only ones that will command support (Lindblom, 1959, p.245).

The Scientific Basis of Social Science Enquiry

A number of other reasons may be suggested for the comparative lack of involvement of British social scientists in policy making. One concerns the doubt as to whether their chosen field of study is a science at all. This problem arises partially from a perception about the meaning of the term 'science' which expects that it deals in 'facts' which can be applied to immutable rules of behaviour that have withstood the test of rigorous and repeated experimentation. However, the social sciences deal with human behaviour which, inevitably, is rather less predictable than inanimate objects. Further, there is a tendency to regard many of the issues with which the social sciences attempt to grapple as essentially 'common sense' – thus explanations by 'experts', in particular explanations which seem to challenge conventional wisdom, tend to be disregarded. Mary Tuck, formerly Head of the Home Office Research and Planning Unit, has noted that 'Most people simply do not know what social science is and in so far as they do, suspect it is a lot of nonsense' (Tuck, 1991, p.2). This is unfortunate since the intransigence of many societal problems indicates that their solutions are anything but common sense and that new perspectives, based on thorough and rigorous research, are urgently required. As Tuck notes, part of the difficulty for social scientists arises from the breadth of their disciplines and from the cross disciplinary nature of many of the problems which they confront (Tuck, *ibid.*). A further related difficulty is that the solutions that social scientists propose are always likely to become the subject of political debate and therefore 'facts' are likely to become subordinated to values. Public administration is a subject on which a number of people may think they have expertise and, consequently, the expertise of specialists is apparently diminished. This is a pity because such an attitude ignores the particular expertise and insights that the academic expert can bring. Finally, many social scientists will have been educated at universities established in the second half of the twentieth century, rather than at longer established universities such as Oxford and Cambridge, and this may undermine their respectability, particularly in the minds of those who have graduated from the older universities.

Attitudes Towards the Outputs of Universities

A particularly important factor concerns the relatively poor public image of university social science education, which feeds a general expectation that the research outputs from university social sciences departments are unlikely to be relevant to the needs of the country. This anti-intellectualism is part of a reaction to a perceived eliteness in universities. It has not been helped by the anti social science bias of some members of the Conservative administrations of 1979-1997. Perhaps this mood is changing. Universities are no longer the preserve of an elite, partly because of the policies of those Conservative governments who have raised the higher education participation rate of 18 and 19 year olds to nearly one in three. Many more students are studying in the social sciences and as a consequence it may be assumed that the population at large will be increasingly aware of both the value of the constituent subjects of the social sciences as areas of inquiry and also of the way in which the results of research in these subjects may inform the policy making process.

Time

There is an additional problem concerning the time taken to produce policies which have an academic input. It takes time to commission a report from a university and even longer for the report to be delivered. But often work is required quickly and for this reason the potential contribution of academics may be ignored. Politicians are frequently too busy to contact academics or only contact those that they know – usually those that are located around London. They are unaware in many cases of the research that is being undertaken in other universities and may be unaware of how this might be found. This is a pity since it may lead to substantive areas of research activity being ignored. For example, it has been evident for some time that 'ethics' is likely to be a major issue in British government. It has emerged in a number of Select Committee enquiries and a number of groups (such as the Association of First Division Civil Servants) have expressed their views on the issue. But there has not been a major conference organised by ministers or officials in the government which has sought to bring together academics and practitioners to explore, on a general level, the implications of ethical behaviour in public service. It may be that the work of academics such as Richard Chapman is scrutinised on this issue and that it contributes to policy making. But there is little evidence that this is the case.

Narrow Specialisms of Academics

It might be argued that academics are too narrowly specialised for many policy decisions and that they are reluctant to work across the boundaries between disciplines. It may also be suggested that they are accustomed to working on their own rather than being members of a team, as is typically the norm in policy making. There may be some truth in these assertions – although the last of them also flies in the face of much of the evidence about current research projects in the academic world. Moreover, the value of academics to the policy making process is precisely that they are experts in particular fields, rather then generalists in the way that many members of the civil service may be regarded as generalists. A different concern relates to the possibility of different expectations about the results of any commissioned research. Academics do not necessarily expect to find answers in any piece of research and may be inclined to treat research projects as part of an on going process of inquiry. However, discovering answers is the principal function of policy makers – it is what they are employed to do. There may also be differences about the focus of any work to be undertaken. As indicated earlier, politicians and officials may have perceptions about the scope of an enquiry and about the facts to be considered that academics may be unwilling to accept. A greater integration between the two would help academics to appreciate the limitations faced by policy makers whilst also allowing the latter to benefit from the ability of academics to put a policy in a slightly wider framework. Graham Mather has suggested that too often academics appear to be good at criticism and analysis whilst not offering workable solutions (Mather, 1993). One of the difficulties here is the problem for the outsider of knowing what solutions are likely to be acceptable. A second is that of actually reaching those who will determine the nature of any accepted solution. A third problem is that academics often raise wide ranging issues only to find that no one in government is directly responsible for dealing with those issues. Far from being irrelevant to society, problems highlighted by academics may not relate to the organizational structure of governments and also may not fit the government's current agenda. In these circumstances their research findings will be ignored.

Problems of Reaching a Wider Audience

There is a further problem of reaching a wider audience which relates to the way in which academic outputs are made public. Because of the difficulties of publishing (and the inordinate cost of books) there is a tendency for academics to find that they are only talking to themselves through learned journals or conferences. Inevitably, these are rarely penetrated by the wider body of public officials who are thus unaware of the outputs or interests of individual academics. Richard Chapman was particularly active, through his work in the Joint University Council's Public Administration Committee and in the now defunct Royal Institute of Public Administration, in constructing links between academics working in the field of public administration and public officials. Whilst he and others have invariably found plenty of officials willing to be 'helpful' to the academic community, this helpfulness and

181

courtesy has rarely developed on a wider level into an exchange between equals. To say that there is mutual suspicion between the two communities would be unfair; it is nevertheless true that too often the two have separate agendas which rarely seem to coincide. In this context, it is perhaps unfortunate that academics are too infrequently involved in the process of setting the agendas for government research, rather than simply picking up proposals for research that have been decided elsewhere.

Academics and the Policy Process

A critical role for the academic in the policy process is that of an informed critic able to comment impartially on current issues. In this task, as the introductory chapter has demonstrated, Richard Chapman has been pre-eminent amongst scholars in the United Kingdom. His extensive publications reflect the work of one who, whilst acknowledging the pressures and demands of the high offices of state, nonetheless recognises the necessity for careful and constructive criticism of some the activities of those called to such office. As noted above, and as the title of this *festschrift* suggests, this critical scholarship can be grouped under the three headings of 'Reform', 'Ethics' and 'Leadership'.

Reform

Reform, in the sense of desired and planned change as well as in the sense of continuous adaptation to the environment, has been a continuous feature of public service activity during the past fifteen years, in Britain as well as in other parts of the world. These reforms of both structures and processes have not been value free; instead, as John Greenaway notes in his chapter, they have been profoundly political in the sense that they have invariably led to the conferring of benefits on some groups of people at the expense of others. The significance of these reforms may hold little interest to those unfamiliar with the subtleties of the changes that have taken place. However their effects may be very important, not least in relation to issues of accountability and ethical behaviour in the public services. Peter Barberis observes in his chapter that the increasing use of special advisers and political aides marks a fundamental change both in the kind of public accountability of those who serve ministers and in expectations of their ethical behaviour. One of the themes of this book, which also provides a link between many of its chapters, is that changes in the public sector should not be undertaken solely in the narrow interests of efficiency or effectiveness, and those who such values serve, but should also respect other fundamental features of the public service, particularly its concern for universality, impartiality and accountability.

182

In his chapter, John Rohr has noted that Richard Chapman's scholarship has 'the abiding presence of the British constitution at the heart of his interpretation of the administrative enterprise' and commended the ability of that constitution to respond flexibly to changes in administrative focus (particularly, in this case, the development of the New Public Management). This was especially evident, for example, in the development of the Next Steps agencies, which raised fundamental issues about the operation of the constitutional convention of ministerial responsibility. In the absence of any written constitutional constraints the government had no difficulty in establishing such agencies without even the need for an Act of Parliament. If such agencies can be created by administrative action there must be real concern about the safeguards in the British system to protect the citizen against arbitrary actions by the state. In this case, administrative action threatened the long standing right of individuals to have their grievances dealt with by an oral response from a minister in Parliament. The only real safeguards are provided by the activities of the opposition (and government backbenchers) in Parliament and by informed commentary by the press and those few academics interested in constitutional issues; these may (with varying degrees of effectiveness) be able to influence public opinion and, possibly, the attitude of the government. However, as Michael Hunt has pointed out, the absence of any real acceptance of the demands of citizenship in this country means that most members of the public do not see it as their responsibility to become fully informed about the constitutional or political implications of reforms to the structure of government. They have not been helped in this by the traditional culture of secrecy in government which is only now challenged by the proposals for a Freedom of Information Act. The result is that the political and constitutional significance of many reforms has been largely ignored by the wider public, many of whom suffer as a consequence.

Ethics

Malcolm Jack's chapter takes as its focus the important issues of corruption and decay in public life. Whilst the British public are, no doubt, sufficiently mature to accept that the occasional scandal is always a possibility in public life, the increasing evidence of unethical behaviour has been of unusual concern. The setting up of the Committee on Standards of Conduct in Public Life and, subsequently, the Committee of Inquiry into the Export of Dual Use Goods to Iran and Iraq, are clear testimonies to that concern which arises from a number of incidents involving holders of public office whose conduct seems to have strayed beyond the boundaries of what would normally be regarded as acceptable. Such incidents appear to have been confined to those who held political office rather than officials and a consequence of this is that discussion of ethical behaviour has focused on the corrupt actions of politicians rather than examining the exercise of discretionary decision making and other aspects of the working behaviour of officials. This is unfortunate since the fragmentation of the civil service in pursuit of the goals of efficiency and effectiveness has raised questions among its members and among external commentators about both the changing core values of the public service and about the way in which they might be reconciled where they conflict. This is not a new problem; the diverse nature of the public service has always allowed the possibility of conflicting interpretations of the 'public interest'. However, in the past, these conflicting interpretations took place within a framework of values which reflected the interests and purposes of a particular class. The recruitment and socialisation processes of the civil service ensured the continuation of those interests. There was no need to discuss these values, they were accepted without debate, not least because of the way in which they were epitomised in the actions of some of the leading public servants of the day. Most importantly, they reflected the values of the leading politicians of the day.

The 1980s have seen a marked change in the cohesion of the civil service as well as in the social origins of politicians and public servants. For a variety of reasons, respect for public officials (as for members of many other professions) has diminished in the past two decades, not helped perhaps by rather public criticisms from some leading members of the Conservative governments. Understandably, many officials have become uncertain about the values (or interests) they should reflect when contributing to the formulation of public policy. Further, as some well publicised cases have demonstrated, they have not been helped by the somewhat cavalier attitude towards public service values (particularly public accountability) adopted by some ministers. Some specification of appropriate values has become essential even if, as Barry O'Toole points out, specifications in the form of a Code of Practice have little value unless they are supported by a firm belief in the principles they espouse. The recent civil service Code of Practice perfectly illustrates this because its somewhat limited considerations do not fully address the discretionary problems that civil servants are likely to encounter. The solution, as O'Toole's chapter suggests, is to return to a belief in the four particular characteristics of public service, which needs to be adopted by both politicians and officials. This does not offer a clear path without problems or snares to trap the unwary. It does, however, offer a sense of purpose which has been lost in the confused world of the New Public Management.

Leadership

The introduction to this book referred to Richard Chapman's early involvement in the selection of RAF officers, and the stimulus that this provided for his subsequent interest in leadership. This has never been an interest in techniques or traits of leadership but more in the relationship between 'leadership' and 'management', seeing both as concerned with style and the encouragement of appropriate ethical behaviour. As Richard Chapman noted in relation to Lord Bridges 'the approved high standards of professional conduct at all levels in the British civil service depends largely on the controls and influence exercised by outstanding civil servants who may be called leaders' (Chapman, 1988a, p.307). Such a style is not learned from books, still less from training courses but, rather, is informed by a lengthy process of apprenticeship. To that extent, it reflects what modern organisation theorists have described as 'situational leadership'. Peter Barberis draws attention to Sir Peter Carey's assertion that nothing in his previous career had prepared him for the managerial tasks associated with being a permanent secretary, and this is no doubt correct in terms of the expectations of the New Public Management current at the time that he became a permanent secretary. Nonetheless, Sir Peter enjoyed a lengthy apprenticeship for leadership that is likely to have been at least as valuable as any formal training in techniques. The critical issue, of course, is whether the style of leadership which he had assimilated was still relevant at the time he became a permanent secretary, or whether it needed to be supplanted by more proactive styles which owe their origins to the success of business leaders, particularly from America. More important is the question of whether these new styles were, in every sense, appropriate for the civil service. The danger of advocating 'new' styles of leadership lies, obviously, in the assumption that the new style is appropriate for all levels of leadership and for leadership in all situations. Where the civil service has changed, particularly in its reorganisation into 'agencies', such new styles may be relevant. But it would be dangerous to assume that such new styles are relevant in all areas of government activity. This raises issues about the nature of public service, about the values that public service represents, and about the degree of change that has taken place in recent years.

Fred Fiedler has commented that 'leadership exists in the context of an organisational environment which determines, in large part, the specific kind of leadership behaviour which the situation requires' (Fiedler, 1978, p.109); this clearly suggests that the requirements of leadership are situational and rejects the notion of universal qualities of leadership. Fiedler's perception is particularly useful in the context of the public service because the service comprises a number of units undertaking a variety of different tasks which may each demand different skills from their leaders. Further, leadership must be sensitive not only to differing tasks but also to different kinds of public servant. Even at a simple level, leadership of a group of staff in (for example) the Meteorological Office is likely to be different from leadership in a local office of the Benefits Agency. In this context, the whole hearted importing of private sector models of leadership runs the risk of ignoring those aspects of the public sector that are unique. This has become apparent, for example, in the wake of the Next Steps reforms. Whilst there may be evidence that the attempt to separate policy making from implementation in order to allow managers greater freedom to determine the work of their agencies has been successful in some of the less publicly significant functions of government, there is abundant evidence that it has been more difficult to apply the distinction in agencies with a higher public profile such as the Child Support Agency and the Prison Service. In the latter, in particular, the evidence would seem to suggest that the problems faced by the Service are in part a reflection of the introduction of reforms that had not been thoroughly thought through and which were, in any case, ill suited to the tasks to be performed. Thus, although the former Home Secretary, Michael Howard, had little hesitation in blaming poor management for some of the problems that occurred in the agency, a more reasoned appraisal would suggest that it was the reform itself that was wrong, and that this led to impossible demands on senior mangers in the Prison Service. The former Director of the Service, Derek Lewis, has drawn attention to the almost intolerable level of requests for information by the Home Secretary which reflected a degree of interference in the running of the Service which, in his view, made it impossible for the Director to exercise the sort of leadership that he would have wished (Lewis, 1997). Sadly, the problem that Derek Lewis has raised was predicted before he became Director of the Service. A number of informed commentators drew attention to the failure of *Improving Management in Government: the Next Steps* to fully define the terms 'policy making' and 'administration' (see, for example, Chapman, 1988b). Embarrassing public problems were always likely to result in political interference. It is a pity that such notes of caution were derided as reflections of old and tired methods of delivering public services rather than as informed commentaries based on theory that had withstood the test of practical experience.

This is not to suggest that modern understandings of modern management are irrelevant to the public service. Far from it; David Morris rightly suggests in his chapter that the scale of change in the public sector in the past twenty years needs to be accompanied by a different set of paradigms for understanding the way in which services are most effectively delivered, including the role of leadership. But some long standing aspects of leadership remain important. One of these relates to the encouragement of trust in the processes of government and the chapters by David Dillman and Edward Warrington have both drawn attention to the critical role played by particular leaders (rather than managers) in this regard. Neither of the two officials studied would be described as charismatic but both, in the examples they set, profoundly influenced their more junior officials and the politicians that they served. David Dillman notes in his chapter that the particular influence of John Macy lay not so much in what he did but in the way he went about it, a point reflected in Richard Chapman's own studies of the role played by civil servants such as Sir Percival Waterfield and Sir Edward Bridges (Chapman, 1984; Chapman, 1988a). All of these studies thus draw attention to the link between leadership and ethics. Whilst public servants are unlikely directly to bear the costs of any public loss of confidence in the process of government they certainly suffer by association. For example, whilst members of the public may hold ministers responsible for the deceptions that occurred at the time of the 'Arms to Iraq' scandal they may also find it hard to understand why public servants were unable to prevent ministers from indulging in behaviour that many would regard as unethical.

Conclusion

Albaek's work, referred to earlier, makes clear that rational, scientific, contributions by social scientists are unlikely to be directly utilised by policy makers, because the political process is not about agreeing on 'truth' but achieving an acceptable consensus between actors with different perceptions of the truth (Albaek, 1995). In such a setting, the contributions of social scientists are most likely to be used to justify policies already decided upon and, to that extent, their principal value is in providing information which, in a general sense, adds to the sum of public knowledge. Work is undertaken and published and gradually seeps through into the conscious minds of the public and policy makers. It is utilised only when there is a perceived need for it. This is not to suggest that this should be the summit of the ambition of academic social scientists. They may reasonably aspire to more than this. However, for their ideas to receive wider and more immediate recognition there needs to be a much greater interchange between academics and practitioners than there is at the moment. The British experience is in marked contrast to that of (say) Australia or the United Sates where interaction seems to take place as a matter of course. Part of the problem in the UK is the absence of neutral territory where such meetings can take place. Another problem simply concerns geography; the locus of power of central government remains largely in London and hence there is little opportunity or incentive for civil servants to meet academics from universities in other parts of the country except on a relatively limited scale and usually in relation to specific purposes. The annual conference of the Public Administration Committee, for example, attracts only a small proportion of practitioners in relation to the number of academics who attend and the reasons for this can only be guessed at. Cost and pressure of work are undoubtedly two factors. So too, no doubt, is a climate of opinion that regards three days of time spent at an 'academic' conference as irrelevant to the immediate needs of public officials. In this context the demise of the Royal Institute of Public Administration which acted as a bridge between academia and the public service, was particularly unfortunate. Richard Chapman's own attempts to limit the damage caused to academic/official inter-relations by the collapse of the RIPA are well known to his immediate colleagues, even if they were not fully appreciated by a wider audience. As a result of his efforts, as well as those of other people, the damage has not been as serious as was once feared.

Some attempts have been made during the last twenty years to try to overcome the dissonance between academics and practitioners. There is, for example, a greater readiness by public officials to commission reports from experts in universities. In a lecture to the 1992 annual conference of the Public Administration Committee the former Cabinet Secretary, Sir Robin Butler, drew attention to a number of exchanges between academia and the civil service (Butler, 1992, p.10) and has subsequently referred to his interest in the 'Whitehall' project of research undertaken by academic staff and funded by the Economic and Social Research Council. Such interest is most welcome and, no doubt, the exchanges referred to are very valuable for both organisations and participants. However, they only respond to the tip of the problem. It has often appeared in the past that officials and academics are unaware of each other's needs. What is required is a culture where it is normal for public officials to seek the advice, where relevant, of academics from a variety of universities and where public officials from a variety of social science disciplines feel able to discuss their work either with academics in seminars or by contributing to taught courses. At the same time, perhaps more academics need to recognise the value of research which is less theoretically based (and therefore less 'respectable' in the eyes of the academic community) than they normally undertake, but which has a greater potential value to inform immediate policy problems. This involves a degree of flexibility which (for good reasons) many academics may find difficult. However, one result of such attitudinal changes might be a greater involvement by academics in determining the agenda of funded research projects, thus allowing them to ensure that projects acknowledge wider issues that may be of public concern rather than just the immediate needs of particular policies. Such projects would also benefit from the realism that would be supplied by practitioners. A further benefit might be an acceptance by the government that better administration is their responsibility and one to which they need to respond with their own commissioned research programmes rather than abdicating such responsibility to cash-starved research councils.

Three areas where the social scientist may have a role to play as disinterested observer are suggested in the title of this book. They are the areas to which Richard Chapman has made such a distinguished contribution during the years that he has taught and researched in universities. The contribution

188

that he has made to the study of the public service (in its many facets) is recognised not only by the numerous cohorts of students who have benefited from his teaching, and by the many academic colleagues who have benefited from the wisdom of his advice and counsel, but also by public officials who have recognised and respected the informed scholarship of his work. There can be no greater testament to the significance of that work than that it has both enhanced the study of public administration, and convincingly demonstrated the case for academics to contribute to its practice.

References

Albaek, Erik (1995), 'Between knowledge and power: Utilisation of social science in public policy making', *Policy Sciences*, Vol. 28, pp.79-100.

Blume, S.S. (1979), 'Policy Studies and Social Policy in Britain', *Journal of Social Policy*, Vol. 8, No. 3, pp.311-334.

Butler, Sir Robin (1992), 'The New Public Management: the contribution of Whitehall and Academia', *Public Policy and Administration*, Vol. 7, No. 3, Winter, pp.3-14.

Chapman, Richard A. (1984), *Leadership in the British Civil Service: a study of Sir Percival Waterfield and the creation of the Civil Service Selection Board*, Croom Helm.

Chapman, Richard A. (1988a), *Ethics in the British Civil Service*, Routledge.

Chapman, Richard A. (1988b), 'The Next Steps', *Public Policy and Administration*, Vol. 3, No. 3, Winter, pp.3-10.

Chapman, Richard A. (1992), 'The End of the Civil Service?' *Teaching Public Administration*, Vol. X11, No. 2, pp.1-5.

Chapman, Richard A. (1996), 'Standards in Public Life: A Valediction', *Teaching Public Administration*, Vol. XV1, No. 1, Spring, pp.1-19.

Chapman, Richard A. & O'Toole, Barry J. (1995). 'The Role of the Civil Service: A Traditional View in a Period of Change', *Public Policy and Administration*, Vol. 10, No. 2, Summer, pp.3-20.

Fiedler, F.E. (1978), 'Situational Control and a Dynamic Theory of Leadership' in King, B. *et al*, *Managerial Control and Organisational Democracy*, Winston: Wiley, pp.107-131.

Frank, J.E & R.A. Smith (1976), 'Social Scientists in the Policy Process', *Journal of Applied Behavioural Studies*, Vol. 12, No. 1, pp.104-117.

Heller, Frank, (1987), 'The cost-effective big bang', *The Times Higher Education Supplement*, 16 January, p.13.

Lewis, D. (1997), *Hidden Agendas: Politics, Law and Disorder*, Hamish Hamilton.

Lindblom, C.E. (1959), 'The Science of Muddling Through', *Public Administration Review*, Spring, reprinted in Pugh, D.S. (Ed), (1984), *Organisation Theory: selected readings*, Penguin, (second edition), pp.238-255.

Mather, G. (1993), 'Viewpoint', *Social Sciences*, No. 19, June, p.2.

Sharpe, L.J. (1975), 'The Social Scientist and Policy Making: Some Cautionary Thoughts and Transatlantic Reflections', *Policy and Politics*, Vol. 4, pp.7-35.

Simon, H. (1957), *Administrative Behavior*, New York: Macmillan, (second edition).

Tuck, Mary (1991), 'Viewpoint', *Social Sciences*, No. 11, August, p.2.

Appendix I
The Career of Richard Arnold Chapman, Emeritus Professor of Politics, University of Durham

University Education
1958-61   University of Leicester
1961-62   Carleton University

Academic Qualifications
B.A. Social Sciences, University of Leicester, 1961
M.A. Public Administration, Carleton University, 1962
Ph.D. University of Leicester, 1966
D. Litt. University of Leicester 1989
F.I.Mgt. (M.B.I.M. elected 1975)
F.R.Hist.S. (elected 1987)

Academic Appointments
1961-62   Assistant in Political Science, Carleton University
1962-63   Assistant Lecturer in Politics and Tutor in Beaumont Hall, University of Leicester
1963-68   Leverhulme Lecturer in Public Administration, University of Liverpool
1968-71   Senior Lecturer in Local Government and Administration, University of Birmingham
1971-85   Reader in Politics, University of Durham
1986-87   Hallsworth Senior Research Fellow, University of Manchester
1986-96   Professor of Politics, University of Durham (Emeritus, since 1996)
1991   British Council Fellow, Hong Kong
1991-92   Sir Norman Chester Senior Research Fellow, Nuffield College, Oxford
1993   Visiting Professor of Public Administration, University of South Africa

1995-96 Sir James Knott Foundation Research Fellow, University of Durham

1997-99 Emeritus Fellow, Leverhulme Trust

Previous Career

1953-55 Air Ministry, London (Clerical Officer)

1955-62 Ministry of Pensions and National Insurance, London (Executive Officer)

1962 (a few months) Inland Revenue, London (H.M. Inspector of Taxes)

1956-58 Royal Air Force: National Service

Major Committee and Administrative appointments in the University of Durham: a selection

1973-76 and 1988-91 Chairman of the Board of Studies in Politics

1975-76 Deputy Dean, Faculty of the Social Sciences

1976-78 Dean of the Faculty of Social Sciences

1977-80 and 1982-85 Member of the Council of the University

1975-77 Member of the Governing Body, University College

1976-79 Hon. Treasurer, St. Chad's College, also Member of the Council and Governing Body of the College

1977-79 Vice-Chairman (effectively Chairman) of the Curators of the Library

1979-96 Convenor of the Public Policy Studies Group of the Faculty of Social Sciences

1981-83 Member of the Committee to Review the Structure and Government of the University of Durham

1982-85 Executive Vice-President of the Society of Fellows of Durham University Research Foundation

1983-85 President, Durham AUT

1973-85 and 1988-91 Member of Senate

1988-91 Member of the Governing Body, Trevelyan College

1994-96 Chairman, SCR, St. Chad's College

1995-96 Member of the Council, St. Chad's College

Selection of other appointments

1964-67 Hon. Treasurer of the Political Studies Association of the United Kingdom

1965-68 Member of the Board of Managers, Northway Schools, Liverpool

1968-71 Editor, *PAC Bulletin*

1969-70 Member of the Review of Activities Committee of the Royal Institute of Public Administration

1969-71 Member of the Council and the Executive Committee of The Birmingham Settlement

1969-73　Associate, Institute of Development Studies, University of Sussex

1970-80 and 1989-95　Member of the Civil Service Commission Final Selection Board for appointments to administrative posts in the Civil and Foreign Services

1972-74, 1980-86 and 1987-92　Member of the Executive Council of the Northern Group of the Royal Institute of Public Administration

1977-81　Chairman of the Public Administration Committee of the Joint University Council for Social and Public Administration

1983-86　Chairman of the Joint University Council for Social and Public Administration

1974-　Member of the International Editorial Advisory Board of *Sage Public Administration Abstracts*

1975-89　Member of the Editorial Committee of the *International Review of Administrative Sciences*

1976-79　Member of the Governing Body of New College, Durham

1977-81　Member of the Civil Service College Advisory Council

1980-86　Member of the Administrative Staff Qualifications Council and, following its re-organisation in 1982, of the Examinations Committee of the Local Government Training Board

1982-85　Member of the Public and Social Administration Board of the CNAA

1982-　Member of the Editorial Board of *Politics, Administration and Change*

1983-　Editor of the Croom Helm (now Routledge) series of books 'Studies in Public Policy Making'

1986-　Member of the Editorial Board of *Public Policy and Administration*

1987-　Honorary Fellow, Institute for Development Policy and Management, University of Manchester

1987-　Editor of the Routledge series of books on 'Public Sector Management'

1988-92　Regional Editorial Associate of *Governance*

1988-　Specialist on the register of the Hong Kong Council for Academic Accreditation

1988-93　Editorial Adviser, *Teaching Public Administration*

1990-　Honorary Life Member of Durham Students' Union

1991-92　Member, on the Register of Members, CNAA

1991-　Member of the International Advisory Board, *Hong Kong Public Administration*

1993-96　Chairman of the International Sub-Committee of the PAC/Joint University Council

1993-98　Member of the Lord Chancellor's Advisory Council on Public Records

1993-　Member of the Publications Steering Committee of the Public Record Office

1993-	Member of the Editorial Board of the *Journal of Public Administration* (SAIPA)
1993-	Member of the Editorial Board of *Teaching Public Administration*
1994-96	Member of the Steering Committee, European Group of Public Administration
1994-96	Member of the Executive Board of the Structure and Organisation of Government Research Committee of the International Political Science Association
1996-97	Specialist Adviser to the House of Lords Select Committee on the Public Service
1997-	Honorary Fellow, Joint University Council

External Examining:
(i) for first degrees or higher degrees or diplomas involving courses

1964-73	Local Government Examinations Board
1971-74	University of Strathclyde
1971-75	University of Kent
1974-76	Durham Technical College
1974-76	University of London
1976-79	Teesside Polytechnic
1976-79	University of Manchester
1979-83	Sheffield City Polytechnic
1980-84	University of Hull
1984-91	Sheffield City Polytechnic
1988-92	Nottingham Polytechnic
1991-97	University of Dublin
1993-	University of the West Indies

(ii) External examiner for doctoral degrees in the Universities of Birmingham, Dublin, Hull, Kent, London, Oxford, Sussex and York.

Research Grants (with titles of major publications resulting from them)

1972-73	SSRC (£750) – *Teaching Public Administration* (1973)
1974-78	SSRC (£575) – *The Dynamics of Administrative Reform* (1980)
1980-85	SSRC (£2,950) – *Leadership in the British Civil Service* (1984); *Ethics in the British Civil Service* (1988)
1986-87	Joseph Rowntree Charitable Trust (£285) – *Open Government* (1987)
1990-91	Joseph Rowntree Charitable Trust (£1,500) – *Ethics in Public Service* (1993)
1991-95	ESRC (£3,230) and
1991-96	Nuffield Foundation (£1,700) – *The Treasury* (1997)
1997-99	Leverhulme Trust – Emeritus Fellowship (£15,500) and
1998-02	ESRC (£62,550)

PUBLICATIONS
Books

1. *Decision Making* (Routledge and Kegan Paul, 1968; reprinted 1971) viii + 118pp.
2. *The Higher Civil Service in Britain* (Constable, 1970) x + 194pp.
3. (Edited, with A. Dunsire) *Style in Administration: Readings in British Public Administration* (RIPA and Allen and Unwin, 1971) 496pp.
4. Contributor and Editor: *The Role of Commissions in Policy Making* (Allen and Unwin, 1973) 206pp.
5. *Teaching Public Administration* (Joint University Council for Social and Public Administration, 1973) 110pp.
6. (with J.R. Greenaway) *The Dynamics of Administrative Reform* (Croom Helm, 1980) 249pp.
7. *Leadership in the British Civil Service* (Croom Helm, 1984) 210pp.
8. Contributor and Editor: *Public Policy Studies: The North East of England* (Edinburgh University Press, 1985) 198pp.
9. Contributor and Co-Editor (with Michael Hunt), *Open Government* (Croom Helm, 1987) 194pp.
10. *Ethics in the British Civil Service* (Routledge, 1988) 338pp.
11. *The Art of Darkness* (Inaugural Lecture: University of Durham, 1988) 28pp.
12. (with Pradeep K. Saxena) *Public Sector Management: India and Britain,* Printwell Publishers, Jaipur, 1990, 142pp.
13. Contributor and Editor: *Ethics in Public Service* (Edinburgh University Press, 1993) xiv + 178pp. Also published by Carleton University Press, Ottawa, 1993.
14. *Verejnáspráva,* Katedra Politológie Filozofickej Fakulty Univerzity Komenského/ Vzdelávacia Nadácia Jána Husa, Bratislava, 1996, 96pp.
15. *The Treasury in public policy-making,* Routledge, 1997, xiv + 204pp.

Articles and Contributions to Books

1. 'Cast your vote', *Inter-Varsity,* Spring 1964, pp.35-36.
2. 'The Significance of Parliamentary Procedure', *Parliamentary Affairs,* 1963, Vol. XVI, pp.179-189.
3. 'The Real Cause of Bureaucracy', *Administration,* 1964, Vol. XII, pp.55-60.
4. 'The Bank Rate Decision of 19 September 1957: A Case Study of Joint Decision Making', *Public Administration,* 1964, Vol. 43, pp.199-213.
5. 'Rousseau on Natural and Unnatural Administration', *Administration,* 1965, Vol. XIII, pp.192-199.
6. 'Thomas Hill Green (1836-1882)', *The Review of Politics,* 1965, Vol. 27, pp.516-531.
7. 'The Basis of T.H. Green's Philosophy', *International Review of History and Political Science,* 1966, Vol. III, pp.72-88 (also reprinted in D.P. Rastogi (Ed.), *Political Essays,* Review Publications, Meerut, 1967, pp.35-51).

8. 'Local Government in Ontario: The Peel Halton Local Government Review', *Administration*, 1966, Vol. XIV, pp.255-263.
9. 'Prismatic Theory in Public Administration: A Review of the Theories of Fred W. Riggs', *Public Administration*, 1966, Vol. 44, pp.415-433.
10. 'The Liverpool University Seminar for Councillors', *The Municipal Review*, 1967, Vol. XVI, pp.197.
11. 'Profile of a Profession: The Administrative Class of the Civil Service', *The Civil Service*, Vol. III, Surveys and Investigations, HMSO, 1968, pp.1-29.
12. 'The Canadian Civil Service', *Administration*, 1968, Vol. XVI, pp.35-55.
13. 'Report on Research in Public Administration', *PAC Bulletin*, No. 5, December 1968, pp.26-40.
14. 'Councillors in Training', *Rural District Review*, 1968, Vol. 74, pp.180-181.
15. 'Local Government: Attitudes and Images', *Parliamentary Affairs*, 1968, Vol. XXI, pp.384-390.
16. 'The Fulton Report: A Summary', *Public Administration*, 1968, Vol. 46, pp.443-451.
17. (with J.D. Stewart) 'Notes of University/Civil Service Collaboration in Research', *PAC Bulletin*, No. 6, June 1969, pp.96-112.
18. 'Report on Teaching of Public Administration in British Universities', *PAC Bulletin*, No. 6, June 1969, pp.130-141.
19. 'Report on Numbers of Students taking Graduate Courses in Public Administration', *PAC Bulletin*, No. 7, December 1969, pp.57-61.
20. 'Official Liberality', *Public Administration*, 1970, Vol. 48, pp.123-136.
21. 'Administrative Reform in Britain', *Administration*, 1970, Vol. 18, pp.326-341. (Also reprinted in the *International Journal of Politics*, 1972, Vol. 2, pp.109-113.)
22. 'Report on Research in Public Administration', *PAC Bulletin*, No. 8, June 1970, pp.66-86.
23. 'The National Coal Board: Notes on Management Training in a Nationalised Industry', *PAC Bulletin*, No. 9, November 1970, pp.67-68.
24. 'The Bank of England: not a nationalised industry or a public corporation, but a nationalised institution', *Parliamentary Affairs*, 1971, Vol. XXIV, pp.208-221.
25. 'The Role of the Minister', *Parliamentary Affairs*, 1972. Vol. XXV, pp.184-185.
26. 'The Vehicle and General Affair: some reflections for public administration in Britain', *Public Administration*, 1973, Vol. 51, pp.273-290.
27. 'Administrative Reform in Saudi Arabia', *Journal of Administration Overseas*, 1974, Vol. 13, pp.332-347.
28. 'Safeguards for protecting the individual', *Parliamentary Affairs*, 1974, Vol. XXVII, pp.410-411.
29. 'The role of central and departmental policy units and planning units in policy making and priority setting: recent developments in Britain',

Public Administration, (Sydney) 1975, Vol. 34, pp.144-155. (Also reprinted in *Policy Co-ordination in Government,* Dunker and Humbolt (Berlin) 1976, pp.209-226 and in *Policy Co-ordination in Government,* Cujas (Paris) 1976, pp.109-123.)

30. 'Efficiency and Effectiveness in the Civil Service', *Eleventh Report from the Expenditure Committee, Session 1976-77, The Civil Service,* Vol. III, Appendices (HC 535 III), (HMSO, 1977), pp.957-959.

31. 'Merger of Ministries in Britain', *Administration,* 1977, Vol. 25, pp.23-34.

32. 'Problems of Modern Democracy', *Parliamentary Affairs,* 1978, Vol. XXXI, pp.228-231.

33. 'Efficiency as Virtu: The Expenditure Committee on the Civil Service', *Public Administration Bulletin,* No. 27, 1978, pp.41-50.

34. 'The development of the academic study of public administration in the United Kingdom, the United States, Canada and Ireland', *International Review of Administrative Sciences,* 1978, Vol. 44, pp.40-49.

35. 'The Process of Social Change through Public Administration', *Revista Mexicana de Ciencias Politicas y Sociales,* 1978, Vol. 24, pp.37-49.

36. (with R. Munroe) 'Public Administration Training in the Civil Service', *Teaching Politics,* 1979, Vol. 8, pp.1-12.

37. 'Preface' in Roy Lewis and Chris Himsworth *Public Administration Teaching in Further and Higher Education,* Joint University Council for Social and Public Administration, 1979, pp.i-iv.

38. 'The Higher Civil Service in Britain: Allegations of "Bias" in Selection for Administrative Posts', *Revue francaise d'Administration publique,* 1979, No 12, pp.19-33.

39. 'The PAC and Teaching Public Administration in the 1970s', *Public Administration Bulletin,* No 34, 1980, pp.9-20.

40. 'Reducing the Public Sector: The Thatcher Government's Approach', *Policy Studies Journal,* 1981, Vol. 9, pp.1152-1163.

41. 'Commentary on civil service reform in the United States government: a United Kingdom perspective', *International Review of Administrative Sciences,* 1982, Vol. 48, pp.315-316.

42. 'Strategies for Reducing Government Activities', in G.E. Caiden and H. Siedentopf (Eds.) *Administrative Reform Strategies,* Lexington Books, 1982, pp.59-69.

43. 'Civil Service Recruitment: Bias Against External Candidates', *Public Administration,* 1982, Vol. 60, pp.77-84.

44. 'Public Administration Education in Britain', *Journal of Further and Higher Education,* 1982, Vol. 6, pp.48-55.

45. 'The Rise and Fall of the CSD', *Policy and Politics,* 1983, Vol. 11, pp.41-61.

46. 'Administrative culture and personnel management: the British Civil Service in the 1980s', *Teaching Public Administration,* 1984, Vol. 4, pp.1-14.

47. 'The Committee on Research into Sandwich Education Report, The

RISE Report and Public Administration: A Review', *Teaching Public Administration*, Vol. VI, 1986, pp.34-54.

48. 'Appendix 13', House of Commons, *Seventh Report from the Treasury and Civil Service Committee, Session 1985-86, Civil Servants and Ministers, Duties and Responsibilities*, Vol. II, Annexes, Minutes of Evidence and Appendices, HC 92-II, HMSO, 1986, pp.293-297.

49. 'Whitehall and Westminster: issues for education and public debate', *Parliamentary Affairs*, Vol. 40, 1987, pp.133-135.

50. 'Civil Service', in V. Bogdanor (Ed.) *The Blackwell Encyclopaedia of Political Institutions*, Blackwell, 1987, pp.104-106.

51. 'The Changing Administrative Culture of the British Civil Service', in Colin Campbell S.J. and B. Guy Peters (Eds.) *Organising Governance: Governing Organisations*, University of Pittsburgh Press, 1988, pp.167-82.

52. 'Obsessive Secrecy and Arbitrary Government', *Teaching Public Administration*, 1988, Vol. 8, pp.47-48.

53. 'The British Civil Service: inward secondments: cause for concern', *Public Policy and Administration*, 1988, Vol. 3, No 2, pp.1-3.

54. 'General Editor's Introduction', in J.A. Chandler, *Public Policy-Making for Local Government*, Croom Helm, 1988, pp.x-xii.

55. '"The Next Steps": A Review', *Public Policy and Administration*, 1988, Vol. 3, No 3, pp.3-10.

56. 'General Editor's Introduction' in Barry J. O'Toole, *Private Gain and Public Service*, Routledge, 1989, pp.xi-xii.

57. 'Edward Bridges' in K.G. Robbins (Ed.) *The Blackwell Biographical Dictionary of British Political Life in the Twentieth Century*, Blackwell, 1990, pp.61-2.

58. 'Decision Making Revisited', *Public Administration*, 1990, Vol. 68, pp.353-67.

59. 'The Civil Service: Changes since Fulton', *Contemporary Record*, 1990, Vol. 4, No 3, pp.28-32.

60. 'General Editor's Introduction', in Kevin Theakston, *Labour and Whitehall*, Routledge, 1991, pp.vii-viii.

61. 'Concepts and issues in public sector reform: the experience of the United Kingdom in the 1980s', *Public Policy and Administration*, 1991, Vol. 6, No 2, pp.1-19. Translated into Japanese and published in *Journal of Law and Political Science*, 1992, Vol. 22, 1, pp.33-58.

62. 'New arrangements for recruitment to the British Civil Service: cause for concern', *Public Policy and Administration*, 1991, Vol. 6, No 3, pp.1-6.

63. 'The End of the British Civil Service?', *Teaching Public Administration*, 1992, Vol. 12, 2, pp.1-5. Reprinted in Peter Barberis (Ed.), *The Whitehall Reader*, Open University Press, 1996, pp.187-91.

64. 'The Demise of the Royal Institute of Public Administration (U.K.)', *Australian Journal of Public Administration*, 1992, Vol. 51, pp.519-20.

65. 'Obituary: Professor Arthur Livingstone 1915-1990', *Public Policy and Administration*, 1992, Vol. 7, No 1, p.59.
66. 'Editorial Advisor's Foreword', *Teaching Public Administration*, 1993, Vol. 13, No 1, pp.1-2.
67. 'Civil Service recruitment: fairness or preferential advantage?', *Public Policy and Administration*, 1993, Vol. 7, No 2, pp.68-73.
68. 'The role of the civil service', Treasury and Civil Service Committee, Sixth Report, Session 1992-93. *The Role of the Civil Service: Interim Report*, Vol. II, Minutes of Evidence and Appendices, HC 390-II, HMSO, 1993, pp.318-19.
69. 'The demise of the RIPA: an idea shattered', *Australian Journal of Public Administration*, 1993, Vol. 52, pp.466-74.
70. 'Public Administration Education in Britain', *Journal of Public Administration*, SAIPA, 1993, Vol. 28, pp.159-76.
71. 'Nuove disposizioni: per il reclutamento nel pubblico impiego Britannico: cause di preoccupazione', *Problemi di Amministrazione Pubblica*, 1993, Vol. 18(1), pp.145-55.
72. 'Ethics in the public sector', *Politeia*, 1993, Vol. 12(2), pp.28-42.
73. (with Barry J. O'Toole) 'The Heroic approach in the historiography of public administration in the United Kingdom', *Yearbook of European Administrative History*, 1994, Vol. 6, pp.65-77.
74. 'Social change through public administration', *Politeia*, 1994, Vol. 13(1), pp.4-16.
75. 'Change in the Civil Service', *Public Administration*, 1994, Vol. 72, pp.599-610.
76. *Public Service Ethics: ideas, institutions and indicators*, LSE, 1994, Public Policy Paper No 9, pp.1-10.
77. (with Barry J. O'Toole) 'The Role of the Civil Service: A Traditional View in a Period of Change', *Public Policy and Administration*, 1995, Vol. 10, No 2, pp.3-20.
78. (with Barry J. O'Toole) 'Parliamentary Accountability and the Next Steps' in Barry J. O'Toole and A. Grant Jordan, *The Next Steps: Improving Management in Government?*, Dartmouth, 1995, pp.118-141.
79. 'The Experience of Public Sector Management in the United Kingdom in the 1980s and Implications for Hong Kong', in Jane C.Y. Lee and Anthony B.L. Cheung, *Public Sector Reform in Hong Kong*, The Chinese University Press, Hong Kong, 1995, pp.157-185.
80. 'The First Nolan Report on Standards in Public Life', *Teaching Public Administration* 1995, Vol. 15, No. 2, pp.1-14.
81. 'Whatever happened to the Civil Servants?', *Durham First*, No 3, Spring 1996, pp.2-4.
82. 'Tragedy and Farce: the decision to privatise the RAS agency', *Public Policy and Administration*, Vol. 11(1), 1996, pp.1-7.

83. 'Standards in Public Life: A Valediction', *Teaching Public Administration,* Vol. XVI, No. 1, 1996, pp.1-19.
84. 'The End of the British Civil Service', in Peter Barberis (Ed.), *The Civil Service in an Era of Change,* Dartmouth, 1997, pp.23-37.
85. 'General Editor's Introduction', in James Elliott *The Politics and Public Sector Management of Tourism,* Routledge, 1997, pp.x-xi.
86. 'Minister-Civil Servant Relationships', in *Sharing Experiences, Training Review, 1996,* Staff Development Office, Malta, pp.26-31.
87. 'From Croquet Mallets to Flamingos: perspectives on change', *Public Policy and Administration,* Vol. 11(4), 1996, pp.1-17.
88. 'Civil Service Recruitment: the Civil Service Commissioners', Annual Report 1996-7', *Public Policy and Administration,* Vol. 12(3), 1997, pp.1-6.
89. 'Standards in Public Life', *Economic and Social Studies* (Malta), Vol. 9, 1997, pp.50-63.
90. 'Public Administration Committee (PAC)', in *International Encyclopaedia of Public Policy and Administration,* Vol. 3, Westview Press, 1998, pp.1788-9.
91. 'Royal Commissions', in *International Encyclopaedia of Public Policy and Administration,* Vol. 4, Westview Press, 1998, pp.2002-4.
92. 'Problems of ethics in public sector management', *Public Money and Management,* Vol. 18(1), 1998, pp.1-5.

Professor Chapman's current major project on The Civil Service Commission 1855-1991 is in its early stages. It is planned to result in a book, expected to be published in 2002. He has an Emeritus Fellowship from the Leverhulme Trust to enable him to undertake the research, as well as a significant personal research grant from the ESRC.

Index

First Division Association (FDA)
35, 130
Fisher, Sir Warren 32, 33, 88, 127,
138
France 58, 62, 72; Constitution of
104, 105, 106, 108-9, 116, 117
Freedom of Information (FOI) (*see
also* open government) chapter
3, in Australia 42, 48, 51; in
Canada 48; in Sweden 41; in the
UK 48-50, 53, 183; in the United
States 42, 50
Freedom of Information, White
Paper on (1997) 53
Friedman, Milton 61
Fulton Committee/ Reforms 13,
14, 26, 34, 35, 36, 125-6, 132

GCHQ Affair 95
de Gaulle, General 108
the Geddes axe 31
generalist administration 14-14, 29,
127
Germany 58
Gladstone, W.E. 27-30
Gore, Al 152
Green, T.H. 6, 28, 69, 70, 84-6, 87,
99-100

Haldane, Lord 32
Hankey, Sir Maurice 32
Harrington, James 71
Harrison, Wilfred 4
Hayek, Frederick 61
Head of the Civil Service 2, 89,
117, 142
Hegel, G.W.F. 55-6, 69
Heiser, Sir Terence 135
Hill, Sir Rowland 137
Hobbes, Thomas 75
Home Office 95, 137, 179
Hookham, Maurice 4
Hoover Commission Reports
(1949, 1955, USA) 144

House of Commons 10, 35, 36
House of Lords Select Committee
on Public Service 5, 96
Howard, Michael, MP 38, 137, 186

Ibbs, Sir Robin 132, 152
INLOGOV 4
Imperial Rome 71
'inverse concensus' 10-11

James II 73
Japan 58, 61
Joint University Council (JUC) 1,
5, 181-2
Johnson, Lyndon B. 146, 147, 148,
150, 151
Jowett, Benjamin 27-30

Kennedy, John F. 146, 147
Keynesianism 59, 61

Labour Party 42, 97
Leadership in Public Service: vii, 2,
6, 7, 12, 16-18, 19-20, 82, 142,
142-5, 150-2, 153, 156-7, 163,
164, 165-9, 172, 184-9 (*see also*
chapter 9 'Leadership in the
American Civil Service' 142-57)
Leverhulme Lectureship in Public
Administration (University of
Liverpool) 4
Lewis, Derek 35, 186
Lloyd George, David 31, 33
Locke, John 78
Lord Chancellor's Advisory
Council on Public Records 5

MacDonnell Royal Commission
1911, The 31
Machievelli, Nicolo 56, 72-3, 74
machinery of government 12
Macy, John W. 142, 145-8, 149-52,
152, 155, 156-7
Major, John 36, 44, 125, 134, 137, 138

'public interest' the 86-7, 92-5, 96
Public Policy and Administration 5, 8
Public Record Office 18
prison service 9, 95, 97, 186
Public Service Commission (Malta)
  160
public service, the ethic of 13-14,
  18, 28, 33, 82, chapter 6, 103,
  125, 127-8, 130, 138, 139, 149,
  157, 185, 186-7
Public Service Reform Commission
  (Malta) 161-64, 168

Quebec 106, 112, 114, 118
Questions of Procedure for Ministers
  94, 99

Ramsay Macdonald, James 33
Rayner, Sir Derek
  (Lord)/Raynerism 26, 33
Reagan, Ronald 107, 111, 112
Recruitment and Assessment
  Services Agency (RAS) 8, 96,
  177
Reform in Public Service vii, 6, 7-
  11, 19-20, chapter 2, 39, 182-3
RAF Uxbridge 2, 3
Robinson Crusoe (by Danel Defoe)
  80, 81
Roosevelt, Franklin D 146
Rousseau, Jean-Jacques 70, 73, 76-
  82, 87; and corruption 76-82, 96;
  and education 78-82
Royal Air Force 2
Royal Institute of Public
  Administration (RIPA) 97, 181,
  188
Russell, the Earl 28, 29
Russell-Smith, Dame Enid 4, 19

Sachsenhausen Case 91
Scott Report (1996) 36, 52, 93, 99,
  137, 177-8, 183
Select Committee on Public

Expenditure (1942) 35
self-fulfilment, self-realization 69,
  85-6, 87, 89
Sharp, Dame Evelyn 133
Smith, Adam 76
Smith, F. E. 33
Social Scientists and Policy Making
  176-82
Social Security, Department of
  (DSS)
Societies for the Reformation of
  Manners 73-4
Soviet Union 61
Sparta 80
Speaker of the House of Commons
  52
Spectator, The 74
Stacey, Frank 6, 14
standards in public life 82, 157,
  175, 177
Stowe, Sir Kenneth 135
Swift, Jonathan 72
Symons, Elizabeth 35

Tatler, The 74
Thatcher, Margaret (Baroness) 26,
  36, 45, 58. 61, 111-12, 115, 124,
  125, 127, 128, 134, 137
Trade and Industry, Department of
  (DTI) 126
Transport, Department of 38
Treasury 29, 30-4, 34-9, 112
Treasury and Civil Service
  Committee (of the House of
  Commons) 10, 125

United States of America 42, 50,
  58, 175, 186; Constitution of
  104, 105, 106-08, 108, 110, 111,
  113, 116, 153; Leadership in
  public service of chapter 9;
  Supreme Court of 111
University of Birmingham 4
University of Cambridge 29, 179